About This Book

Here, in one volume that you can keep by your desk to read, reference, and squish spiders with, is nearly all the information you need to create your own Web pages—everything from how to write them to how to link them together to how to set up your own Web server and use it to manage forms and create special programs to process them.

In addition, this book provides hints, suggestions, and examples of how to structure your overall presentation—not just the words within each page. This book won't just teach you how to create a Web presentation—it'll teach you how to create a good Web presentation.

Who Should Read This Book

Is this book for you? It is if:

- ☐ You've seen what's out on the Web, and you want to contribute your own content.
- ☐ You're representing a company that wants to create an Internet "presence" and you're not sure where to start.
- ☐ You're an information developer, such as a technical writer, and you want to learn how the Web can help you present your information online.
- ☐ You're doing research or polling and you're interested in creating a system that allows people to "register" comments or vote for particular suggestions or items.

How This Book Is Structured

This book is intended to be read and absorbed over the course of a week (and it's a real week, 7 days, not a business week). On each day you'll read two chapters, which describe one or two concepts related to Web presentation design. With this book in hand you should be able to go from a simple idea for a Web presentation to writing and putting that presentation up on the Web—and all this in a week, maybe even less!

Conventions

 Note: A Note box presents interesting pieces of information related to the surrounding discussion.

 Tip: A Tip box offers advice or teaches an easier way to do something.

 Warning: A Warning box advises you about potential problems and helps you steer clear of disaster.

 Input: An Input icon identifies some new HTML code that you can type in yourself.

 Output: An Output icon highlights what the same HTML code looks like when viewed by either Mosaic or Lynx.

Teach Yourself Web Publishing with HTML

in a Week

Teach Yourself
Web Publishing
with HTML
in a Week

Laura Lemay

SAMS
PUBLISHING

201 West 103rd Street
Indianapolis, Indiana 46290

Overview

Contents

14   HTML Assistants: Editors and Converters   345

Appendixes

A   Sources for Further Information   357

Acknowledgments

To Sams Publishing, for letting me write my first "real" book.

To the Coca-Cola company, for creating Diet Coke and selling so much of it to me.

To all the folks on the comp.infosystems.www newsgroups, the www-talk mailing list, and the Web conference on the WELL, for answering questions and putting up with my late night rants.

And to Eric, for moral support when I was sure I would never make my deadlines (and for encouraging me to go back to work), for accepting that I wasn't going to spend more than ten minutes outside the computer room for two months, and for setting up an enormous amount of UNIX and networking equipment for me to muck with. I think I would have simply exploded weeks ago without you.

About the Author

Laura Lemay

Laura Lemay is a technical writer, computer nerd, and part-time motorcycle mechanic, who has been writing and designing software documentation and online help systems for six years. She has been involved with the Internet for more than ten years, the World Wide Web for close to a year. You can reach her on the Net at lemay@lne.com, or by pointing your Web browser at http://slack.lne.com/lemay/theBook/index.html.

Introduction

So you've browsed the Web for a while, and you've seen the sort of stuff that people are putting up on the Net. And you're noticing that more and more stuff is going up all the time, and that more and more people are becoming interested in it. "I want to do that," you think. "How can I do that?" If you have the time and you know where to look, you could find out everything you need to know from the information out on the Web. It's all there; it's all available, and it's all free. Or, you could read this book instead. Here, in one volume that you can keep by your desk to read, reference, and squish spiders with, is nearly all the information you need to create your own Web pages—everything from how to write them to how to link them together to how to set up your own Web server and use it to manage forms and create special programs to process them.

But wait, there's more. This book goes beyond the scope of other books on how to create Web pages, which just teach you the basic technical details such as how to produce a boldface word. In this book, you'll learn why you should be producing a particular effect and when you should use it, as well as how. In addition, this book provides hints, suggestions, and examples of how to structure your overall presentation—not just the words within each page. This book won't just teach you how to create a Web presentation—it'll teach you how to create a good Web presentation.

Also, unlike many other books on this subject, this book doesn't focus on any one computer system. Regardless of whether you're using a PC running Windows, a Macintosh, or some dialect of UNIX (or any other computer system), the concepts in this book will be valuable to you, and you will be able to apply them to your Web pages regardless of your platform of choice.

Sound good? Glad you think so. I thought it was a good idea when I wrote it, and I hope you get as much out of this book reading it as I did writing it.

Who Should Read This Book

Is this book for you? That depends:

- ☐ If you've seen what's out on the Web, and you want to contribute your own content, this book is for you.
- ☐ If you represent a company that wants to create an Internet "presence" and you're not sure where to start, this book is for you.
- ☐ If you're an information developer, such as a technical writer, and you want to learn how the Web can help you present your information online, this book is for you.

☐ If you're doing research or polling and you're interested in creating a system that allows people to "register" comments or vote for particular suggestions or items, this book is for you.

☐ If you're just curious about how the Web works, some parts of this book are for you, although you might be able to find what you need on the Web itself.

☐ If you've never seen the Web before but you've heard this Mosaic thing is really nifty and want to get set up using it, this book isn't for you. You'll need a more general book about getting set up and using Mosaic before moving on to actually producing Web documents yourself.

What This Book Contains

This book is intended to be read and absorbed over the course of a week—and it's a real week, 7 days, not a business week. On each day you'll read two chapters, which describe one or two concepts related to Web presentation design.

☐ On Day 1, you get a general overview of the World Wide Web and what you can do with it and come up with a plan for your Web presentation.

☐ On Day 2, you learn about the HTML language and how to write simple documents and link them together using hypertext link.

☐ On Day 3, you do more with HTML, including working with lists and character formatting as well as more with links.

☐ Day 4 tells you all about adding multimedia capabilities to your Web presentations: using images, sounds, and video to enhance your material.

☐ On Day 5 you get some hints for creating a well-constructed Web presentation, and you explore some examples of Web presentations to get an idea of what sort of work you can do.

☐ Day 6 falls into two parts. First, you learn how to put your presentation up on the Web, including how to set up a Web server and advertise the work you've done. In the second part of the day, you learn about gateway scripts that can be used to extend the capabilities of your Web presentation to include interactivity and link your presentation with other programs such as databases.

☐ Finally, on Day 7, you learn about forms and how to process the input you get from them, as well as how to create clickable image maps. To finish off the book and the week, you learn about HTML editors that can help you construct Web pages, as well as converter tools that enable you to translate documents written in other applications to HTML.

With this book in hand you should be able to go from a simple idea for a Web presentation to writing that presentation and putting it up on the Web—and all this in a week, maybe even less!

What You Need Before You Start

There are seemingly hundreds of books on the market about how to get connected to the Internet, and lots of books about how to use the World Wide Web. This book isn't one of them. I'm assuming that if you're reading this book, you already have a working connection to the Internet, that you have a World Wide Web browser such as Mosaic or Lynx available to you, and that you've used it at least a couple of times. You should also have at least a passing acquaintance with some other portions of the Internet such as electronic mail, Gopher, and Usenet news, as I may refer to them in general terms in this book. Although you won't need to explicitly use them to work through the content in this book, some parts of the Web may refer to these other concepts.

In other words, you need to have used the Web in order to provide content for the Web. If you have this one simple qualification, then read on!

DAY 1

1

The World of the World Wide Web

A journey of a thousand miles begins with a single step, and here you are at Day 1, Chapter 1, of a journey that will show you how to use HyperText Markup Language to produce documents on the World Wide Web. In this chapter, you learn the following basics:

☐ What the World Wide Web is and why it's terribly cool

☐ How to use a browser to explore the Web

☐ What a Web server is and why you need one

☐ What a Uniform Resource Locator is

☐ What home pages are used for

If you've already spent time exploring the Web, you may already be familiar with much of the content in this chapter, if not all of it. If so, by all means skip ahead to the next chapter, where you'll find an overview of the more general things to think about when you design and organize your own Web documents.

Note: In case you haven't used the Web before, here's a real quick jump start: In several places in this chapter, and throughout this book, I tell you to point your browser (the application that you use to explore the Web, for example, Mosaic or Lynx) at a particular Web page, and give you an address that looks something like this:

```
http://www.ncsa.uiuc.edu/SDG/Software/Mosaic/Docs/whats-new.html
```

That thing with all the slashes in it is called a URL, pronounced either spelled out ("U R L") or as "earl," depending on your preference. I explain specifically what it is later in this chapter. Think of URLs as addresses to interesting places on the Web. You use a URL by starting up your browser, and then selecting the Open... menu item (sometimes called Open URL..., or just Go). At that point you can enter in that URL and your browser will link up to the information contained at that address.

What Is the World Wide Web?

I have a friend who likes to describe things with lots of meaningful words strung together in a chain, so that it takes several minutes to sort out what he's just said.

If I were he, I'd describe the World Wide Web as a global, interactive, dynamic, cross-platform, distributed, graphical hypertext information system that runs over the Internet. Whew! Unless you understand each of those words and how they fit together, that isn't going to make much sense. (My friend often doesn't make much sense, either.)

So let's take each one of those words and see what they mean in the context of how you'll be using the Web as a publishing medium.

The Web Is a Hypertext Information System

If you've used any sort of basic online help system, you're already familiar with the primary concept behind the World Wide Web: hypertext.

The idea behind hypertext is that instead of reading text in a rigid, linear structure (such as a book), you can easily skip from one point to another, get more information, go back, jump to other topics, and navigate through the text based on what interests you at the time.

Online help systems or help stacks such as those provided by Microsoft Windows Help, Sun Microsystems' AnswerBook, or HyperCard on the Macintosh use hypertext to present information. To get more information on a topic, just click on that topic. A new screen (or another window, or a dialog box, however the program defines a jump) appears with that new information. Perhaps there are links on that screen that take you to still other screens, and links on those screens that take you even further away from your original topic. Figure 1.1 shows a simple diagram of how that kind of system works.

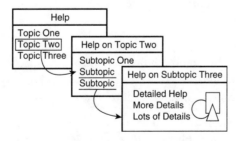

Figure 1.1. *A simple online help system.*

Now imagine that your online help system is linked to another online help system on another application related to yours; for example, your drawing program's help is linked to your word processor's help. Your word processor's help is then linked to an

encyclopedia, where you could look up any other concepts that you don't understand. The encyclopedia is hooked into a global index of magazine articles that enables you to get the most recent information on the topics that the encyclopedia covers; the article index is then also linked into information about the writers of those articles, and some pictures of their children. (See Figure 1.2.)

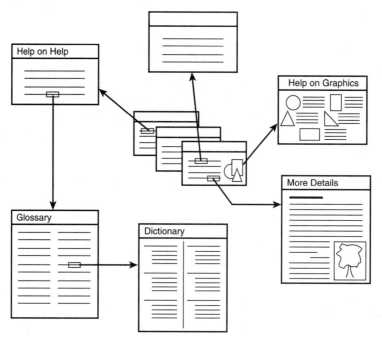

Figure 1.2. *A more complex online help system.*

With all these interlinked systems available with the simple help system you got with the program you bought, you'd rapidly run out of disk space, and you'd question whether you needed all this information when all you wanted to know was how to do one simple thing in your simple application. All that information could be expensive, too.

But if the information didn't take up much disk space, and if it were freely available, and you could get it reasonably quickly and anytime you wanted to, then things would be more interesting. In fact, the information system might very well end up more interesting than the software you bought in the first place.

That's just what the World Wide Web is: more information than you could ever digest in a lifetime, linked together in various ways, out there on the Net, available for you to browse whenever you want to. It's big, and deep, and easy to get lost in. But it's also an immense amount of fun.

The Web Is Graphical and Easy To Navigate

One of the best parts of the Web, and arguably the reason it has become so popular over other Internet services such as Gopher, is the capability the Web has to display both text and graphics in full color on the same page. Before the Web, using the Internet involved simple text-only connections, and you had to navigate the Internet's various services using command-line interfaces and arcane tools. Although there was lots of really exciting information on the Net, it wasn't necessarily pretty to look at.

The Web provides capabilities for graphics, sound, and video to be incorporated with the text, and the interface is easily navigable—just jump from link to link, from page to page, across sites and servers.

Note: If the Web incorporates so much more than text, why do I keep calling the Web a Hyper*Text* system? Well, if you're going to be absolutely technically correct about it, the Web is not a hypertext system—it's a hyper*media* system. But, on the other hand, one could argue that the Web began as a text-only system, and much of the content is still text-heavy, with extra bits of media added in as emphasis. There are many very educated people arguing these very points at this moment, and presenting their arguments in papers and discursive rants as educated people like to do. Whatever. I prefer the term hypertext, and it's my book, so I'm going to use it. You know what I mean.

The Web Is Cross-Platform

If you can access the Internet, you can access the World Wide Web. It doesn't matter what system you're running on or whether you think Windows widgets look better than Macintosh widgets or vice versa (or if you think both Mac and Windows people are weenies). The World Wide Web is not limited to any one kind of machine. The Web doesn't care about user-interface wars between companies with too much money anyway.

You get access to the Web through an application called a *browser,* like Mosaic. I explain more about what the browser actually does later in this chapter. There are lots of browsers out there, for most popular platforms. And once you've got a browser and a connection to the Internet, you've got it made. You're on the Web.

There is one small catch, however. The Web, like most Internet applications, started on UNIX systems, and much of the use of the Web still takes place on UNIX systems, although personal computers are rapidly catching up. Because UNIX is still the dominant platform, most of the newer advances in Web technology are taking place on UNIX first. But wait around a bit; if something turns out to work really well on UNIX, you can bet that it'll hit the personal computer side sooner or later. And with more and more people getting involved in developing for the Web, it'll probably be more sooner than later.

The Web Is Distributed

Information takes up an awful lot of space, particularly when you include multimedia capabilities such as images, sounds, and video. To store all the information that the Web provides, you'd need an untold amount of disk space, and managing it would be almost impossible. Imagine being prompted to insert CD-ROM #456 ALP through ALR into your drive when you looked something up in your online encyclopedia and wanted to find out more information about Alpacas.

The Web is successful in providing so much information because that information is distributed globally across thousands of different sites, each of which contributes the space for the information it publishes. You, as a consumer of that information, go to that site to view the information, and when you're done you go somewhere else, and your system reclaims the disk space that the original information took up. You don't have to install it, or change disks, or do anything other than point your browser at that site.

The Web Is Dynamic

Because information on the Web is contained on the site that published it, people who published it in the first place can update the information on the fly at any time.

If you're browsing that information, you don't have to install a new version of the help, buy another book ("The Second Edition"), or call technical support to find out why the diagram on page 324 of your book does not match what the window on your screen says. Just bring up your browser and check out what's up there.

If you're publishing information on the Web, you can make sure the information you're publishing is up-to-date all the time. You don't have to spend a lot of time re-releasing documents as maintenance releases or change notes. There is no cost of materials. You don't have to get bids on number of copies or quality of output. Color is free. And you won't get calls from hapless customers who have a version of the book that was obsolete four years ago.

An excellent example of how information can be dynamically updated on the Web is the "What's New on the Web" page at NCSA. If you have a Web browser, point it at `http://www.ncsa.uiuc.edu/SDG/Software/Mosaic Docs/whats-new.html` or see Figure 1.3.

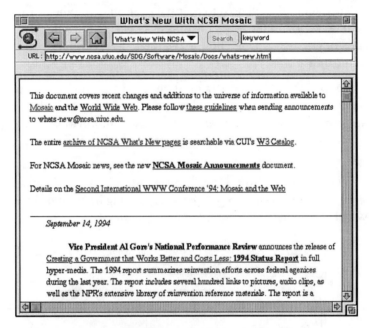

Figure 1.3. *What's New on the Web (from NCSA).*

The What's New page, which is updated every couple of days, contains descriptions of new Web servers that have appeared on the Net with links to those servers. It's often a good place to start browsing the Web because it contains much of the new stuff out there as it appears.

The Web Can Access Many Forms of Internet Information

When the World Wide Web was created, one of the new features it provided was a new Internet protocol for managing hypertext information across the Internet: HTTP, or HyperText Transfer Protocol. HTTP is a simple protocol that allows for the hypertext documents to be transferred quickly over the Net between Web browsers and servers. Unless you are writing your own server, or are overly curious about the innards of the Web, you won't really need to know much more about HTTP than what it's there for.

In addition to providing a new system for publishing and distributing information, the World Wide Web supports the forms of information distribution that already existed on the Internet.

And there are lots of them: FTP, Gopher, Usenet news, WAIS, telnet, e-mail. They all use different tools (that all need to be installed separately), and all those tools operate in different ways. It makes for a nice beefy book on How to Use the Internet, but remembering all the tools and how to use them makes exploring the Internet considerably more difficult.

The Web fixes that. Using the same application that you use to read hypertext Web information, you can get to files and information contained in these other information systems. And, even better, you can create links to information on those systems just as you would create links to other Web information. It's all seamless and all available through a single application.

To use a Gopher server from a Web browser, use a URL that looks something like this: `gopher://name_of_gopher_server`. For example, Figure 1.4 shows the Gopher server on the WELL, a popular Internet service in San Francisco.

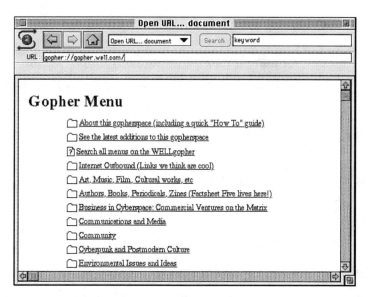

Figure 1.4. *The WELL's Gopher server.*

To use FTP from the Web, use a URL that looks like this: `ftp://name_of_site/directory/filename`. You can also use just a directory and your Web server will show you a list of the files, as in Figure 1.5, which shows my own FTP directory at `ftp://ftp.netcom.com/pub/lemay`.

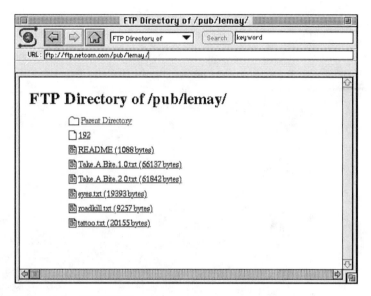

FTP Directory of /pub/lemay/

FTP Directory of ▼   Search keyword

URL : ftp://ftp.netcom.com/pub/lemay/

FTP Directory of /pub/lemay/

📁 Parent Directory
📄 192
📄 README (1088 bytes)
📄 Take_A_Bite_1.0.txt (66137 bytes)
📄 Take_A_Bite_2.0.txt (61842 bytes)
📄 eyes.txt (19393 bytes)
📄 roadkill.txt (9257 bytes)
📄 tattoo.txt (20155 bytes)

Figure 1.5. *The author's FTP Directory.*

You learn how to use the World Wide Web to get access and to link to other forms of Internet information in Chapter 6, "More About Links and URLs."

The Web Is Interactive

The Web is interactive by nature; the act of selecting a link and retrieving another screen of information is a form of interactivity. In addition to this simple interactivity, however, the Web enables you to design screens that look like forms; people browsing these screens can select from several choices (radio buttons), fill in information in slots, or select a button to perform a particular operation. You, as the publisher of the form, can then take the information supplied through the form and do whatever you want with it—build another page of information on the fly, add the current information to a database, or display a particular picture.

> **Note:** Forms have been a relatively recent addition to browsers on the World Wide Web. If you have an older browser, it may not support forms, and you may not be able to take advantage of this feature. If your browser doesn't support forms, consider upgrading to a new version or switching to a different browser. Forms are too much fun to miss out on.

If your browser can handle forms, try exploring `http://www.ugcs.caltech.edu/~werdna/sttng/vote/`. This page provides "Star Trek: The Next Generation" fans a way to vote for their favorite episodes by rating them on a scale from 1 to 10. The votes are correlated and distributed via the Web (of course). Figure 1.6 shows the main voting page.

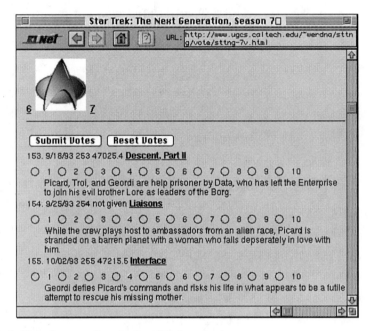

Figure 1.6. *Vote for your favorite* Star Trek *episodes.*

Who Owns the Web?

No single entity "owns" the World Wide Web. The World Wide Web Initiative is a cooperative organization based at CERN, the European Particle Physics Laboratory in Switzerland. (CERN was the original birthplace of the Web in 1990.) The World Wide Web Initiative supports and defines the languages and protocols that make up the Web (HTTP, HTML, and so on). This is the closest anyone gets to setting the standards for and enforcing rules about the World Wide Web.

You can visit CERN's WWW home page at `http://info.cern.ch/hypertext/WWW/TheProject.html`. Figure 1.7 shows that home page.

Figure 1.7. *The WWW home Page.*

Web Browsers: More than Just Mosaic

To access the World Wide Web, you use what is called a *browser*. Browsers are sometimes also called *clients*, since they get information from a *server*.

The most popular browser for the World Wide Web is Mosaic, developed at the National Center for Supercomputing Applications (NCSA) at the University of Illinois. Mosaic was the first browser that was able to use color and graphics, and the first browser that made the Web look really interesting. Mosaic has become so popular that using Mosaic and using the World Wide Web have become almost synonymous to many people.

Mosaic may be the most popular Web browser, but it is far from the only browser, and it is important to make a distinction between the information you're browsing and what you use to view it. (This will become very important when you design your Web pages.) Mosaic isn't the only story in town, and assuming it is will limit the audience you have for the information you want to present.

13

A wide array of Web browsers is available, and more are popping up all the time. Most browsers available now are freeware or shareware ("try before you buy"), but browsers with enhanced capabilities from commercial companies should be out by the time you read this book. Browsers exist for most platforms and are available for both graphical user-interface based systems (Mac, Windows, X11), and text-only for dial-up UNIX connections.

What Does a Browser Do?

The browser's job is twofold: given a pointer to a piece of information on the Net (called a URL—I explain this in the next section), it has to be able to access that piece of information or operate in some way based on the contents of that pointer. For hypertext Web documents, this means being able to speak to the server using the HTTP protocol. Since the Web can also manage information contained on FTP and Gopher servers, in news postings, in mail, and so on, the browser has to speak the language of those tools as well.

What the browser does most often, however, is deal with Web documents. Each "page" that you load from the Web is a single document, written in a language called HTML (HyperText Markup Language), that includes the text of the document, its structure, any links to other documents, and images and other media. (You'll learn all about HTML on days two and three, since you need to know it in order to write your own Web pages.)

The browser talks to the Web server over the Net and retrieves a document from that server. If the document is an HTML file, it then interprets the HTML code contained in that document and formats and displays the document. If the document contains images or links to other documents, it manages those parts as well.

A Short Overview of Popular Browsers

This section describes a few of the more popular browsers that people are using to view Web documents, based on the number of questions I've seen asked about them and statistics posted to the `comp.infosystems.www` Usenet newsgroups. These are in no way all the browsers available, and if the browser you're using isn't here, don't feel that you have to use one of these. Whatever browser you have is fine as long as it works for you.

Note: The pictures throughout this book are generally taken from a browser on the Macintosh (Mosaic or MacWeb), or using the text-only browser Lynx, for the sole reason that I'm writing this book on a Macintosh, so it's

easier this way. If you're using Windows or a UNIX system, don't feel left out. As I noted earlier, the glory of the Web is that you see the same information regardless of the platform you're on. So ignore the buttons and window borders and focus on what's inside the window.

This list may very well be obsolete as soon as I write it. Appendix A, "Sources For Further Information," contains an address you can look at for a more up-to-date list of available browsers.

Different browsers support different features. Although most support basic hypertext documents and links, a few more recent features, such as forms and sending electronic mail, are not yet supported by many browsers. (This may have changed by the time you read this.)

Note: If the only connection you have to the Internet is through a dial-up text-only UNIX (or other) account, you are limited to using text-only browsers such as Lynx. You will not be able to view documents in color or view graphics online.

For fully graphical browsing on the Web, you need a direct connection to the Internet such as those provided by SLIP or PPP. Getting your machine connected to the Internet is beyond the scope of this book, but there are plenty of books out there to help you do so.

NCSA Mosaic

As I mentioned earlier, Mosaic is the most popular of the full-color graphical browsers. Mosaic is provided and supported by NCSA at the University of Illinois.

Mosaic comes in versions for X11 (UNIX), MS Windows, and Macintosh; each version is colloquially called XMosaic, WinMosaic, and MacMosaic, respectively. The development support for the X version tends to be somewhat ahead of the PC and Macintosh versions. For example, MacMosaic is only now beginning to support forms.

You can get all three versions of NCSA Mosaic via FTP at `ftp://ftp.ncsa.uiuc.edu/Mosaic`, although because the server is extremely busy, it may be difficult to connect. Try during non-primetime hours (evenings after 5 p.m. and weekends).

As of this writing, Mosaic does not support sending e-mail on any platform. Figure 1.8 shows NCSA Mosaic for X11.

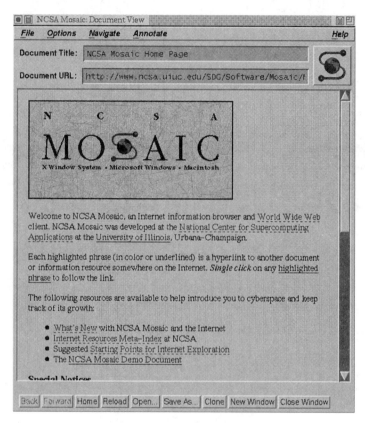

Figure 1.8. *Mosaic (for X).*

Lynx

Lynx ("links," get it?), developed by The University of Kansas, is an excellent browser for text-only Internet connections such as dial-up UNIX accounts. It requires VT100 terminal emulation, which most terminal programs should support. Lynx enables you to use arrow keys to select and navigate links within Web documents. It's quite fast and supports both forms and electronic mail, making it even more useful than many graphical browsers.

A version of Lynx is also available for DOS systems. Lynx is available at `ftp://ftp2.cc.ukans.edu/pub/lynx`. Figure 1.9 shows Lynx running on a UNIX system.

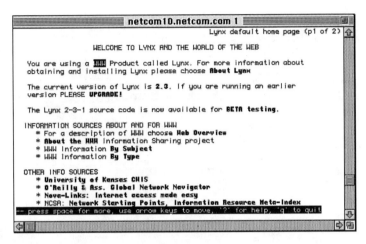

Figure 1.9. *Lynx.*

MacWeb and WinWeb

EINet, the Enterprise Integration Network, provides the browsers MacWeb and WinWeb for Macintosh and Windows, respectively. Both are in alpha release, but both provide many features such as forms, and both tend to be smaller, faster, and more stable than their counterparts from Mosaic.

MacWeb is available from `ftp://ftp.einet.net/einet/mac/macweb`, and WinWeb from `ftp://ftp.einet.net/einet/pc/winweb`. Figure 1.10 shows MacWeb.

Cello

Cello is a browser for Microsoft Windows. Cello does not yet handle forms, but support is expected in the next version. Cello, shown in Figure 1.11, is available from `ftp://ftp.law.cornell.edu/pub/LII/Cello/Cello.zip`.

Netscape

New in town, and stomping over less adequate browsers, is Netscape from Netscape Communications Corp., formerly Mosaic Communications Corp, a company founded by many members of the original NCSA Mosaic programming team. Netscape is free for personal use and is available for X11, Windows, and Macintosh. Netscape provides up-to-the-minute features for all three platforms, including full forms support and an integrated Usenet news reader, as well as speed optimizations for browsing using slower Net connections (such as a 14.4K bps modem).

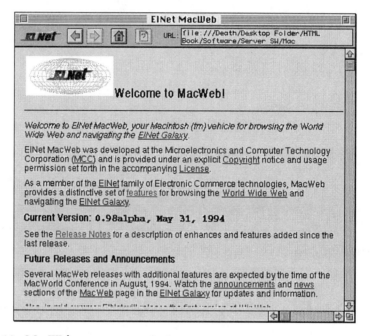

Figure 1.10. *MacWeb.*

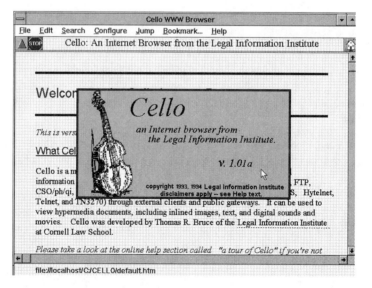

Figure 1.11. *Cello.*

Note: Netscape Communications has also proposed several additions to the HTML language to better manage screen layout; for example, to control font sizes and image handling. These new extensions have met with some controversy amongst the Web community, as up to this point the elements of the HTML language had been defined by an Internet-wide committee. The status of the Netscape HTML extensions, and whether browsers besides Netscape will support them, is still up in the air. In this book I focus only on the standard HTML language—the basic common denominator that most browsers support. See Appendix C for a description of the Netscape extensions.

Web Servers

To publish documents on the Web, you need some sort of server, which feeds documents and media to the browsers that request them. Whenever you point your browser at a Web document, the browser talks to the server to get at that document. Since the Web can read files from services such as FTP or Gopher, you can use those tools to serve Web documents. (Most browsers can figure out that they're reading a hypertext document even if it doesn't come over the wire specifically using HTTP.) The best way to publish Web pages, however, is through the use of a dedicated Web server.

A Web server uses the HTTP protocol to listen for requests for files from browsers. It then delivers the files and any included images those files refer to. Web servers can also be set up to handle commands sent back from the browser; for example, in the case of forms or other interactive Web pages. You can't do that with FTP or Gopher.

Several Web servers are available, although as I already noted, much of the server technology is focused on the UNIX side. I describe more about the available servers in Chapter 11, "Putting It All Online."

Uniform Resource Locators

A URL is a pointer to some bit of data on the Web, be it a Web document, a file on FTP or Gopher, a posting on Usenet, or a data record in a database. When someone tells you to point your browser at a particular location on the Web, he or she will give you a URL that indicates where you're pointing. You've seen several URLs already in this chapter; you've been using them to get to the pages I've been pointing out along the way.

The URL provides a universal, consistent method for finding and accessing information, not necessarily for you, but mostly for your Web browser. (If they were for you they would be in a format that would make them easier to remember.) If someone tells you to check out a particular URL, you use the Open command (sometimes called Go or Open URL), then type in the URL (or copy and paste it if you can), and the browser goes to the document contained at that URL.

Besides this immediate use of URLs, you also use URLs when you create a hypertext link within a document to another document. So any way you look at it, URLs are important to how you and your browser get around on the Web.

URLs contain information about how to get at the information (what protocol: FTP, gopher, HTTP), the Internet host name to look on (`www.ncsa.uiuc.edu`, or `ftp.apple.com`, or `netcom16.netcom.com`, and so on), and the directory or other location on that site to find the file. There are also special URLs for things like sending mail to people (called "mailto" URLs), and for using the telnet program.

You'll learn all about URLs and what each part of them means as the book progresses.

> **Note:** URLs are actually part of a larger group of uniform resource objects defined by the World Wide Web initiative. There are also Uniform Resource Names (URNs) and Uniform Resource Identifiers (URIs). (Both URNs and URLs are a form of URIs. Got it?) I won't talk about either of these in this book, since all of the documents I have seen use URLs. You can get more information on the URL specification (and the specifications for all the WWW concepts) directly from CERN. Appendix A, "Sources for Further Information," contains the URL you need to find that information.

Home Pages

You'll see the term "home page" a lot when you browse the Web, used in several different ways.

If you are reading and browsing the Web, the home page is the Web page that loads when you start your browser. Each browser has its own default home page, which is often the

same page for the site that developed the browser. (For example, the Mosaic home page is at NCSA, and the Lynx home page is at the University of Kansas.)

Within your browser you can change your default home page to start up any page you want—a common tactic I've seen many people use is to create a simple page of links to other interesting places or pages that they visit a lot. The procedure for changing your home page varies from browser to browser, so I won't explain it here. See the documentation that came with your browser for more information on changing your local home page.

The second use of a home page is more important to people publishing information on the Web—and since you bought this book, I assume you are one of those people. To a provider of information to the Web, the home page is the entry point for your readers to the content you've provided for the Web.

A common assumption to make if you are new to the Web is that there is some kind of starting point to begin browsing at, some sort of top-level index. The Web itself doesn't have a "top"; there is no central index or starting point on the Web. There's no central authority controlling the Web, so there's no place a top-level index could go.

Because Mosaic is such a popular browser, the NCSA Mosaic home page is often considered the "top" of the Web, and the NCSA home page has been written to provide several launching points for Web exploration in general. But if you're not using the Mosaic browser, then you won't see the Mosaic home page unless you explicitly load it. So the Mosaic home page is not the top either.

What the Web does have are thousands of little "tops": entry points for each server (and often for multiple places on single servers) that provide some information about what that server contains or what interrelated information it contains links to. That's what home pages are used for.

The home page you provide for your content may contain a menu of items available deeper within your web, an index to the contents of the server, or some other general information. Figure 1.12 shows a typical home page; this one is for the English department at Carnegie Mellon University, and can be found at URL `http://english-server.hss.cmu.edu/`.

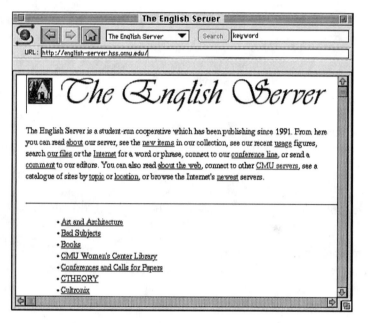

Figure 1.12. *The English Server home page.*

Summary

In this chapter you've learned the basics for what the World Wide Web is, how it can be used, why it's useful, and the various features and terminology used to describe the Web and its tools. In particular, after reading this chapter, you should be able to use your browser to open any arbitrary URL (and know what a URL is), know the difference between a browser and a server (and name several available browsers), and know what a home page is and how to recognize one in the wild.

Q&A

Q I use Gopher a lot. How is the Web different?

A Although Gopher and the Web are similar in the sense that they both distribute information to the Web in a distributed and easily browsable fashion, they differ in their philosophy. Gopher provides information in a strict menu fashion: you either have an index or a document, so you search the indexes to find the information you want, and then read or download the document.

With the Web, everything is a page, and everything on that page can potentially be linked to other pages. There isn't any significant difference between indexes and documents on the Web; an index can be a document, and vice versa. Also, since you can get to Gopher on the Web, you can look at Gopher indexes and documents using the Web, too.

The Web also has the significant advantage of allowing mixed text and graphics on each "page," making the Web less of a huge information kiosk, as Gopher tends to be, and more of a huge interactive hyperlinked magazine.

Q How fast is the Web growing?

A Very fast. Very, very fast. Various pundits have claimed that Web traffic across the Internet is growing by 20 percent a month, and that twelve new Web servers are added to the Net every day. A year ago at this time, Web traffic on the Net accounted for 1 percent of all Internet traffic. In July it was 6 percent, and it is expected to grow even more in the coming year. This is faster growth than any other service on the Internet.

With the rapid growth comes a lot of rapid change, however. Expect more and more new services—including new browsers, new servers, new tools for development, and other new features—to appear as time passes quickly by.

Q Why would anyone use a text-only browser like Lynx when there are graphical browsers available?

A You need a special Internet connection in order to use a graphical browser on the Web. If your machine isn't directly hooked up to the Internet, you'll need to use a modem with a special network account to make your machine think it's on the Net—and these kinds of accounts aren't cheap, even if you live in an area where there are lots of companies that provide them. Even then, unless you have a very fast modem, Web pages can take a long time to load, particularly if there are lots of graphics on the page.

Lynx is the ideal solution for people who either don't have a direct Internet connection or don't want to take the time to use the Web graphically. It's fast and it enables you to get ahold of just about everything on the Web; indirectly, yes, but it's there.

Q I've heard there's a home page about ice sculpture on the Web. How do I find it?

A Well, good luck. Although some indexes of the Web exist (a good one is the CERN Virtual Library at `http://info.cern.ch/hypertext/DataSources/bySubject/Overview.html`), most are incomplete, and with the Web changing so fast, it's difficult to keep up with all the new information appearing on the Web. Appendix A contains a few pointers to these indexes.

NCSA provides the "What's New on the Web" page at NCSA (`http://www.ncsa.uiuc.edu/SDG/Software/Mosaic/Docs/whats-new.html`; see Figure 1.3 for a picture), which provides information on new servers out there as they appear. Other sites may provide "What's New" pages as well.

There are also what are called Web "robots" or "spiders" (spiders in the Web—get it?), which search the Web and build an index of what's out there. Appendix A contains more information about searchable Web indexes and URLs for where to find them.

The best resource I've found for locating Web pages about a particular subject is to ask other people if they've seen one. The Usenet newsgroup `comp.infosystems.www.users` is a good place to ask if anyone has seen your ice sculpture home page.

2

Getting Organized

When you write a book, a paper, an article, or even a memo, you usually don't just jump right in with the first sentence and then write it through to the end. Same goes with the visual arts—you don't normally start from the top left corner of the canvas or page and work your way down to the bottom right.

A better way to write or draw or design a work is to do some planning beforehand—to know what it is you're going to do and what you're trying to accomplish, and to have a general idea or rough sketch of the structure of the piece before you jump in and work on it.

Just as with more traditional modes of communication, writing and designing Web pages takes some amount of planning and thought before you start flinging text and graphics around and linking them wildly to each other. Perhaps even more so, because trying to apply the rules of traditional writing or design to online hypertext often results in documents that are either difficult to understand and navigate online or that simply don't take advantage of the features that hypertext provides. Poorly organized Web documents are also difficult to revise or to expand.

In this chapter I describe some of the things you should think about before you jump in and start developing your Web pages. Specifically, you

☐ Learn the difference between a Web presentation, a Web page, and a Web document

☐ Think about the sort of information (content) you want to put on the Web

☐ Set your goals for the presentation

☐ Organize your content into main topics

☐ Come up with a general structure for pages and topics

After you have an overall idea of how you're going to construct your Web pages, you'll be ready to actually start writing and designing those pages tomorrow in Chapter 3, "Begin with the Basics."

Anatomy of a Web Presentation

First, let's look at some simple terminology that you'll be using throughout this book. You need to know what the following terms mean and how they apply to the body of work you're developing for the Web:

☐ Web presentations

☐ Web pages or documents

☐ Home pages

A Web *presentation* consists of one or more Web *pages* containing text and graphics, linked together in a meaningful way, which, as a whole, describe a body of information or create an overall consistent effect. (See Figure 2.1.)

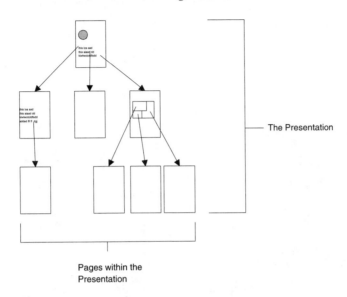

The Presentation

Pages within the
Presentation

Figure 2.1. *Web presentations and pages.*

Web pages are sometimes called Web *documents;* I refer to them as both pages and documents interchangeably in this book. Unlike in the hard copy world, where a document is a single body of work such as a book and a page is an element within that work, the terms page and document refer to the same thing on the Web: a single file on disk, retrieved and formatted by a Web browser.

The *home page,* as I mentioned briefly in the last chapter, is the "top" of your set of Web pages. It is the place where most people start exploring your Web presentation, and it is the URL of that home page you will give people when you tell them to check out your Web site. (See Figure 2.2.)

The home page generally contains an overview of the content available from that starting point, often in the form of a table of contents. Although the home page usually contains a more general overview of specific information contained on other pages, if your content is small enough you may very well include everything on that single home page.

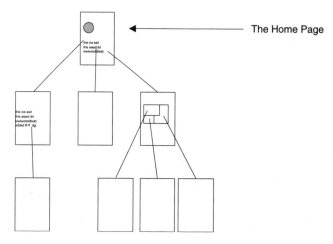

The Home Page

Figure 2.2. *The home page.*

What Do You Want to Do on the Web?

This may seem like a silly question. You wouldn't have bought this book if you didn't have some idea of what you want to put online already. But maybe you don't really know what it is you want to put up on the Web, or you have a vague idea but nothing concrete. Maybe you just want to do something similar to some other Web page you've seen that you thought was particularly cool.

What you want to put on the Web is what I'll refer to throughout this book as your *content*. Content is a general term that can refer to text, or graphics, or media, or interactive forms, or anything. If you were to tell someone what your Web pages are "about," you would be describing your content.

What sort of content can you put on the Web? Just about anything you want to. Here are some of the kinds of content that are popular on the Web right now:

- ☐ **Personal Information.** You can communicate everything anyone could ever want to know about you and how incredibly marvelous you are—your hobbies, your resume, your picture, things you've done.

- ☐ **Hobbies or Special Interests.** A Web document could contain information about a particular topic or hobby or something you're interested in; for example, music, Star Trek, motorcycles, cult movies, hallucinogenic mushrooms, or upcoming concerts in your city.

- ☐ **Publications.** Newspapers, magazines, and other publications lend themselves particularly well to the Web, and they have the advantage of being more immediate and easier to update than their print counterparts.

☐ **Company Profiles.** This could offer information about what a company does, where it is located, job openings, data sheets, white papers, marketing collateral, who to contact; such a page might even present demonstration software, if that's what the company does.

☐ **Online Documentation.** The term online documentation can refer to everything from quick reference cards to full reference documentation to interactive tutorials or training modules. And it doesn't have to refer to product documentation; anything task-oriented (changing the oil in your car, making a souffle, creating landscape portraits in oil) could be described as online documentation.

☐ **Shopping Catalogs.** If your company offers items for sale, making your lists available on the Web is a quick and easy way to let your customers know what you have available and your prices—and if prices change, you can just update your Web documents to reflect that. With interactive forms you can even let your readers order your product online, although it would be best to wait for browsers with better security features before asking for someone's credit card number over the net—it's too easy for unscrupulous individuals to pick up the account number in transit from the customer's site to yours.

☐ **Polling and Opinion Gathering.** Interactivity and forms on the Web allow you to get feedback on nearly any topic from your readers, including opinion polls, suggestion boxes, comments on your Web pages or your products, and so on.

☐ **Anything Else that Comes to Mind.** Hypertext fiction, online toys, media archives, collaborative art...anything!

The Web is limited only by what you want to do with it. In fact, if what you want to do with it isn't in this list, or seems especially wild or half-baked, then that's an excellent reason to try it. The most interesting Web pages out there are the ones that stretch the boundaries of what the Web is supposed to be capable of.

If you really have no ideas of what to put up on the Web, then don't feel that you have to stop here, put this book away, and come up with something before continuing. Maybe by reading through this book you'll get some ideas (and this book will be useful even if you don't have ideas). I've personally found that the best way to come up with ideas is to spend an afternoon browsing on the Web itself and exploring what other people have done.

Set Your Goals

What do you want people to be able to accomplish in your presentation? Are they looking for specific information on how to do something? Are they going to read through each page in turn, going on only when they're done with the page they're on? Are they just

going to start at your home page and wander aimlessly around, exploring your "world" until they get bored and go somewhere else?

As an exercise, come up with a list of several goals that your readers might have for your Web pages. The clearer your goals, the better.

For example, say you were creating a Web presentation describing the company you work for. Some people reading that presentation may want to know about job openings. Others may want to know where you're actually located. Still others may have heard that your company makes technical white papers available over the Net and they want to download the most recent version of a particular one. Each of these is a valid goal, and you should list each one.

For a shopping catalog Web presentation, you might only have a few goals: to allow you readers to browse the items you have for sale by name or by price, and to order specific items once they're done browsing.

For a personal or special interest home page you may have only a single goal: to allow your reader to browse and explore the information you've provided.

The goals do not have to be lofty ("this Web presentation will bring about world peace") or even make much sense to anyone except you, but coming up with goals for your Web documents equips you to design, organize, and write your Web pages specifically to reach those goals, and helps you resist the urge to obscure your content with extra information.

Break Up Your Content into Main Topics

With your goals in mind, now try to organize the content you have into main topics or sections, chunking related information together under a single topic. Sometimes the goals you came up with in the previous section and your list of topics will be closely related; for example, if you're putting together a Web page for a bookstore, the goal of being able to order books fits nicely under a topic called, appropriately, "Ordering Books."

You don't have to be exact at this point in development; your goal here is just to try to come up with an idea of *what*, specifically, you'll be describing in your Web pages. You can organize things better later, as you write the actual pages.

For example, say you were designing a Web presentation about how to tune your car. This is a simple example, since tune-ups consist of a concrete set of steps that fit neatly into topic headings. In this example, your topics might be

- [ ] Change the oil and oil filter
- [ ] Check and adjust engine timing
- [ ] Check and adjust valve clearances
- [ ] Check and replace the spark plugs
- [ ] Check fluid levels, belts, and hoses

Don't worry about the order of the steps, or how you're going to get your reader to go from one section to another. Just list the things you want to describe in your presentation.

How about a less task-oriented example? Say you wanted to create a set of Web pages about a particular rock band because you're a big fan and you're sure there are other fans out there who would benefit from your extensive knowledge of the band. Your topics might be

- [ ] The history of the band
- [ ] Biographies of each of the band members
- [ ] A "discography"—all the albums and singles the band has released
- [ ] Selected lyrics
- [ ] Images of album covers
- [ ] Information about upcoming shows and future products

You can come up with as many topics as you want, but try to keep each topic reasonably short; if a single topic seems too large, try to break it up into subtopics. If you have too many small topics, try to group them together into some sort of more general topic heading. For example, if you were creating an online encyclopedia of poisonous plants, having individual topics for each plant would be overkill; you could just as easily group each plant name under a letter of the alphabet (A, B, C, and so on) and use each letter as a topic. That's assuming, of course, that your readers will be looking up information in your encyclopedia alphabetically. If they want to look up poisonous plants using some other method, then you would have to come up with different topics.

Your goal is to have a set of topics that are roughly the same size and that group together related bits of the information you have to present.

Ideas for Organization and Navigation

At this point you should have a good idea about what you want to talk about, and a list of topics. The next step is to actually start structuring the information you have into a set of Web pages. But before you do that, consider some "standard" structures that have been used in other help systems and online tools. This section describes some of those structures, their various features, and some important considerations, including

- [ ] The kinds of information that work well for each structure
- [ ] How readers find their way through the content of each structure type to find what they need
- [ ] How to make sure readers can figure out where they are within your documents (context) and find their way back to a known position

Think, as you read this section, how your information might fit into one of these forms, or how you can combine these forms to create a new structure for your Web presentation.

Note: Many of the forms I describe in this section were drawn from a book called *Designing and Writing Online Documentation* by William K. Horton (John Wiley & Sons, 1990). Although Horton's book was written primarily for technical writers and developers working specifically with online help systems, it's a great book for ideas on structuring documents and for dealing with hypertext information in general. If you start doing a lot of work with the Web, you might want to pick up this book; it provides a lot of insight beyond what I have to offer.

Hierarchies

Probably the easiest and most logical way to structure your Web documents is in a hierarchical or menu fashion, illustrated in Figure 2.3. Hierarchies and menus lend themselves especially well to online and hypertext documents. Most online help systems, for example, are hierarchical. You start with a list or menu of major topics; selecting one leads you to a list of subtopics, which then leads you to discussion about a particular topic. Different help systems have different levels, of course, but most follow this simple structure.

In a hierarchical organization, it is easy for readers to know their position in the structure; choices are to move up for more general information, or down for more specific information. Providing a link back to the top level enables your reader to get back to some known position quickly and easily.

In hierarchies, the home page provides the most general overview to the content below it and defines the main links for the pages further down in the hierarchy.

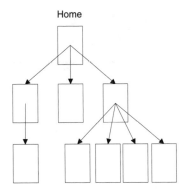

Figure 2.3. *Hierarchical organization.*

For example, a Web presentation about gardening might have a home page with the topics shown in Figure 2.4.

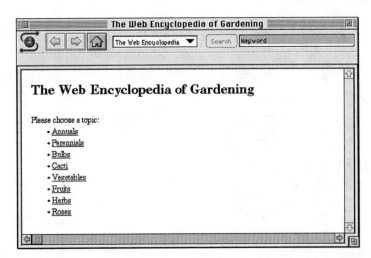

Figure 2.4. *Gardening home page.*

If you selected Fruits, you would then be linked "down" into the hierarchy to a page about fruits (Figure 2.5). From there you can go back to the home page or select another link and go further down into more specific information about particular fruits.

Selecting Soft Fruits takes you to yet another menu-like page, where you have still more categories to choose from (Figure 2.6). From there you can go up to Fruits, back to the home page, or down to one of the choices in this menu.

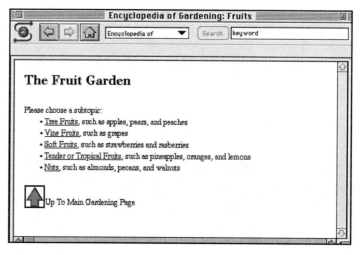

Figure 2.5. *Fruits.*

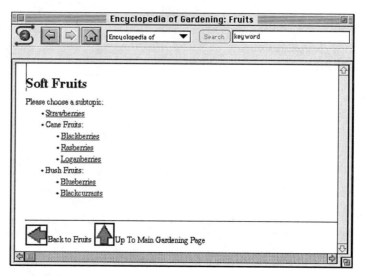

Figure 2.6. *Soft fruits.*

Note that each level has a consistent interface (up, down, back to index), and that each time you have a limited set of choices for basic navigation. Hierarchies are structured enough that the chance for getting lost is minimal (especially with clues about where "up" is; for example, a link that says "Up to Soft Fruits" as opposed to just "Up"). Additionally, if you organize each level of the hierarchy and avoid overlap between topics (and the

content you have lends itself to a hierarchical organization), hierarchies can be easy to traverse to find particular bits of information. If that was one of your goals for your readers, using a hierarchy may work particularly well.

Avoid including too many levels and too many choices, however, as you can easily annoy your reader. Too many menu pages results in "voice mail syndrome"; after having to choose from too many menus you forget what it was you originally wanted, and you're too annoyed to care. Try to keep your hierarchy two to three levels deep, combining information on the pages at the leaf nodes of the hierarchy if necessary.

Linear

Another way to organize your documents is to use a linear or sequential organization, much like printed documents are written. In a linear structure, illustrated in Figure 2.7, the home page is the title, or introduction, and each page follows sequentially from that structure. In a strict linear structure, there are links that move from one page to another, typically forward and back. You may also want to include a link to "Home" that takes you quickly back to the first page.

Context is generally easy to figure out in a linear structure simply because there are so few places to go.

Home

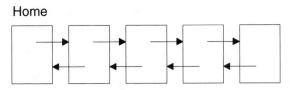

Figure 2.7. *Linear organization.*

A linear organization is very rigid and limits both the freedom that your readers have to explore and that you have to present your information. Linear structures are good for putting material online that has a very linear structure offline (such as short stories, step-by-step instructions, or computer-based training), or when you explicitly want to prevent your reader from skipping around.

For example, consider teaching someone how to make cheese using the Web. Cheese-making is a complex process that involves several steps that must be followed in a specific order.

Describing this process using Web pages lends itself to a linear structure rather well. When navigating a set of Web pages on this subject, you would start with the home page, which might have a summary or an overview of the steps to follow; then using the links for "forward," move on to the first step, "Choosing the Right Milk"; to the next step, "Setting and Curdling the Milk"; all the way through to the last step, "Curing and Ripening the Cheese." If you needed to review at any time, you could use the link for "back." Since the process is so linear, there would be little need for links that branch off from the main stem or links that join together different steps in the process.

Linear with Alternatives

You can improve the rigidity of a linear structure by allowing the reader to deviate from the main path. For example, you could have a linear structure that has alternatives that branch out from a single point in the main branch. (See Figure 2.8.) The branches can then rejoin the main branch at some point further down, or they can continue down that separate track until they reach an "end."

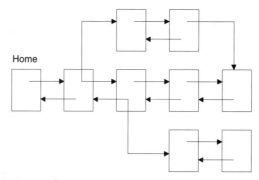

Figure 2.8. *Linear with alternatives.*

For example, say you had an installation procedure for a software package that was similar in most ways, except for one step, which uses different procedures depending on the system the software is being installed on. At that point in the linear installation, you could branch out to cover each system, as shown in Figure 2.9.

After the system-specific part of the installation, you could then link back to the original branch and continue on with the generic installation.

In addition to branching from a linear structure, you could also provide links that allow readers to skip forward or back in the chain if they need to review a particular step or if they already understand some content. (See Figure 2.10.)

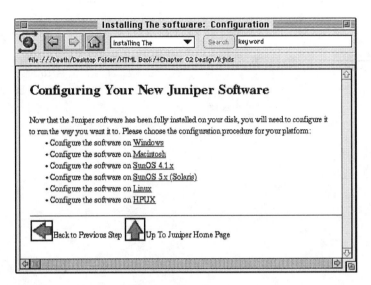

Figure 2.9. *Different steps for different systems.*

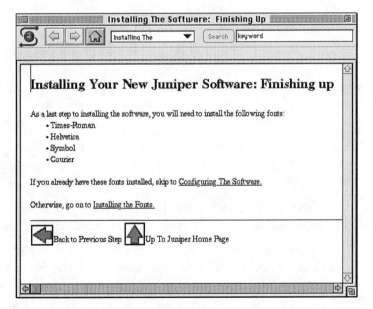

Figure 2.10. *Skip ahead or back.*

Combination of Linear and Hierarchical

A popular form of document organization on the Web is a combination of a linear structure and a hierarchical one, shown in Figure 2.11. This structure occurs most often when very structured but linear documents are put online; the popular FAQ (Frequently Asked Questions) files use this structure.

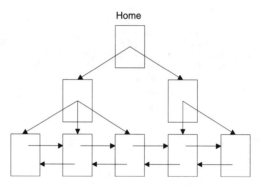

Figure 2.11. *Combination of linear and hierarchical.*

The combination of linear and hierarchical documents works well as long as there are appropriate clues regarding context. Because the reader can either move up and down OR forward and back, it's easy to lose one's mental positioning in the hierarchy when one crosses hierarchical boundaries by moving forward or back.

For example, say you were putting the Shakespearean play *Macbeth* online as a set of Web pages. In addition to the simple linear structure that the play provides, you could create a hierarchical table of contents and summary of each act linked to appropriate places within the text, something like that shown in Figure 2.12.

Because this is both a linear and hierarchical structure, on each page of the script you provide links to go forward, back, return to beginning, and up. But what is the context for going up?

If you've just come down into this page from an Act summary, the context makes sense. "Up" means go back to the summary you just came from.

But say you went down from a summary, and then went forward, crossing an act boundary (say from Act 1 to Act 2). Now what does "up" mean? The fact that you're moving up to a page that you may not have seen before is disorienting given the nature of what the reader expects from a hierarchy. Up and down are supposed to be consistent.

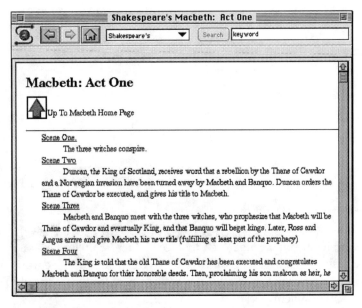

Figure 2.12. *Macbeth hierarchy.*

Consider two possible solutions:

- [ ] Do not allow "forward" and "back" links across hierarchical boundaries. In this case, in order to read from Act 1 to Act 2 in *Macbeth*, you would have to move up in the hierarchy and then back down into Act 2.

- [ ] Provide more context in the link text. Instead of just "Up" or an icon for the link that moves up in the hierarchy, include a description of what you're moving up to.

Web

A web is a set of documents with little or no actual overall structure; the only thing tying each page together is a link. (See Figure 2.13.) The reader drifts from document to document, following the links around.

Web structures tend to be free-flowing and allow the reader to wander aimlessly through the content. Web structures are excellent for content that is intended to be meandering or unrelated, or when you want to encourage browsing. The World Wide Web itself is, of course, a giant web structure.

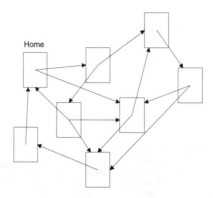

Figure 2.13. *A web structure.*

An example of content organized in a web structure might be a set of virtual "rooms" created using Web pages. If you've ever played an old text-adventure game like Zork or Dungeon, or if you've used a MUD (Multi-User Dungeon), you are familiar with this kind of environment.

Designed in the context of a Web presentation, the environment is organized so that each page is a specific location (and usually contains a description of that location), and from that location you can "move" in several different directions, exploring the environment much in the way you would move from room to room in a building in the real world (and getting lost just as easily). For example, the initial home page might look something like what's shown in Figure 2.14.

From that page you can then explore one of the links, say, to go into the building, which would take you to the page shown in Figure 2.15.

Each room has a set of links to each "adjacent" room in the environment. By following the links, you can explore the rooms in the environment.

The problem with web organizations is that it's too easy to get lost in them—just as you might in the "world" you were exploring in the example. Without any overall structure to the content, it's difficult to figure out the relationship between where you are and where you're going, and, often, where you've been. Context is difficult, and often the only way to find your way back out of a Web structure is to retrace your steps. Web structures can be extremely disorienting and immensely frustrating if your reader has a specific goal in mind.

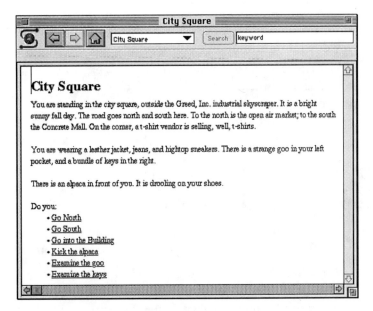

Figure 2.14. *The home page for a Web-based virtual environment.*

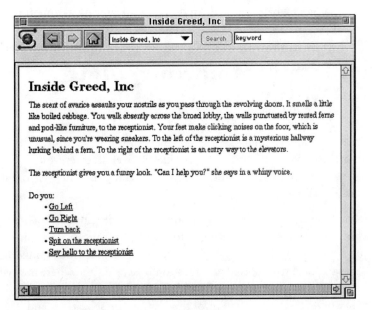

Figure 2.15. *Another page in the Web environment.*

To solve the problem of disorientation, you can use clues on each page. Two ideas:

☐ Provide a way out. "Return to home page" is an excellent link.

☐ Include a map of the overall structure on each page, with a "you are here" indication somewhere in the map. It doesn't have to be an actual visual map, but providing some sort of context will go a long way towards preventing your readers from getting lost.

Storyboarding Your Web Presentation

The next step in planning your Web presentation is to figure out what content goes on what page, and to come up with some simple links for navigation between those pages.

If you're using one of the structures described in the previous section, much of the organization may arise from that structure, in which case this section will be easy. If you want to combine different kinds of structures, however, or if you have a lot of content that needs to be linked together in sophisticated ways, sitting down and making a specific plan of what goes where will be incredibly useful later on as you develop and link each individual page.

What Is Storyboarding and Why Do I Need It?

Storyboarding a presentation is a concept borrowed from filmmaking in which each scene and each individual camera shot is sketched and roughed out in the order in which it occurs in the movie. Storyboarding provides an overall structure and plan to the film that allows the director and his staff to have a distinct idea of where each individual shot fits into the overall movie.

The storyboarding concept works quite well for developing Web pages as well. The storyboard provides an overall rough outline of what the presentation will look like when it's done, including which topics go on which pages, the primary links, maybe even some conceptual idea of what sort of graphics you'll be using and where they will go. With that representation in hand, you can develop each page in turn without trying to remember exactly where that page fits into the overall presentation and its often complex relationships among other pages.

In the case of really large sets of documents, such a representation allows different people to develop different portions of the same Web presentation. With a clear storyboard, you can minimize duplication of work and reduce the amount of contextual information each individual person needs to remember.

For smaller or simpler Web presentations, or presentations with a simple logical structure, storyboarding may be unnecessary. But for larger and more complex projects, the existence of a storyboard can save enormous amounts of time and frustration. If you can't keep all the parts of your content and their relationships in your head, consider doing a storyboard.

So what does a storyboard for a Web presentation look like? It can be as simple as a couple of sheets of paper, each one representing a page, with a list of topics that each page will describe and some thoughts about the links that page will include. I've seen storyboards for very complex hypertext systems that involved a really large bulletin board, index cards, and string. Each index card had a topic written on it, and the links were represented by string tied on pins from card to card. (See Figure 2.16.)

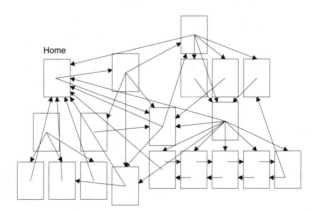

Figure 2.16. *A complex storyboard.*

The point of a storyboard is that it organizes your Web pages in a way that works for you. If you like index cards and string, work with it. If a simple outline on paper or on the computer works better, use that instead.

Hints for Storyboarding

Some things to think about when developing your storyboard:

☐ Which topics will go on each page?

A simple rule of thumb is to have each topic represented by a single page. But if you have a large number of topics, maintaining and linking them can be a daunting task. Consider combining smaller, related topics onto a single page instead. But don't go overboard and put everything on one page; your reader still has to download your document over the Net. It's better to have several medium-sized pages (say, the size of two to ten pages in your word processor) than to have one monolithic page or hundreds of little tiny pages.

☐ What are the primary forms of navigation between pages?

What links will you need for your reader to navigate from page to page? These are the main links in your document that allow your reader to accomplish the goals you defined in the first section. Links for forward, back, up, down, or home all fall under the category of primary navigation.

☐ What alternative forms of navigation are you going to provide?

In addition to the simple navigation links, some Web presentations contain extra information that is parallel to the main Web content, such as a glossary of terms, an alphabetical index of concepts, or a credits page. Consider these extra forms of information when designing your plan and think about how you are going to link them into the main content.

☐ What will you put on your home page?

Since the home page is the starting point for the rest of the information in your presentation, consider what sort of information you're going to put on the home page. A general summary of what's to come? A list of links to other topics?

☐ Review your goals.

As you design the framework for your Web presentation, keep your goals in mind, and make sure you are not obscuring your goals with extra information or content.

Summary

Designing a Web presentation, like designing a book outline, a building plan, or a painting, can sometimes be a complex and involved process. Having a plan before beginning can help you keep the details straight and help you develop the finished

product with fewer false starts. In this chapter, you've learned how to put together a simple plan and structure for creating a set of Web pages, including

☐ Deciding what sort of content to present

☐ Coming up with a set of goals for that content

☐ Deciding on a set of topics

☐ Organizing and storyboarding the presentation

With that plan in place, you can now move on to the next few chapters and learn the specifics of how to write individual Web pages, create links between them, and add graphics and media to enhance the presentation for your audience.

Q&A

Q This all seems like an awful lot of work. All I want to do is do something simple, and you're telling me I have to have goals and topics and storyboards.

A If you are doing something simple, then no, you won't need to do much, if any, of the stuff I recommend in this chapter. But once you're talking about two or three interlinked pages or more, it really helps to have a plan before you start. If you just dive in you may discover that keeping everything straight in your head is a daunting task. And the result may not be what you expected, making it difficult for people to get the information that they need out of your presentation, and difficult for you to reorganize it so that it makes sense. Having a plan before you start can't hurt, and it may save you time in the long run.

Q You've talked a lot in this chapter about organizing topics and pages, but you've said nothing about the design and layout of individual pages.

A I discuss that later in this book, after you've learned more about the sorts of layout HTML (the language Web pages are written in) is capable of, and the stuff that it just can't do. There's a whole chapter and more about page layout and design on Day Five: Chapter 9, "Writing and Designing Web Pages: Do's and Don'ts."

Q What if I don't like any of the basic structures you talked about in this chapter?

A Then design your own. As long as your readers can find what they want to find or do what you want them to be able to do, there are no rules that say you MUST use a hierarchy or a linear structure. I only presented those structures as potential ideas for organizing your Web pages.

DAY
2

3

Begin with the Basics

So after yesterday, with lots of text to read and digest, you're probably wondering when you're actually going to get to write an actual Web page.

Welcome to Day 2! Today you'll learn about HTML, the language WWW hypertext documents are written in, and specifically about the following things:

- [ ] What HTML is and why you have to use it
- [ ] What you can and cannot do when you design HTML documents
- [ ] HTML tags: what they are and how to use them
- [ ] Tags for overall document structure: <HTML>, <HEAD>, <BODY>
- [ ] Tags for titles and headings, and paragraphs: <TITLE>, <H1>...<H6>, <P>
- [ ] Tags for comments

What HTML Is...and What It Isn't

Before you dive into actually writing some HTML, you should know what HTML is, what it can do, and most specifically what it can't do.

HTML stands for HyperText Markup Language. HTML is based on SGML (the Standard Generalized Markup Language), which is used to describe the general structure of various kinds of documents. It is not a page description language like PostScript, nor is it a language that can be easily generated from your favorite page layout program. The focus of HTML is the content of the document, not its appearance. This section explains a little bit more about that.

HTML Describes the Structure of a Document

HTML, by virtue of its SGML heritage, is a language for describing *structured documents*. The theory behind this is that most documents have common elements—for example, titles, paragraphs, or lists—and if you define a set of elements that a document has before you start writing, you can label those parts of the document with the appropriate names. (See Figure 3.1.) After you've labeled a document in terms of its structure, you can write tools that do things like automatic indexing, or footnotes, or cross-references.

If you've worked with word processing programs that use style sheets (such as Microsoft Word) or paragraph catalogs (such as FrameMaker), then you've done something similar; each section of text conforms to one of a set of styles that are pre-defined before you start working.

A Sample Document

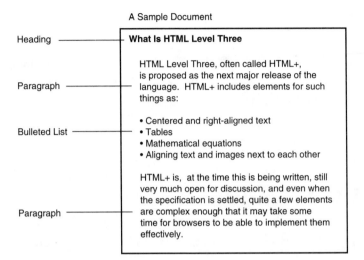

Heading	**What Is HTML Level Three**
Paragraph	HTML Level Three, often called HTML+, is proposed as the next major release of the language. HTML+ includes elements for such things as:
Bulleted List	• Centered and right-aligned text • Tables • Mathematical equations • Aligning text and images next to each other
Paragraph	HTML+ is, at the time this is being written, still very much open for discussion, and even when the specification is settled, quite a few elements are complex enough that it may take some time for browsers to be able to implement them effectively.

Figure 3.1. *Document elements.*

The elements of a document are labeled through the use of HTML tags. It is the tags that describe the document; anything that it not a tag is part of the document itself.

HTML Does Not Describe Page Layout

What style sheets and templates do provide that HTML doesn't is the appearance of each part of the document on the page or screen. For example, styles in Microsoft Word not only have a name ("heading1," for example, for a heading), they also describe the font, the size, and the indentation, among other things, of that heading.

With a few minor exceptions, HTML does not describe the appearance or layout of a document. The designers of HTML did this on purpose. Why? Because if you separate the structure of a document and its appearance, you can then quickly and easily change the appearance of that document without a lot of tinkering. You can format the document in different ways for different audiences or for different purposes (printed or online documents, quick reference cards, help systems). Also, you or the readers of your document can reformat any text on the fly to different styles as desired. All that is needed is a formatting tool that can interpret the tags.

Web browsers, in addition to providing the networking functions to retrieve documents over the Net, are also HTML formatters. When you load an HTML document into a browser such as Mosaic or Lynx, that browser reads, or *parses*, the HTML information and formats the text and images on the screen. If you use different browsers, you may

notice that the same document may appear differently in each browser—the headings may be centered in one, or in a larger font.

This does put a wrinkle in how you write and design your Web documents, however, and it may often frustrate you. The number one prevailing rule of designing documents for the Web, as I mention throughout this book, is this:

> *Do NOT design your documents based on what they look like in one browser. Focus instead on providing clear, well-structured content that is easy to read and understand.*

HTML Is Limited

So now you've realized that you won't be able to do really interesting visual things on the World Wide Web; that someone else is controlling what your document will look like. There's more bad news.

In the current state of HTML, the choices you have for the elements in your document (the tags) are also very limited. There are very few kinds of elements you have to choose from: headings, paragraphs, a few lists are essentially it. You can include images, but you can't align a column of text next to an image. You can't indent text, or center it, or format it into tables.

You also cannot make up your own elements (tags); if you could, how would browsers know how to interpret them?

So the answer is, this is what you're stuck with.

HTML's Advantages (Yes, There Are Some)

Working in a text-only markup language, with little control over the appearance of the text and limited tags to choose from, may seem frustratingly archaic in this age of fully-WYSIWYG desktop publishing. But for the kind of environment that the Web provides, HTML does have advantages over other forms of document publishing language that would include more features and allow you more control. For example:

☐ Each HTML document is small, so it can be transferred over the Net as fast as possible. You don't have to include font or formatting information that would slow down the time it would take to load and display the document.

☐ HTML documents are device-independent. This is a fancy way of saying that they can be displayed on any platform; all you need is a browser for that platform that understands HTML. You don't have to worry about font formats (or font names or whether a font is installed), or display resolutions, or whether you have a color monitor or not. The browser worries about that.

Also, although HTML is a markup language, it is an especially small and simple-to-learn markup language. There are very few tags to memorize, and there are simple editors that can even insert HTML tags into text for you. Other markup or page layout languages (such as the PostScript page description language, or troff on the UNIX system) are much larger and require a lot of initial learning before you can write simple documents. With HTML you can get started right away, as you'll find out later in this chapter.

Will It Get Better?

Yes, it will.

Most browsers available now support what is called HTML Level One—the first version of the HTML specification (consider it to be something like the 1.0 release of a software program). HTML Level One is the base standard for Web documents; a browser must support most, if not all, HTML Level One tags. This book focuses primarily on HTML Level One.

Two other levels of HTML have been proposed: HTML Level Two is similar to HTML Level One, but has additional features to support interactive forms. (You'll learn more about forms in Chapter 13, "Forms and Image Maps.") By the time you read this, most browsers should be able to handle HTML Level Two; many of the more popular browsers support them now.

HTML Level Three, often called HTML+, is proposed as the next major release of the language. HTML+ includes elements for such things as

☐ Centered and right-aligned text
☐ Tables
☐ Mathematical equations
☐ The alignment of text and images next to each other

HTML+ is, at the time this is being written, still very much open for discussion, and even when the specification is settled, quite a few elements are complex enough that it may take some time for browsers to be able to implement them effectively. But the future looks bright for a more flexible and general HTML language.

What HTML Files Look Like

Documents written in HTML are in plain text (ASCII), and contain two things:

☐ The text of the document itself

☐ HTML *tags* that indicate document elements, structure, formatting, and hypertext links to other documents or to included media.

Most HTML tags look something like this:

```
<TheTagName> affected text </TheTagName>
```

The tag name itself (here, `TheTagName`), is enclosed in brackets (<>).

HTML tags generally have a beginning and an ending tag, surrounding the text that they affect. The beginning tag "turns on" a feature (such as headings, bold, and so on), and the ending tag turns it off. Closing tags generally have the tag name preceded by a slash (/).

Not all HTML tags have a beginning and an end. Some tags are only one-sided, and still other tags are "containers" that hold extra information and text inside the brackets. You'll learn about these tags as the book progresses.

All HTML tags are case-insensitive; that is, you can specify them in upper or lower case, or in any mixture. So, `<HTML>` is the same as `<html>` is the same as `<HtMl>`. I like to put my tags in all caps (`<HTML>`) so I can pick them out from the text better. That's how I show them in the examples in this book.

◢▼ Exercise 3.1. Take a look at HTML sources.

Before you actually start writing your own HTML documents, it helps to get a feel for what an HTML document looks like. Luckily, there's plenty of source out there for you to look at—every document that comes over the wire to your browser is in HTML format. (You usually only see the formatted version after the browser gets done with it.)

Most Web browsers have a way of viewing the HTML source of the Web page you're currently looking at. You may have a menu item or a button for View Source or View HTML. In Lynx, the \ (backslash) command toggles between source view and formatted view.

Some browsers do not have the capability to directly view the source of a Web document, but do allow you to save the current page as a file to your local disk. Under a dialog box for saving the file, there may be a menu of formats; for example, Text, PostScript, or HTML. You can save the current page as HTML and then open that file in a text editor or word processor to see the HTML source.

Try going to a typical home page, then viewing the source for that page. For example, Figure 3.2 shows what the normal NCSA Mosaic home page (URL `http://www.ncsa.uiuc.edu/SDG/Software/Mosaic/NCSAMosaicHome.html`) looks like.

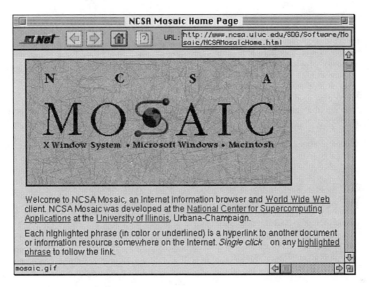

Figure 3.2. *Mosaic home page.*

The HTML source of that page should look something like Figure 3.3.

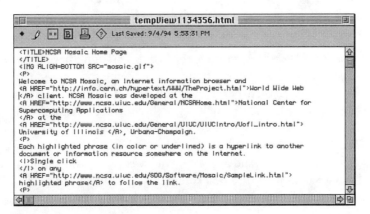

Figure 3.3. *Some HTML source.*

Try viewing the source of your own favorite Web pages. You should start seeing some similarities in the way pages are organized, and get a feel for the kinds of tags that HTML uses. You can learn a lot about HTML by comparing the text on the screen with the source for that text.

Exercise 3.2. Creating an HTML document.

You've seen what HTML looks like—now it's your turn. Let's start with a really simple example so you can get a basic feel for HTML.

To write an HTML document, all you really need is an editor that can write text (ASCII) files. You can use a plain old text editor (for example, TeachText on the Mac or vi on UNIX), or you can use a full-featured word processor, as long as it can save the files as text only, with no control codes or funny characters.

Open up that text editor, and type the following code. You don't have to understand what any of this means at this point; you'll learn about it later in this chapter. This is just a simple example to get you started:

```
<HTML><HEAD>
<TITLE>My Sample HTML Document</TITLE></HEAD>
<BODY>
<H1>This is an HTML Document</H1>
</BODY></HTML>
```

After you create your HTML file, save it to disk—and remember to save it as a text-only file if you're using a word processor. One other thing to note when you save your file: Many HTML browsers use an extension to determine whether the file is an HTML or a plain file. So when you name the file, give it an extension of .html (.htm on DOS systems); for example, `myexample.html` or `homepage.htm`.

Now, start up a Web browser such as Mosaic. You don't have to be connected to the network since you're not going to be opening documents at any other site (although your browser may require you to be on a network; this varies from browser to browser, so give it a try and see what happens). Look in your browser for a menu item or button for Open Local.... (In Lynx simply use the command `lynx myfile.html` from a command line.) The Open Local command (or its equivalent) tells the browser to read in an HTML file from a local disk, parse it, and display it, as if it were a page already out on the Web. Using your browser and the Open Local command, you can write and test your HTML files on your computer in the privacy of your own home.

Try opening up the little file you just created in your browser. You should see something like the picture shown in Figure 3.4.

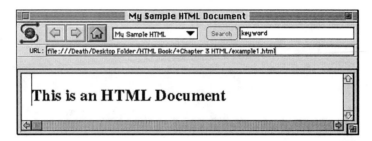

Figure 3.4. *The sample HTML file.*

If you don't see something like what's in the picture, go back into your text editor and make the change. You don't have to quit your browser; just fix the file and save it again under the same name.

Then, in your browser, choose Reload or its equivalent. (In Lynx, it's Control+R.) The browser will read the new version of your file, and voilà, you can edit and preview and edit and preview until you get it right.

A Note About Formatting

When an HTML document is parsed by a browser, any formatting you may have done by hand—that is, any extra spaces, tabs, returns, and so on—are all ignored. The only thing that formats an HTML document is an HTML tag. If you spend hours carefully editing a plain text file to have nicely formatted paragraphs and columns of numbers, but do not include any tags, then when you read the document into an HTML browser, all the text will flow all into one paragraph, and all your work will have been in vain.

Note: There's one exception to this rule: a tag called `<PRE>`. You'll learn about this tag tomorrow in Chapter 5, "Still More HTML."

The advantage of having all white space (spaces, tabs, returns) ignored is that you can put your tags wherever you want to. The following examples all produce the same output. (Try it!)

```
<H1>If music be the food of love, play on.</H1>

<H1>
If music be the food of love, play on.
</H1>
```

```
<H1>
If music be the food of love, play on.                    </H1>

<H1>      If      music     be      the      food     of
love,
play      on. </H1>
```

Programs to Help You Write HTML

You may be thinking that all this tag stuff is a real pain, especially if you didn't get that small example right the first time. (Don't fret about it; I didn't get that example right the first time, and I created it.) You have to remember all the tags. And you have to type them in right and close each one. What a hassle.

There are programs that can help you write HTML. These programs tend to fall into two categories: editors in which you write HTML directly, and converters, which convert the output of some other word processing program into HTML.

Editors

Many freeware and shareware programs are available for editing HTML files. Most of these programs are essentially text editors with extra menu items or buttons that insert the appropriate HTML tags into your text. HTML-based text editors are particularly nice for two reasons: You don't have to remember all the tags, and you don't have to take the time to type them all in.

I discuss some of the available HTML-based editors in Chapter 14, "HTML Assistants: Editors and Converters." For now, if you have an HTML editor, feel free to use it for the examples in this book. If all you have is a text editor, no problem; it just means you'll have to do a little more typing.

What about WYSIWYG editors? The problem is that there's really no such thing as WYSIWYG when you're dealing with HTML, since WYG varies wildly based on the browser that someone is using to read your document. So you could spend hours in a so-called WYSIWYG HTML editor (say, one that makes your documents look just like Mosaic), only to discover that when the output of that editor is read on some other browser, it looks truly awful.

The best way to deal with HTML is not to get too hung up on its appearance. Write clear HTML code and make sure your writing is clear and well-organized, and the appearance will take care of itself.

Converters

In addition to the HTML editors, there are also converters, which take files from many popular word-processing programs and convert them to HTML. This is the closest thing HTML gets to being WYSIWYG; with a simple set of templates, you could write your documents entirely in the program that you're used to, and then convert the result, and almost never have to deal with all this non-WYSIWYG text-only tag nonsense.

In many cases, converters can be extremely useful, particularly for putting existing documents on the Web as fast as possible.

However, converters are in no way an ideal environment for HTML development. What converter programs exist (and most of them are shareware or public domain, with little support) are fairly limited, not necessarily by their own features, but mostly by the limitations in HTML itself. No amount of fancy converting is going to make HTML do things that it can't yet do. If a particular capability doesn't exist in HTML, there's nothing the converter can do to solve that.

The other problem with converters is that even though you can do most of your writing and development in a converter with a simple set of formats and low expectations, you will eventually have to go "under the hood" and edit the HTML text yourself. Most converters do not convert images. No converter that I have seen will automate links to documents out on the Web, although a few do links to related local documents.

In other words, even if you've already decided that you want to do the bulk of your Web work using a converter, you'll need to know HTML anyhow. So press onward; there's not that much to learn.

Structuring Your HTML

HTML defines three tags that are used to describe the document's overall structure and provide some simple "header" information that browsers or HTML parsers can use to figure out what your document is, or to find out simple information about the document (such as its title or who wrote it) before loading the entire thing. The document structure tags don't affect what the document looks like when its formatted; they're only there to help tools that interpret or filter HTML files.

Although a "correct" HTML document will always contain these structure tags, if your document does not contain them, most browsers will be able to read it anyway. However, because it is possible that in the future the document structure tags might become required elements, or that tools may come along that require them, if you get in the habit of including the document structure tags now, you won't have to worry about updating all your files later on.

<HTML>

The first document structure tag in every HTML document is the <HTML> tag, which indicates that the content of this file is in the HTML language.

All the text and HTML commands in your HTML document should go within the beginning and ending HTML tags, like this:

```
<HTML>
...your document...
</HTML>
```

<HEAD>

The <HEAD> tag specifies that the lines within the beginning and ending points of the tag are the prologue to the rest of the file. There are generally only a few tags that go into the <HEAD> portion of the document (most notably, the document title, described below). You should never put any of the text of your document into the header.

Here's a typical example of how you would properly use the <HEAD> tag (you'll learn about </TITLE> later):

```
<HTML>
<HEAD>
<TITLE>This is the Title.</TITLE>
</HEAD>
....
</HTML>
```

<BODY>

The remainder of your HTML document, including all the text and other content (links, pictures, and so on) is enclosed within a <BODY> tag. In combination with the <HTML> and <HEAD> tags, this looks like this:

```
<HTML>
<HEAD>
<TITLE>This is the Title. It will be explained later on</TITLE>
</HEAD>
<BODY>
....
</BODY>
</HTML>
```

The Title

Each HTML document needs a title. To give a document a title, use the `<TITLE>` HTML tag. `<TITLE>` tags always go inside the document header (the `<HEAD>` tags), and describe the contents of the page, like this:

```
<HTML>
<HEAD>
<TITLE>The Lion, The Witch, and the Wardrobe</TITLE>
</HEAD>
<BODY>
...
</BODY>
</HTML>
```

You can only have one title in the document, and that title can only contain plain text; that is, there shouldn't be any other tags inside the title.

When you pick a title, try to pick one that is both short and descriptive of the content on the page. Additionally, your title should also be relevant out of context. If someone browsing on the Web followed a random link and ended up on this page, or if they found your title in a friend's browser history list, would they have any idea what this page is about? You may not intend the page to be used independently of the documents you specifically linked to it, but because anyone can link to any page at any time, be prepared for that consequence and pick a helpful title.

Additionally, because many browsers put the title in the title bar of the window, you may have a limited number of words available. (Although the text within the `<TITLE>` tag can be of any length, it may be cut off by the browser when it's displayed.) Here are some other examples of good titles:

```
<TITLE>Poisonous Plants of North America</TITLE>

<TITLE>Image Editing: A Tutorial</TITLE>

<TITLE>Upcoming Cemetery Tours, Summer 1995</TITLE>

<TITLE>Installing The Software: Opening the CD Case</TITLE>

<TITLE>Laura Lemay's Awesome Home Page</TITLE>
```

And some not-so-good titles:

```
<TITLE>Part Two</TITLE>

<TITLE>An Example</TITLE>

<TITLE>Nigel Franklin Hobbes</TITLE>

<TITLE>Minutes of the Second Meeting of the Fourth Conference of the Committee
for the Preservation of English Roses, Day Four, After Lunch</TITLE>
```

```
<TITLE>Poisonous Plants of North America</TITLE>
```

The title is displayed in the window's title bar

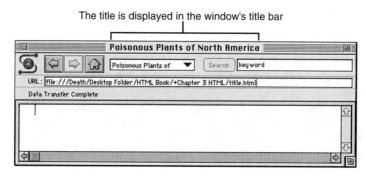

Figure 3.5. *The output in Mosaic.*

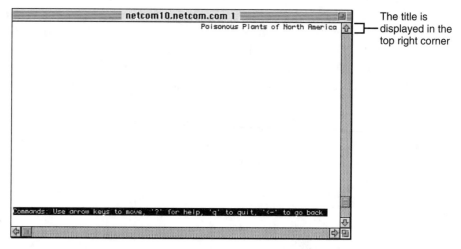

The title is displayed in the top right corner

Figure 3.6. *The output in Lynx.*

Headings

Headings are used to divide sections of text, just like this book is divided. ("Headings," above, is a heading.) HTML defines six levels of headings. Heading tags look like this:

```
<H1>Installing Your Safetee Lock</H1>
```

The numbers indicate heading levels (H1 through H6). The headings themselves, when they're displayed, are not numbered; they're displayed either in bigger or bolder text or centered or underlined or in all caps—in some way that makes them stand out from regular text.

Think of the headings as though they were items in an outline; if the text you're writing about has a structure, use the headings to indicate that structure, as shown in the next code lines. (Note that here I've indented the headings in this example to show the hierarchy better. They don't have to be indented in your document, and, in fact, the indenting will be ignored by the browser.)

```
<H1>Engine Tune-Up</H1>
    <H2>Change The Oil</H2>
    <H2>Adjust the Valves</H2>
    <H2>Change the Spark Plugs</H2>
        <H3>Remove the Old Plugs</H3>
        <H3>Prepare the New Plugs</H3>
            <H4>Remove the Guards</H4>
            <H4>Check the Gap</H4>
            <H4>Apply Anti-Seize Lubricant</H4>
            <H4>Install the Plugs</H4>
    <H2>Adjust the Timing<H2>
```

Note that unlike titles, headings can be any length you want them to be, including lines and lines of text (although because headings are emphasized, having lines and lines of emphasized text may be tiring for your reader).

It's a common practice to use a first-level heading at the top of your document to either duplicate the title (which is usually displayed elsewhere), or to provide a shorter or less contextual form of the title. For example, if you had a page that showed several examples of folding bedsheets, part of a long document on how to fold bedsheets, the title might look something like this:

```
<TITLE>How to Fold Sheets: Some Examples</TITLE>
```

The top-most heading, however, might just say:

```
<H1>Examples</H1>
```

Don't use headings to do boldface, or to make certain parts of your document stand out more. Although it may look cool on your browser, you don't know what it'll look like when other people use their own browsers to read your document (and, in fact, it may look really stupid).

Also, it's a good idea to use headings hierarchically; that is, to start your document with a first-level heading and to use the headings in order. Don't skip levels. If you follow a first-level head with a fourth-level head, for example, readers will probably wonder what

happened to the second and third level headings in between. Even though you may prefer the look of certain headings in certain places in your browser, they may look entirely different and be confusing to someone else using another browser.

```
<H1>Engine Tune-Up</H1>
    <H2>Change The Oil</H2>
    <H2>Change the Spark Plugs</H2>
        <H3>Prepare the New Plugs</H3>
            <H4>Remove the Guards</H4>
            <H4>Check the Gap</H4>
```

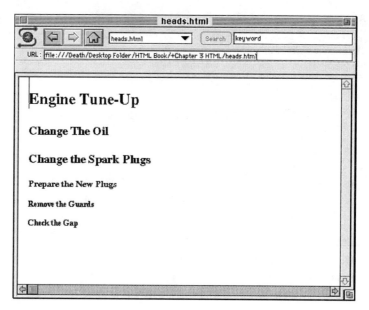

Figure 3.7. *The output in Mosaic.*

```
                    ENGINE TUNE-UP

Change The Oil

Change the Spark Plugs

    PREPARE THE NEW PLUGS

        Remove the Guards

        Check the Gap
```

Figure 3.8. *The output in Lynx.*

Paragraphs

Now that you have a document title and several headings, let's add some ordinary paragraphs to the document.

Unfortunately, paragraphs in HTML are slippery things. Between the three versions of HTML, the definition of a paragraph has changed. The only thing they agree on is that you indicate a plain text paragraph using the <P> tag.

The first version of HTML specified the <P> tag as a one-sided tag. There was no corresponding </P>, and the <P> tag was used to indicate the *end* of a paragraph, not the beginning. So paragraphs in the first version of HTML looked like this:

```
The blue sweater was reluctant to be worn, and wrestled with her as she attempted to
put it on. The collar was too small, and would not fit over her head, and the arm
holes moved seemingly randomly away from her searching hands.<P>
Exasperated, she took off the sweater and flung it on the floor. Then she vindictively
stomped on it in revenge for its recalcitrant behavior.<P>
```

Most browsers that were written at the time of HTML 1 assume that paragraphs will be formatted this way. When they come across a <P> tag, they start a new line and add some extra vertical space between the line they just ended and the one that they just began, as shown in Figure 3.9.

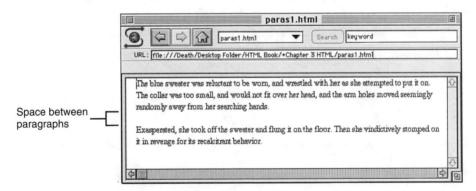

Space between paragraphs

Figure 3.9. *How paragraphs are formatted.*

In the HTML Level two specification and the proposed Level three (HTML+) tags, the paragraph tag has been revised. In these versions of HTML, the paragraph tags are two-sided (<P>...</P>), but <P> indicates the *beginning* of the paragraph. Also, the closing tag (</P>) is optional, presumably to be backwards-compatible with the original version of HTML. So the sweater story would look like this in the newer versions of HTML:

```
<P>The blue sweater was reluctant to be worn, and wrestled with her as she attempted
to put it on. The collar was too small, and would not fit over her head, and the arm
holes moved seemingly randomly away from her searching hands.</P>
<P>Exasperated, she took of the sweater and flung it on the floor. Then she
vindictively stomped on it in revenge for its recalcitrant behavior.</P>
```

The good news is that if you want to use the new version of the paragraph tag (as I do in all the examples throughout this book), most, if not all, browsers will accept it without complaint. (I haven't found any that have a problem with it.)

However, note that because many browsers expect <P> to indicate the *end* of a paragraph, if you use it at the beginning you may end up with extra space in between the first paragraph and the element before it, as shown in Figure 3.10.

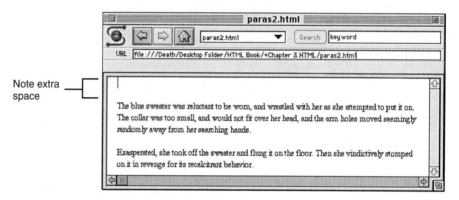

Figure 3.10. *Extra space before paragraphs.*

If this bothers you overly much, you can do one of the following:

- ☐ Go back to the old style of defining paragraphs.
- ☐ Use <P> as a paragraph separator, rather than indicating the beginning or ending of a paragraph.
- ☐ Leave off the first <P> in each set of paragraphs.

Some people like to use <P> tags to pad extra space around other tags to spread out the text on the page. Once again, the cardinal reminder: Design for content, not for appearance. Someone with a text-based browser is not going to care much about the extra space you so carefully put in.

```
<P>The sweater lay quietly on the floor, seething from its ill treatment. It
wasn't its fault that it didn't fit right. It hadn't wanted to be purchased
by this ill-mannered woman</P>
```

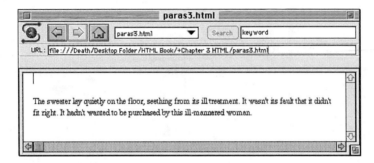

Figure 3.11. *The output in Mosaic.*

```
The sweater lay quietly on the floor, seething from its ill treatment.
It wasn't its fault that it didn't fit right. It hadn't wanted to be
purchased by this ill-mannered woman.
```

Figure 3.12. *The output in Lynx.*

Comments

You can put comments into HTML documents to describe the document itself or to provide some kind of indication of the status of the document; some source code control programs can put document status into comments, for example. Text in comments is ignored when the HTML file is parsed; comments don't ever show up on screen—that's why they're comments. Comments look like this:

```
<!— This is a comment —>
```

Each line should be individually commented, and it's usually a good idea not to include other HTML tags within comments. (Although this practice isn't strictly illegal, many browsers may get confused when they encounter HTML tags within comments and display them anyway.)

Here are some examples:

```
<!— Rewrite this section with less humor —>
<!— Neil helped with this section —>
<!— Go Tigers! —>
```

3

Exercise 3.3. Creating a real HTML document.

At this point, you should know enough to get started creating simple HTML documents: You understand what HTML is, you've been introduced to a handful of tags, and you've even tried browsing an HTML file. You haven't done any links yet, but you'll get to that soon enough, in the next chapter.

This exercise shows you how to create an HTML file that uses the tags you've learned about in this chapter, so you can get a feel for what they look like when they're displayed on-screen and for the sorts of typical mistakes you're going to make. (Everyone makes them, and that's why it's often useful to use an HTML editor that does the typing for you. The editor doesn't forget the closing tags, or leave off the slash, or misspell the tag itself.)

So, create a simple example in that text editor of yours. It doesn't have to say much of anything; in fact, all it needs to include are the structure tags, a title, a couple of headings, and a paragraph or two, Here's an example:

Input
```
<HTML>
<HEAD>
<TITLE>Company Profile, Camembert Incorporated</TITLE>
</HEAD>
<BODY>
<H1>Camembert Incorporated</H1>
"Many's the long night I dreamed of cheese — toasted, mostly." — Robert
Louis Stevenson
<H2>What We Do</H2>
We make cheese. Lots of cheese; more than eight tons of cheese a year. Your
Brie, your Gouda, your Havarti, we make it all.
<H2>Why We Do It</H2>
<P>We are paid an awful lot of money by people who like cheese. So we make
more.</P>
</BODY>
</HTML>
```

Save it to an HTML file, and open it in your browser and see how it came out.

If you have access to another browser on your platform, or on another platform, I highly recommend that you try opening the same HTML file there so you can see the differences in appearance between browsers. Sometimes the differences can surprise you; lines that looked fine in one browser will look strange in another browser.

For example, the cheese factory example looks like Figure 3.13 in NCSA Mosaic (the Macintosh version) and like Figure 3.14 in Lynx.

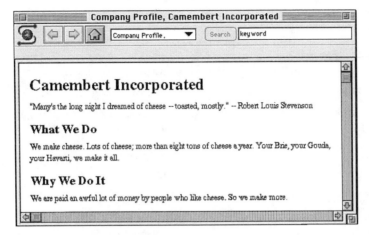

Figure 3.13. *The cheese factory in Mosaic.*

3

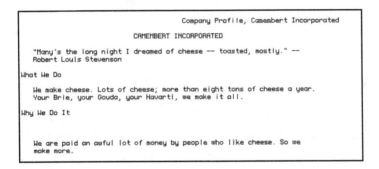

Figure 3.14. *The cheese factory in Lynx.*

See what I mean?

Summary

HTML, a text-only markup language used to describe hypertext documents on the World Wide Web, describes the structure of a document, not its appearance.

In this chapter, you've learned what HTML is and how to write and preview simple HTML files. You've also learned about the HTML tags shown in Table 3.1.

Table 3.1. HTML tags from Chapter 3.

Tag	Use
`<HTML> ... </HTML>`	The entire HTML document
`<HEAD> ... </HEAD>`	The head, or prologue, of the HTML document
`<BODY> ... </BODY>`	All the other content in the HTML document
`<TITLE> ... </TITLE>`	The title of the document
`<H1> ... </H1>`	First-level heading
`<H2> ... </H2>`	Second-level heading
`<H3> ... </H3>`	Third-level heading
`<H4> ... </H4>`	Fourth-level heading
`<H5> ... </H5>`	Fifth-level heading
`<H6> ... </H6>`	Sixth-level heading
`<P>... </P>`	Paragraph
`<!— ... —>`	Comment

Q&A

Q Why was HTML chosen as the language for the WWW when it's so limited?

A At the time, the goal was simply to put hypertext information up on the Net so that it could be easily downloaded and formatted on the fly in a simple, device-independent way. Given those goals, HTML was an ideal language: simple, small, fast to download, and easy to parse. Since then, new features like images and forms and other media have been added. The limitations of HTML didn't become readily apparent until these new browsers and capabilities came along, and more and more people wanted to publish other kinds of information. And it happened so fast!

HTML Level Three should solve many of these limitations. But there's a long way to go yet before HTML allows full control over formatting and layout, simply because of the speed with which it needs to be downloaded over the Net and formatted. If each Web page you viewed took half an hour to load, would you want to read it?

Q Can I do *any* formatting of text in HTML?

A You can do some formatting to strings of characters; for example, making a word or two **bold**. You'll learn about this tomorrow, in Chapter 5.

Q I've noticed in most Web pages that the document structure tags (`<HTML>`, `<HEAD>`, `<BODY>`) aren't often used. Do I really need to include them if pages work just fine without them?

A You don't need to, no. Most browsers will handle plain HTML without the document structure tags. But including the tags will allow your documents to be read by more general SGML tools, and to take advantage of features of future browsers. And, it's the "correct" thing to do if you want your documents to conform to true HTML format.

Q I've seen comments in some HTML files that look like this:

```
<!— this is a comment
>
```

Is that legal?

A That's the old form of comments that was used in very early forms of HTML. Although many browsers may still accept it, you should use the new form (and comment each line individually) in your documents.

4

Putting the Hyper in Hypertext: All About Links

After finishing the last chapter, you have two documents that have some headings and text in them. This is all well and good, but rather boring. The real fun starts when you learn how to do hypertext links and link up all your documents to the Web. This chapter starts you going on creating links. Specifically, you'll learn

☐ All about the HTML link tag (<A>) and its various parts

☐ How to link to other documents on your local disk using relative and absolute path names

☐ How to link to other documents on the Web using URLs

☐ How to organize links in menus and in text so that your readers can find what they need and the links do not distract from the document's content

Creating Links

To create a link in HTML, you need two things:

☐ The name of the file (or the URL of the file) you want to link to

☐ The text that will serve as the "hot spot"—that is, the text that will be highlighted in the browser, which your readers can then select to follow the link

Only the second element is actually visible in your document. When your reader selects the text that points to a link, the browser uses the first element to "jump" to the appropriate document; that is, to retrieve it from the disk or from over the Net, to parse the HTML that document contains (if necessary), and to display it.

The Link Tag: <A>

To create a link in an HTML document, you use the HTML link tag <A>...</A>. The <A> tag is also often called an anchor tag, as it can also be used to create anchors for links. (You'll learn more about creating anchors in Chapter 6, "More About Links and URLs.") The most common use of the link tag, however, is to create links to other documents.

Unlike the simple tags you learned about in the last chapter, the <A> tag has some extra features: the opening tag, <A>, includes both the name of the tag ("A"), and extra information about the link itself. (The extra features are called "attributes" of the tag.) So instead of the opening tag just having a name inside of brackets, it looks something like this:

```
<A NAME="Up" HREF="../menu.html" TITLE="Ostrich Care">
```

The extra attributes (in this example, NAME, HREF, and TITLE) describe the link itself. Most of those parts are only useful for special HTML tools and browsers that can do fancy

things with the links; most of the time you'll be writing the links yourself, so you won't need to use most of them.

The attribute you'll probably use the most often is the HREF attribute, which is probably short for "Hypertext REFerence." (The original HTML documentation doesn't explain what HREF actually means.) The HREF is used to specify the name or URL of the file this link points to.

Like most HTML tags, the link tag also has a closing tag, </A>. All of the text between the opening and closing tags of the link (but not including the link attributes) is the text that will become the actual link on the screen and be highlighted or underlined or blue or red when the Web page is displayed. That's the text you or your reader will click on (or select, in browsers that don't use mice) to jump to the document specified by the HREF attribute.

Figure 4.1 shows the parts of a typical link using the <A> tag, including the HREF, the text of the link, and the closing tag:

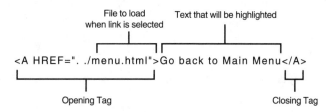

Figure 4.1. *An HTML link using the <A> tag.*

Figure 4.2. *The output in Mosaic.*

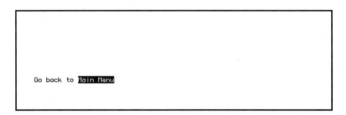

Figure 4.3. *The output in Lynx.*

Exercise 4.1: Link two documents.

Let's go through a really simple example, with two HTML documents on your local disk. You'll need your text editor and a Web browser for this, but since both the documents you'll be fooling with are on your local disk, you won't need to be connected to the network. (Be patient; you'll get to do network stuff in the next section of this chapter.)

First, create two HTML documents, and save them in separate files. Here's the code for the two HTML files I created for this section, which I called menu.html and feeding.html. It really doesn't matter what your two documents look like or what they're called, but make sure you put in your own file names if you're following along with this example.

The first file is called menu.html file, and it looks like this:

```
<HTML>
<HEAD>
<TITLE>How To Care For Your Ostrich</TITLE>
</HEAD><BODY>
<H1>Caring for Your New Ostrich</H1>
<P>Your new ostrich is a delicate and sensitive creature. This document describes how
to care for your ostrich so that he can be a happy and healthy ostrich and give you
hours of fun and friendship.</P>
<P>Feeding Your Ostrich</P>
<P>Grooming Your Ostrich</P>
<P>Cleaning Up After Your Ostrich</P>
<P>Taunting Your Ostrich</P>
</BODY>
</HTML>
```

The list of menu items ("Feeding Your Ostrich," "Grooming Your Ostrich," and so on) will be links to other documents. For now, just type them as regular text; you'll turn them into links later.

Note: The list of menu items would look better on the screen if they were a bulleted list of items or some other menu-like entity. You'll learn how to do lists in the next chapter. For now, individual paragraphs will work fine.

The second file, `feeding.html`, looks like this:

```
<HTML>
<HEAD>
<TITLE>How To Care For Your Ostrich: Feeding Your Ostrich</TITLE>
</HEAD><BODY>
<H1>Feeding Your Ostrich</H1>
<P>This section describes what, how often, and how to feed your ostrich
</P>
<H2>What to Feed Your Ostrich</H2>
Ostriches benefit best from a balanced diet such as that provided by United Bird
Food's Ostrich Kibble 102. We recommend feeding your ostrich a cup of kibbles once a
day, with ample water.
<H2>How to Feed Your Ostrich</H2>
<P>To feed your ostrich, leave the ostrich kibbles in a container by the edge of the
ostrich's pen.</P>
<P>NOTE: Ostriches do not like being watched while eating, and may attack you if you
stand too close. We recommend leaving your ostrich to eat in peace.</P>
<P>Go back to Main Menu</P>
</BODY>
</HTML>
```

Make sure both your files are in the same directory or folder, and if you haven't called them `menu.html` and `feeding.html`, make sure that you take note of the names because you'll need them later.

First, create a link from the menu file to the feeding file. Edit the `menu.html` file, and put the cursor at the line that says `<P>Feeding Your Ostrich</P>`.

Link tags do not define the format of the text itself, so leave in the paragraph tags and just add the link inside the paragraph. First, put in the link tags themselves (the `<A>` and `</A>` tags) around the text that you want to use as the link:

```
<P><A>Feeding Your Ostrich</A></P>
```

Now add the name of the file you want to link to as the HREF part of the opening link tag. Enclose the name of the file in quotes, with an equals sign between HREF and the name. Here I've used `feeding.html`; if you used different files, use a different file name.

```
<P><A HREF="feeding.html">Feeding Your Ostrich</A></P>
```

Note: When you include tags inside other tags, make sure that the closing tag closes the tag that you most recently opened. That is, do this:

```
<P><A> .... </A> </P>
```

Instead of this:

```
<P> <A> ... </P> </A>
```

Some browsers may become confused if you overlap tags in this way, so it's best to always make sure that you close the most recently opened tag first.

Now, start up your browser, select Open Local (or its equivalent), and open the menu.html file. The paragraph that you used as your link should now show up as a link that is in a different color, underlined, or otherwise highlighted. Figure 4.4 shows how it looked when I opened it in the Macintosh version of Mosaic:

Figure 4.4. *The* menu.html *file with link.*

And now, when you click on the link, your browser should load in and display the feeding.html document, as shown in Figure 4.5.

If your browser can't find the file, make sure that the name of the file in the HREF part of the link tag is the same as the name of the file on the disk and that both of the files are in the same directory. Remember to close your link, using the </A> tag, at the end of the text that serves as the link. Also, make sure that you have quotes at the end of the file name (sometimes its easy to forget). All of these things can confuse the browser and make it not find the file or display the link properly.

Now, let's create a link from the feeding document back to the menu. There is a paragraph at the end of the feeding.html document intended for just this purpose:

```
<P>Go back to Main Menu</P>
```

Figure 4.5. *The feeding.html document.*

Add the link tag with the appropriate HREF to that line, like this, where menu.html is the original menu file:

```
<P><A HREF="menu.html">Go back to Main Menu</A></P>
```

Now when you reload the "feeding" file, the link will be active, and you can jump between the menu and the feeding file by selecting those links.

Linking Local Documents: Relative and Absolute Path Names

The example in the previous section shows how to link together documents that are contained in the same folder on your local disk (called, appropriately, *local* documents). This section continues that thread, linking documents that are still on the local disk, but may be contained in different directories on that disk.

When you specify the path name of a file to be linked to as a single filename, within quotes, the browser looks for the listed file in the same directory as the current file, even if that browser is looking at that file over the Net from some faraway place. This is the simplest form of relative path name.

Relative path names can also include directories, or they can point to the path you would take to navigate to that file if you started at the current directory or folder. A path name might include directions, for example, to go up two directory levels, and then go down two other directories to get to the file.

To specify relative path names in links, use UNIX-style path names, regardless of the system you are actually working on. This means that directory or folder names are separated by forward slashes (/), and you use two dots to refer to the directory above the current one (".."). If upper- and lower-case are not relevant on the local system, you don't have to worry about it in the path name, either.

Table 4.1 shows some examples of relative path names and what they mean.

Table 4.1. Relative path names.

Path name	Means
HREF="file.html"	file.html is located in the current directory.
HREF="files/file.html"	file.html is located in the directory (or folder) called file (and the files directory is located in the current directory).
HREF="files/morefiles/file.html"	file.html is located in the morefiles directory, which is located in the files directory, which is located in the current directory.
HREF="../file.html"	file.html is located in the directory (or folder) above the current directory—the same directory the current directory is in.
HREF="../../files/file.html"	file.html is located two directory levels up, in the directory files.

If you're linking files on a personal computer (Mac or PC) and you want to link to a file on a different disk, use the name of the disk as just another directory name in the relative path.

On the Macintosh, the name of the disk is used just as it appears on the disk itself. Assume you have a disk called Hard Disk 2, and your HTML files are contained in a folder called, appropriately, `HTML Files`. If you wanted to link to a file called `jane.html` in a folder called `Public` on a disk called `Jane's Mac`, you would use the following relative path name:

```
HREF="../../Jane's Mac/Public/jane.html"
```

On DOS systems, the disks are referred to by letter, just as you would expect them to be, but instead of being c:, d:, and so on, substitute a vertical bar (|) for the colon (the colon has a special meaning in link path names). So, if the current file is located in `C:\FILES\HTML\`, and you want to link to `D:\FILES.NEW\HTML\MORE\INDEX.HTM`, the relative path name to that file would be:

```
HREF="../../d¦/files.new/html/more/index.htm"
```

Absolute Path Names

You can also specify the link to another document on your local system using an absolute path name. Whereas relative path names point to the document you want to link to by describing its relation to the current document, absolute path names point to the document by starting at the top level of your directory hierarchy and working downward through all the intervening directories to reach the file.

Absolute path names always begin with a slash, which is the way they are differentiated from relative path names. Following the slash are all directories in the path from the top level to the file you are linking to.

> **Note:** "Top" has different meanings depending on how you're publishing your HTML files. If you're just linking to files on your local disk, the "top" is the top of your file system (/ on UNIX, or the disk name on a Mac or PC). When you're publishing files using a Web server, the "top" may or may not be the top of your file system (and generally isn't). You'll learn more about absolute path names and Web servers in Chapter 11, "Putting it All Online."

Table 4.2 shows some examples of absolute path names and what they mean.

Table 4.2. Absolute path names.

Path name	Means
HREF="/u1/lemay/file.html"	file.html is located in the directory /u1/lemay.
HREF="/~lemay/file.html"	file.html is located in the home directory of the user lemay (UNIX systems). (Note that you still need the leading slash.)
HREF="/d¦/files/html/file.html"	file.html is located on the D: disk in the directories files/html (DOS systems).
HREF="/Hard Disk 1/HTML Files/file.html"	file.html is located on the disk Hard Disk 1, in the folder HTML Files (typically a Macintosh).

Should You Use Relative or Absolute Path Names?

To link together your own documents, 99 percent of the time you should use relative path names instead of the absolute path names. Using absolute path names may seem easier for complicated links between lots of documents, but absolute path names are not portable. If you specify your links as absolute path names and you move your files elsewhere on the disk, or rename a directory or a disk listed in that absolute path, then all your links will break and you'll have to laboriously edit all your HTML files and fix them all. Using absolute path names also makes it very difficult to move your files to a Web server when you decide to actually make them available on the Web—and that's what you're reading this book for, isn't it?

Specifying relative path names allows you to move your documents around on your own system and to move them to other systems with little to no file modifications to fix the links. It's much easier to maintain HTML documents with relative path names, so the extra work of setting them initially is often well worth the effort.

Links to Other Documents on the Web

So now you have a whole set of documents, all linked to each other. In some places in your documents, however, you would like to refer to a page somewhere else on the Net; for example, to the Palo Alto Zoo home page for more information on the socialization of ostriches. You can also use the link tag to link to those other documents on the Net, which I'll call *remote* documents.

The HTML code you use to link to documents on the Web looks exactly the same as the code you used for links between local documents. You still use the <A> tag with an HREF attribute, and include some text to serve as the link on your Web page. But instead of a filename or a path in the HREF, use the URL of that document on the Web, as Figure 4.6 shows.

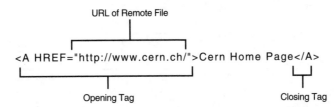

Figure 4.6. *Link to remote files.*

Exercise 4.2: Linking your ostrich pages to the Web.

So let's go back to those two documents you linked together earlier in this chapter, the ones about ostriches. The menu.html file contained several links to other local documents that described how to take care of your ostrich.

Now let's say you want to add a link to the bottom of the menu file to point to the ostrich archives at the Palo Alto Zoo (the world's leading authority on the care of ostriches), whose URL is http://www.zoo.palo-alto.ca.us/ostriches/home.html.

Note: I'm making this all up. Although the city of Palo Alto, California has a Web page (URL `http://www.city.palo-alto.ca.us/home.html`), Palo Alto doesn't have a zoo, and I've never seen any ostriches there. For the purposes of this example, just pretend that there's a Web page for the nonexistent Palo Alto Zoo.

First, add the appropriate text for the link to your menu page:

```
<P>The Palo Alto Zoo has more information on ostriches</P>
```

What if you don't know the URL of the home page for the Palo Alto Zoo (or the document you want to link to), but you do know how to get to it by following several links on several different people's home pages? Not a problem. Use your browser to find the home page for the document you want to link to. (Figure 4.7 shows what the home page for the Palo Alto Zoo might look like, if it existed.)

Figure 4.7. *The Palo Alto Zoo home page.*

Most browsers display the URL of the file they're currently looking at in a box somewhere near the top of the page. This makes it particularly easy for you to link to other

documents; all you have to do is go there with your browser, copy the URL from the window, and paste it into the HTML page you're working on. No typing!

Once you have the URL of the zoo (the URL for that page is in the box in the top corner, and you can usually copy from that box), you can construct a link tag in your menu file and paste the appropriate URL into the link:

```
<P>The <A HREF="http://www.zoo.palo-alto.ca.us/ostriches/home.html">Palo Alto Zoo</A>
has more information on ostriches</P>
```

Of course, if you already know the URL of the page you want to link to, you can just type it into the HREF part of the link, but keep in mind that if you make a mistake that your browser won't be able to find the file on the other end. Most URLs are a little too complex for normal humans to be able to remember them; I prefer to copy and paste whenever I can to cut down on the chances of typing it wrong.

Figure 4.8 shows how the menu.html file, with the new link in it, looks when it is displayed by MacMosaic.

Figure 4.8. *The Palo Alto Zoo link.*

Note that in this link, only some of the text ("Palo Alto Zoo") is serving as the actual link text. The rest of the text is just plain text. This is a common way to specify links; that is, to limit the link text to that which actually describes the link itself. You'll learn about how to write link text in the next section.

Link Text and Organizing Your Links

If you've reached this point, you now know all the technical basics for linking documents together. There are some other details you'll learn about in Chapter 6, such as URLs and creating links to places within documents, but for the most part you can start linking all your documents together and linking them to other Web documents right now.

But before you start doing that, I'd like to talk for a bit about the part of the link tag I haven't mentioned: the actual highlighted text that activates the link.

There are no requirements in HTML for the text you can use for a link. That text can be a single word or an entire paragraph, or even an image, which you'll learn about on Day 4. But be aware that some simple hints on writing and organizing your links will make those links easier to find and use, and keep those links from distracting your reader from the other content on the page.

In particular, I like to follow these simple rules for writing link text:

☐ **Keep the link text short.**

Because links are highlighted on the page, don't overwhelm your Web page by having too big a link. Keep the text that refers to a link short and concise.

☐ **Be descriptive.**

It is possible to create links that are too short; a link is only useful if it tells the reader what they're linking to.

☐ **Use link menus.**

By organizing your links into menus, or lists, you allow your reader to scan the links for the information they need and to find it more easily. Link menus are much easier to scan and read than links embedded in text. The next section talks about link menus.

☐ **If you use links in body text, make those links transparent.**

Body text—that is, text that is arranged in paragraphs—should be just as easily read in hardcopy as it is online. If you put links into body text, word the text such that you don't make the links explicit. "Using Links in Text," later in this chapter, describes links in body text in greater detail.

Using Link Menus

Link menus are links that are arranged in list form or in some other short, easy-to-read and easy-to-understand format. Link menus are terrific for pages that are organized in a hierarchy, for table-of-contents lists of the contents of a document, or for navigation among several documents. Web pages that consist of nothing but links often organize those links in menu form.

The idea of a link menu is that you use short, descriptive terms as the links, with little to no other text directly following the link. (Further description could follow the link on the same line or somehow set off from that text.) Link menus look best in a bulleted or unordered list format, but since you haven't learned how to do that yet in HTML (that's covered tomorrow), just using a set of paragraphs will work fine.

Link menus enable your reader to scan the list of links quickly and easily to find what they're looking for, something that may be difficult to do if you bury your links in body text.

The `menu.html` file for the care and feeding of ostriches was an example of a link menu; each item in the list is itself a link and describes what you'll be linking to. Figure 4.9 shows another example from a list of available browsers (at `http://info.cern.ch/hypertext/WWW/Clients.html`). This example shows how each link is set off in menu form, but also includes some descriptive text explaining what each link is for.

Be Careful of Vague Links

Make sure when you arrange your links into menus that you aren't too short in your descriptions. It's tempting to use menus of filenames or other only slightly descriptive links in menus, like the menu shown in Figure 4.10.

Well, that is a menu of links, and the links are descriptive of the actual document they point to, but they don't really describe that the *content* of that document is. How do readers know what's on the other side of that link, and how can they make a decision about whether they're interested in it or not from the limited information you've given them? Of the three links here, only the last (`pesto.recipe`) gives you a hint about what readers will see when they jump to that file.

A better plan is either to provide some extra text describing the content of the file (Figure 4.11), or to avoid the filenames altogether (who cares?) and just describe the contents of the files in the menu, with the appropriate text highlighted. (See Figure 4.12.)

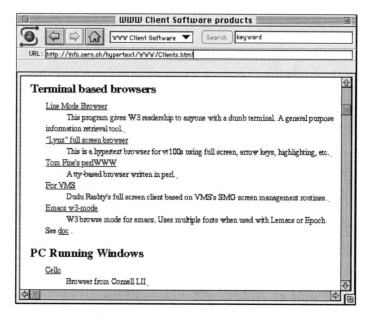

Figure 4.9. *Another link menu.*

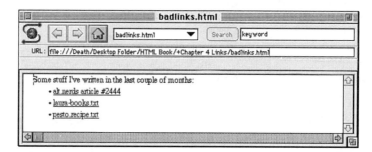

Figure 4.10. *A poor link menu.*

Figure 4.11. *A better link menu.*

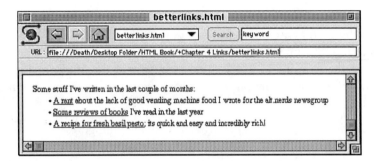

Figure 4.12. *Another better link menu.*

Either one of these forms is better than the first; both give your reader more of a clue of what's on the other side of the link.

Using Links in Text

Instead of putting links on their own lines in menu form, you can also put links directly into paragraphs on the page—to show a footnote-like tangent, for example, or to describe an actual cross-reference to some other document. ("For more information on fainting goats, see The Fainting Goat Primer.") Also, some link menus (like the one shown in Figure 4.14) work better with some extra text, in which some of the words are highlighted as a link. Figure 4.13 shows an example of links in body text. This page is from the documentation for setting up the CERN version of a Web server at `http://info.cern.ch/hypertext/WWW/Daemon/User/Guide.html`.

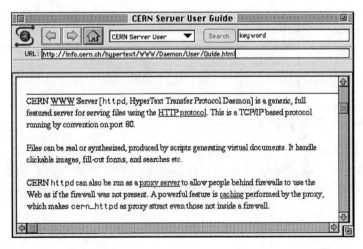

Figure 4.13. *Links in text.*

The best way to provide links in text is to first write the text without the links, and then highlight the appropriate words that point to the linked document. Make sure that you don't interrupt the flow of the document when you include a link. The idea of links in text is that the text should stand on its own, so that the links provide additional or tangential information that your readers can choose to ignore or follow based on their own whims.

Here's another example of using links in text (shown in Figure 4.14), but one in which the text itself isn't overly relevant—it's just there to support the links. If you're using text like this just to describe links, consider using a link menu instead of a paragraph. It'll be easier for your readers to find the information they want; instead of having to read the entire paragraph, they can skim for the links that interest them.

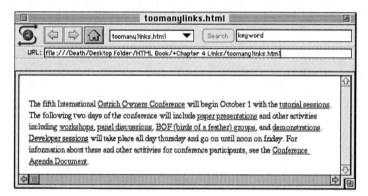

Figure 4.14. *Links in text that don't work well.*

Probably the easiest way to figure out if you're doing links within text properly is to print out the formatted Web page from your browser. In hardcopy, without hypertext, would the paragraph still make sense? If the page reads funny on paper, it'll read funny online as well. Some simple rephrasing of sentences can often help enormously in making the text on your pages more readable and more usable both online and when printed out.

"Here" Syndrome

A common mistake that many Web authors make in creating links in body text is "here" syndrome. "Here" syndrome is the tendency to create links with a single highlighted word ("here"), and to describe the link somewhere else in the text. Here are a couple of examples:

Information about ostrich socialization is contained **here**.

Select **this link** for a tutorial on the internal combustion engine.

Because links are highlighted on the Web page, those links visually "pop out" more than the surrounding text (or "draw the eye" in graphic design lingo). Your reader will see the link first, before reading the text. Try it. Here's a picture of a particularly heinous example of "here" syndrome, in Figure 4.15. Close your eyes, and then open them quickly, pick a "here" at random, and see how long it takes you to find out what the "here" is for.

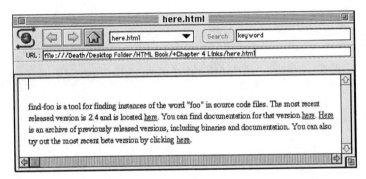

Figure 4.15. *Here syndrome.*

Now try the same thing with a well-organized link menu of the same information, shown in Figure 4.16.

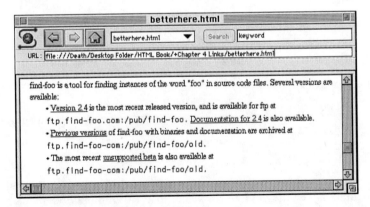

Figure 4.16. *The same page, reorganized.*

Since "here" says nothing about what the link is there for, your poor reader has to search the text before and after the link itself to find out just what is supposed to be Here. In paragraphs that have lots of "here" or other nondescriptive links, it becomes difficult to match up the links with what they are supposed to link to, forcing your reader to work harder to figure things out.

So instead of a link like this:

> Information about ostrich socialization is contained <u>here</u>.

A much better choice of wording would be something like this:

> The Palo Alto Zoo has lots of information about ostrich socialization.

or just

> The Palo Alto Zoo has lots of information about **ostrich socialization.**

Make Links Transparent

Your links should also not broadcast their existence as links when they're used in paragraphs. Here's a link that does just that:

> If you're interested in the text of all patents that have been granted since the beginning of the year, here's a link to the `patent office archives.`

This isn't quite "here" syndrome, since the link text itself is actually descriptive of the link, but you're still telling your reader explicitly that this is a link. This sentence could be reworded such that you can show the link without disrupting the flow of the text:

> `The patent office archives` contain the text of all patents that have been granted since the beginning of the year.

Summary

To create links between documents, you use the `<A>...</A>` tag, called the link or link tag, which has three parts:

1. The tag itself, `<A>...</A>`
2. The `HREF` attribute, which specifies the path name of the file to load (for local documents), or the URL of the file to load (for remote documents)
3. The text in between the opening and closing tags, which is the text that will be highlighted (and able to be selected using a browser) to activate the link

When linking documents that are all stored on the local disk, you can specify their path names as relative or absolute paths. Relative path names indicate the location of the file relative to the current file; absolute path names indicate the location of the file starting from the topmost level of the system (/ on UNIX, a disk name or letter on Macintosh and PC systems).

For local links, relative path names are preferred over absolute path names because they allow those local documents to be moved around more easily to another directory or to another system; if you use absolute path names, your links will break if you change anything in that hard-coded path.

To link to a document on the Web (a remote document), the HREF attribute is the URL of that document. You can easily copy the URL of the document you want to link to by going to that document using your favorite Web browser and then copying and pasting the URL from your browser into the appropriate place in your link tag.

When organizing links in a document, consider using a link menu, a list of documents that your document is linked to. Use short descriptive names for the links, and include extra text describing what the link points to, if necessary.

If you use links in body text, make sure that the text reads well in hard-copy as well as online. Don't refer explicitly to links on text or use the word "here" as the text of a link; use more descriptive phrases instead.

Q&A

Q I put a URL into a link, and it shows up as highlighted in my browser, but when I click on it, the browser says "unable to access document." If it can't find the document, why did it highlight the text?

A The browser highlights text within a link tag whether or not the link is valid. In fact, you can even be not connected to the network and load in a local document full of links and have them all highlighted, even though there's no way to get to them. The only way a you can tell if a link is valid to select it and try to load the document it points to.

As to why the browser couldn't find the document you linked to—make sure you're connected to the network and that you entered the URL into the link correctly. Try opening that URL directly in your browser and see if that works. If directly opening the link doesn't work either, there might be several reasons why. Two common ones are

☐ The server is overloaded or is not on the Net.

4

Machines go down, as do network connections. If a particular URL doesn't work for you, perhaps there's something wrong with the machine or the network. Or maybe its a popular site, and too many people are trying to access it at once. Try again later, or during nonpeak hours for that server. If you know the people who run the server, you can try sending them electronic mail or calling them.

☐ The URL itself is bad.

Sometimes URLs become invalid. Since a URL is a form of absolute path name, if the file to which it refers to moves around, or if a machine or directory name gets changed, the URL itself won't be any good any more. Try contacting the person or site you got the URL from in the first place and see if they have a more recent link.

Q   **Can I put any URL in a link?**

A   You bet. If you can get to a URL using your browser, you can put that URL in a link. Note, however, that some browsers support URLs that others don't. For example, Lynx is really good with mailto URLs (URLs that allow you to send electronic mail to a person's e-mail address); when you select a mailto URL in Lynx, it prompts you for a subject and the body of the message. When you're done, it sends the mail.

Mosaic, on the other hand, can't currently handle mailto URLs, and will insist that a link containing the mailto URL is invalid. The URL itself may be fine, but the browser can't handle it.

Q   **You haven't talked about all the different URLs (mailto, FTP, Gopher, file, WAIS) very much.**

A   You'll learn all about all the different URLs and how to use them in Chapter 6. I have to leave something interesting for the later chapters.

Q   **Can I change the color of the link in HTML?**

A   The color of the link, just like the font and the size of the text on the page, is determined by the browser, not by the HTML code. You can change it in your browser for your documents (see the documentation that came with your browser for more information), but you can't control how the link will look from the HTML side.

Q   **Can I use images as links?**

A   Yup. You'll learn how to do this in Chapter 7, "Including Images on your Web Pages."

DAY
3

5

Still More HTML

Now that you know the basics of laying out HTML pages and linking them together, you are ready to learn more about what HTML can do. This chapter explains most of the remaining tags in the HTML language, including tags to

☐ Create numbered lists, unnumbered lists, and other forms of lists

☐ Format the appearance of individual characters (bold, italic, typewriter)

☐ Include special characters

☐ Create preformatted text (text with spaces and tabs retained)

☐ Create other miscellaneous elements including line breaks, rule lines, addresses, and quotations

In addition, at the end of this chapter, you'll create a complete Web page that uses many of the tags presented in this chapter as well as the information from the previous four chapters.

This chapter covers several tags, and it's all going to be a bit overwhelming. But don't worry about remembering everything now; just get a grasp of what sorts of formatting you can do in HTML and then you can look up the specific tags later.

Things slow down again in the next chapter, so you can catch your breath as you finish the day.

Lists, Lists, and More Lists

In the last chapter, I noted several times that link menus look best in list form, but I didn't explain how to create a list. After working through this section, you'll know not only how to create a list, but how to create five kinds of lists; a list for every occasion!

HTML defines five kinds of lists:

☐ Numbered, or ordered lists, typically labeled with numbers

☐ Unordered, or bulleted lists, typically labeled with bullets or some other symbol

☐ Glossary lists, in which each item in the list has a term and a definition for that term, arranged so that the term is somehow highlighted or drawn out from the text

☐ Menu lists, a list of paragraphs, typically with only one line per paragraph

☐ Directory lists, lists of very short items that can be arranged vertically or horizontally if the browser can handle it

Note: The menu and directory forms of lists are defined by HTML Level One, but are generally considered obsolete in Level Two and Level Three. I explain more about this in the upcoming section about menu and directory lists.

List Tags

All the list tags have common elements:

☐ The entire list is surrounded by the appropriate opening and closing tag for the kind of list (for example, `<OL>` and `</OL>`, or `<MENU>` and `</MENU>`).

☐ Each element within the list has its own tag: `<DT>` and `<DD>` for the glossary lists and `<LI>` for all the other lists.

Although the tags and the list items can appear in any arrangement in your HTML code, I prefer to arrange list code so that the list tags are on their own lines, and each new item also starts on a new line. This makes it easy to pick out the list itself as well as the individual elements. In other words, I find an arrangement like this:

```
<P>Dante's Divine Comedy consists of three books:</P>
<UL>
<LI>The Inferno
<LI>The Purgatorio
<LI>The Paradiso
</UL>
```

easier to read than an arrangement like this:

```
<P>Dante's Divine Comedy consists of three books:</P>
<UL><LI>The Inferno<LI>The Purgatorio<LI>The Paradiso
</UL>
```

even though both result in the same output in the browser.

Numbered Lists

In numbered lists, the elements occur in a particular order; for example, steps to follow to set up a computer or to find the library. Numbered lists are surrounded by the `<OL>`...`</OL>` tags (OL stands for Ordered List), and each item within the list begins with the `<LI>` (List Item) tag.

The <LI> tag is one-sided; you do not have to specify the closing tag. The existence of the next <LI> (or the closing </OL> tag) indicates the end of that item in the list.

When the browser interprets an ordered list, it numbers (and often indents) each of the elements sequentially. You do not have to do the numbering yourself, and if you add or delete items, the browser will renumber them the next time the document is loaded.

```
<P>Laura's Awesome Nachos</P>
<OL>
<LI>Warm up Refried beans with chili powder and cumin.
<LI>Glop refried beans on tortilla chips.
<LI>Grate equal parts Jack and Cheddar cheese, spread on chips.
<LI>Chop one small onion finely, spread on chips.
<LI>Heat under broiler 2 minutes.
<LI>Add guacamole, sour cream, fresh chopped tomatoes, and cilantro.
<LI>Drizzle with hot green salsa.
<LI>Broil another 1 minute.
<LI>Nosh.
</OL>
```

Use numbered lists only when you want to indicate that the elements are ordered; that is, that they must appear or occur in that specific order. If you just want to indicate that something has some number of elements that can appear in any order, use an unordered list instead.

```
<P>To summon the demon, use the following steps:</P>
<OL>
<LI>Draw the pentagram
<LI>Sacrifice the goat
<LI>Chant the incantation
</OL>
```

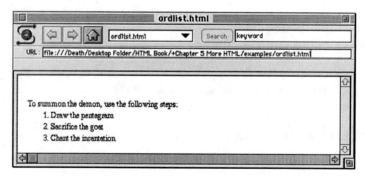

Figure 5.1. *The output in Mosaic.*

```
To summon the demon, use the following steps:
  1. Draw the pentagram
  2. Sacrifice the goat
  3. Chant the incantation
```

Figure 5.2. *The output in Lynx.*

Unordered Lists

Unordered lists are lists in which the elements can appear in any order. Unordered lists look just like ordered lists in HTML, except that the list is indicated using `<UL>....</UL>` tags instead of `OL`. The elements of the list are separated by `<LI>`, just as with ordered lists.

Browsers usually format unordered lists using bullets or with some other symbolic marker; Lynx uses an asterisk (*).

```
<P>Lists in HTML</P>
<UL>
<LI>Ordered Lists
<LI>Unordered Lists
<LI>Menus
<LI>Directories
<LI>Glossary Lists
</UL>
```

```
<P>The three Erinyes, or Furies, were:</P>
<UL>
<LI>Tisiphone
<LI>Megaera
<LI>Alecto
</UL>
```

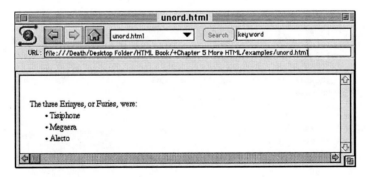

Figure 5.3. *The output in Mosaic.*

```
The three Erinyes, or Furies, were:
   * Tisiphone
   * Megaera
   * Alecto
```

Figure 5.4. *The output in Lynx.*

Menu and Directory Lists

Menus are lists of items or short paragraphs with no bullets or numbers or other label-like things. They are similar to simple lists of paragraphs, except that some browsers may indent them or format them in some way differently from normal paragraphs.

Directory lists are for items that are even shorter than menu lists, and are intended to be formatted by browsers horizontally in columns—like doing a directory listing on a UNIX system.

> **Note:** HTML Level One and Two define menu and directory lists, but the initial draft HTML Level Three does not. (There are other available tags that produce the same effects.) Considering that most browsers seem to format menus and directories in similar ways to the glossary lists (or as unordered lists), and not in the way they are described in the specification, the real state of menu and directory lists as usable elements in the HTML language is unknown. For compatibility with future versions of HTML, it is probably best to stick with the other three forms of lists.

```
<MENU>
<LI>Canto 1: The Dark Wood of Error
<LI>Canto 2: The Descent
<LI>Canto 3: The Vestibule
<LI>Canto 4: Circle One: Limbo
<LI>Canto 5: Circle Two: The Carnal
</MENU>

<DIR>
<LI>files/
<LI>applications/
<LI>mail/
<LI>stuff/
<LI>phone_numbers
</DIR>
```

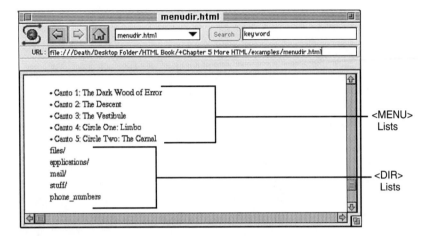

Figure 5.5. *The output in Mosaic.*

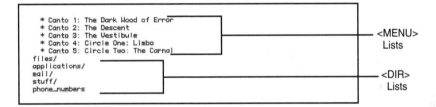

Figure 5.6. *The output in Lynx.*

5

Glossary Lists

Glossary lists, sometimes called definition lists, are slightly different from other lists. Each element of a glossary list has two parts:

☐ A term

☐ That term's definition

Each part of the glossary list has its own tag: `<DT>` for the term, and `<DD>` for its definition. `<DT>` and `<DD>` are both one-sided tags, and they generally occur in pairs, although most browsers can handle single terms or definitions.

The entire glossary list is indicated by the tags `<DL>` ... `</DL>`, in the same way the ordered and unordered tags were used:

```
<DL>
<DT>Basil<DD>Annual. Can grow four feet high; the scent of its tiny white flowers is
heavenly
<DT>Oregano<DD>Perennial. Sends out underground runners and is difficult to get rid of
once established.
<DT>Coriander<DD>Annual. Also called cilantro, coriander likes cooler weather of
spring and fall.
</DL>
```

Glossary lists are generally formatted with the terms and definitions on separate lines, and the left margins of the definitions are indented.

Glossary lists don't have to be used for terms and definitions, of course. They can be used anywhere an indented list is needed. Here's an example:

```
<DL>
<DT>Macbeth<DD>I'll go no more. I am afraid to think of what I have done; look on't
again I dare not.
<DT>Lady Macbeth<DD>Infirm of purpose! Give me the daggers. The sleeping and the dead
are as but pictures. 'Tis the eye if childhood that fears a painted devil. If he do
bleed, I'll gild the faces if the grooms withal, for it must seem their guilt. (Exit.
Knocking within)
<DT>Macbeth<DD>Whence is that knocking? How is't wit me when every noise apalls me?
What hands are here? Ha! They pluck out mine eyes! WIll all Neptune's ocean wash this
blood clean from my hand? No. This my hand will rather the multitudinous seas
incarnadine, making the green one red. (Enter lady Macbeth)
<DT>Lady Macbeth<DD>My hands are of your color, but I shame to wear a heart so white.
</DL>
```

HTML also defines a "compact" form of glossary list in which less white space is used, perhaps by placing the terms and definitions on the same line and highlighting the term, or by lessening the amount of indent used by the definitions.

Note: Most browsers seem to ignore the COMPACT attribute and format compact glossary lists in the same way that normal glossary lists are formatted.

To use the compact form of the glossary list, use the COMPACT attribute inside the opening <DL> tag, like this:

```
<DL COMPACT>
<DT>Capellini<DD>Round and very thin (1-2mm)
<DT>Vermicelli<DD>Round and thing (2-3mm)
<DT>Spaghetti<DD>Round and thin, but thicker than vermicelli (3-4mm)
<DT>Linguine<DD>Flat, (5-6mm)
<DT>Fettucini<DD>flat, 8-10mm)
</DL>
```

```
<DL>
<DT>Basil<DD>Annual. Can grow four feet high; the scent of its tiny white
flowers is heavenly
<DT>Oregano<DD>Perennial. Sends out underground runners and is difficult to
get rid of once established.
<DT>Coriander<DD>Annual. Also called cilantro, coriander likes cooler weather
of spring and fall.
</DL>
```

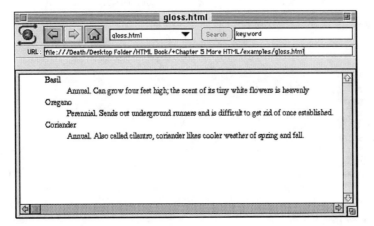

Figure 5.7. *The output in Mosaic.*

5

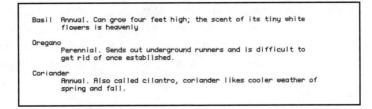

Figure 5.8. *The output in Lynx.*

Nesting Lists

What happens if you put a list inside another a list? This is fine as far as HTML is concerned; just put the entire list structure inside another list as one of its elements. The nested list just becomes another element of the first list, and it is formatted indented from the rest of the list. Lists like this work especially well for menu-like entities in which you want to show hierarchy (for example, in tables-of-contents), or as outlines.

Indenting nested lists in HTML code itself helps show their relationship to the final layout:

```
<OL>
<LI>WWW
<LI>Organization
<LI>Beginning HTML
     <UL>
     <LI>What HTML is
     <LI>How to Write HTML
     <LI>Doc structure
     <LI>Headings
     <LI>Paragraphs
     <LI>Comments
     </UL>
<LI>Links
<LI>More HTML
</OL>
```

Many browsers format nested ordered and unordered lists differently from their enclosing lists; for example, they might use a symbol other than a bullet for a nested list, or number the enclosing list with letters (a, b, c) instead of numbers. Don't assume that this will be the case, however, and refer back to "paragraph 8, subsection b" in your text, as you cannot determine what the exact formatting will be in the final output.

Input

```
<H1>Peppers</H1>
<UL>
<LI>Bell
<LI>Chile
     <UL>
     <LI>Serrano
     <LI>Jalapeno
     <LI>Habanero
     <LI>Anaheim
     </UL>
<LI>Schezuan
<LI>Cayenne
</UL>
```

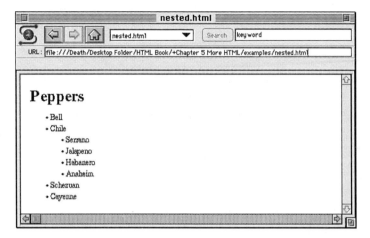

Figure 5.9. *The output in Mosaic.*

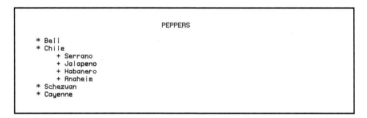

Figure 5.10. *The output in Lynx.*

Exercise 5.1. Creating a link menu.

Now that you've learned how to do lists, in this chapter, and links, in the last chapter, you can create those link menus I was talking about yesterday.

In this exercise , you'll create a Web page for a set of restaurant reviews. This page will serve as the index to the reviews, so the link menu you'll create is essentially a menu of restaurant names.

Start with a simple page framework: a first-level head and some basic explanatory text:

```
<HTML>
<HEAD>
<TITLE>Laura's Restaurant Guide</TITLE>
</HEAD><BODY>
<H1>Laura's Restaurant Reviews</H1>
<P>I spend a lot of time in restaurants in the area, having lunches or dinners with
friends or meeting with potential clients. I've written up several reviews of many of
```

the restaurants I frequent (and a few I'd rather not go back to). Here are reviews for the following restaurants:
```
</BODY></HTML>
```

Now add the list that will become the links, without the link tags themselves. It's always easier to start with link text and then attach actual links afterwards. For this list, we'll use a `<UL>` tag to create a bulleted list of individual restaurants. You could use a `<MENU>` tag here just as easily, but the `<OL>` tag wouldn't be appropriate, because the numbers would imply that you were ranking the restaurants in some way. Here's the HTML list of restaurants; Figure 5.11 shows the page in Mosaic as it currently looks.

```
<UL>
<LI>Schezuan Supreme
<LI>Mel's Pizza
<LI>Tomi
<LI>The Summit Inn
<LI>Cafe Milieu
</UL>
```

Figure 5.11. *A list of restaurants.*

Now, modify each of the list items so that they include link tags. You'll need to keep the `<LI>` tag in there, since that indicates where the list items begin. Just add the `<A>` tags around the text itself. Here we'll link to filenames on the local disk in the same directory as this file, with each individual file containing the review for the particular restaurant:

```
<UL>
<LI><A HREF="schezuan.html">Schezuan Supreme</A>
<LI><A HREF="mels.html">Mel's Pizza</A>
<LI><A HREF="tomi.html">Tomi</A>
<LI><A HREF="summitinn.html">The Summit Inn</A>
<LI><A HREF="millieu.html">Cafe Milieu</A>
</UL>
```

Figure 5.12. *The final link menu.*

The menu of restaurants looks fine, although it is a little sparse: your reader doesn't know what kinds of food each restaurant serves (although some of the restaurant names indicate the kind of food they serve), or if the review is good or bad. An improvement would be to add some short explanatory text after the links to provide a hint of what is on the other side of the link itself:

```
<UL>
<LI><A HREF="schezuan.html">Schezuan Supreme</A>. Chinese food. Prices are
excellent, but service is slow
<LI><A HREF="mels.html">Mel's Pizza</A>. Thin-crust New York style pizza.
Awesome, but loud.
<LI><A HREF="tomi.html">Tomi</A>. Sushi. So-so selection, friendly chefs.
<LI><A HREF="summitinn.html">The Summit Inn</A>. California food. Creative
chefs, but you pay extra for originality and appearance.
<LI><A HREF="millieu.html">Cafe Milieu</A>. Lots of atmosphere, sullen
postmodern waitrons, but an excellent double espresso none the less.
</UL>
```

The revised list then looks like Figure 5.13.

5

Figure 5.13. *The final menu listing.*

Character Styles

When you use an HTML tag for paragraphs, headings, and lists, those tags affect the text as a whole, changing the font, changing the spacing above and below the line, or adding characters (in the case of bulleted lists). *Character styles* are tags that affect words or characters within other HTML entities and have the effect of changing the appearance of that text so that it is somehow different from the surrounding text—making it boldface or underline, for instance.

To change the appearance of a set of characters within text, you can use one of two kinds of tags. The first kind, *logical* style tags, are named after the way the text is used: for emphasis, citation, code, and so on. Logical styles do not indicate the kind of formatting the browser should do for that text; they merely imply that some kind of emphasis should take place.

The second kind of character styles, physical style tags, indicate exactly how the text is to be formatted, such as bold or italic.

Because not all browsers can handle boldface or underline, the logical tags are preferred over the tags that indicate formatting. The logical style tags allow the browser to decide how to format the text to best fit the presentation of the rest of the document.

Logical Styles

Logical style tags indicate how the given highlighted text is to be used, *not* how it is to be displayed. This is similar to the common element tags for paragraphs or headings; they don't indicate how the text is to be formatted, just how it is to be used in a document. Logical style tags indicate text that is a definition, or code, or emphasized from the text around it.

It is up to the browser to determine the actual way text within these tags is presented, be it in boldface, italic, or any other change in appearance. You cannot guarantee that text highlighted using these tags will always be in boldface, or always be italic (and, therefore, you should not depend on it, either).

Each character style tag has both opening and closing sides, and affects the text within those two tags. There are eight styles:

☐ `<EM>`: indicates that the characters are to be emphasized in some way; that is, they are formatted differently from the rest of the text. In graphical browsers, `<EM>` is typically italic. For example:

```
<P>We'd all get along much better if you'd stop being so

<EM>silly.</EM>
```

☐ `<STRONG>`: the characters are to be more strongly emphasized than with `<EM>`. `<STRONG>` text is highlighted differently from `<EM>` text, for example, in boldface. For example:

```
<P>You <STRONG>must </STRONG> open the can before drinking</P>
```

☐ `<CODE>`: a code sample (a fixed-width font such as Courier in graphical displays):

```
<P><CODE>#include "trans.h"</CODE></P>
```

☐ `<SAMP>`: example text, similar to `<CODE>`:

```
<P>The URL for that page is <SAMP>http://www.cern.ch/</SAMP></P>
```

☐ `<KBD>`: text intended to be typed by a user:

```
<P>Type the following command: <KBD>find . -name "prune" -print</KBD></P>
```

☐ `<VAR>`: the name of a variable, or some entity to be replaced with an actual value. Often displayed as italic or underline, for example:

```
<P><CODE>chown </CODE><VAR>your_name the_file</VAR></P>
```

☐ `<DFN>`: highlights a word or phrase that is to be defined (or has just been defined, for example:

```
<P>Styles that are named on how they are used are called    <DFN>character
styles</DFN></P>
```

☐ `<CITE>`: a citation:

```
<P>Eggplant has been known to cause nausea in many unsuspecting
people<CITE> (Lemay, 1994)</CITE></P>
```

Got all those memorized now? Good! There will be a pop quiz at the end of the chapter. Figures 5.14 and 5.15 illustrate how all eight tags are displayed in Mosaic and Lynx.

```
<P>We'd all get along much better if you'd stop being so <EM>silly.</EM>
<P>You <STRONG>must</STRONG> open the can before drinking</P>
<P><CODE>#include "trans.h"</CODE></P>
<P>Type the following command: <KBD>find . -name "prune" -print</KBD></P>
<P><CODE>chown </CODE><VAR>your_name the_file</VAR></P>
<P>The URL for that page is <SAMP>http://www.cern.ch/</SAMP></P>
<P>Styles that are named on how they are used are called <DFN>character
styles</DFN></P>
<P>Eggplant has been known to cause extreme nausea in many unsuspecting
people<CITE> (Lemay, 1994)</CITE></P>
```

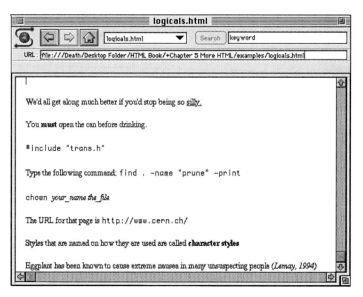

Figure 5.14. *The output in Mosaic.*

```
We'd all get along much better if you'd stop being so silly.

You must open the can before drinking.

#include "trans.h"

Type the following command: find . -name "prune" -print

chown your_name the_file

The URL for that page is http://www.cern.ch/

Styles that are named on how they are used are called character styles

Eggplant has been known to cause extreme nausea in many unsuspecting
people (Lemay, 1994)
```

Figure 5.15. *The output in Lynx.*

Physical Styles

In addition to the tags for style in the previous section, there is also a set of tags that change the actual presentation style of the text—to make it bold, italic, or monospaced.

Like the character style tags, each formatting tag has a beginning and ending tag. There are three physical style tags:

- ☐ <B>, for boldface
- ☐ <I>, for italic
- ☐ <TT>, for monospaced typewriter font

In addition, the <U> tag, for underlining, is proposed, but few browsers currently handle it.

If you choose to use the physical style tags, be forewarned that if a browser cannot handle one of the physical styles, it may substitute another style for the one you're using.

You can nest character tags—for example, use both bold and italic for a set of characters—like this:

```
<B><I>Text that is both bold and italic</I></B>
```

However, the result on the screen, like all HTML tags, is browser-dependent. You will not necessarily end up with text that is both bold and italic. You may end up with one or the other.

113

```
<P>In Dante's <I>Inferno</I>, malaboge was the eighth circle of hell, and
held the malicious and fraudulent</P>
<P>All entries must be received by <B>September 26, 1994</B>.</P>
<P>Type <TT>lpr -Pbirch myfile.txt</TT> to print that file.</P>
```

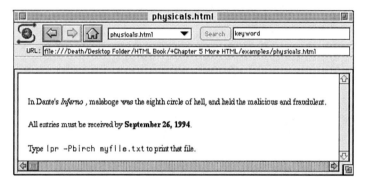

Figure 5.16. *The output in Mosaic.*

```
In Dante's Inferno, malaboge was the eighth circle of hell, and held
the malicious and fraudulent.

All entries must be received by September 26, 1994.

Type lpr -Pbirch myfile.txt to print that file.
```

Figure 5.17. *The output in Lynx.*

Preformatted Text

Most of the time, text in an HTML file is formatted based on the HTML tags used to mark up that text. As I mention in Chapter 3, "Begin with the Basics," any extra white space (spaces, tabs, returns) that you put in your text are stripped out by the browser.

The one exception to this rule is the preformatted text tag <PRE>. Any white space that you put into text that is surrounded by <PRE> and </ PRE> is retained in the final output, so you can format the text the way you want it to look, and it will be presented in that same formatting.

The one catch is that preformatted text is also rendered (in graphical displays, at least), in a monospaced font such as Courier. Preformatted text is excellent for things like code examples, where you want to indent and format lines appropriately. Because it also

enables you to align text by padding it with spaces, you can also use the <PRE> tag for tables, although the fact that those tables are presented in a monospaced font may make them less than ideal (real tables will not be supported in HTML until HTML Level Three). Here's an example of a table created with <PRE>. (Figure 5.18 shows how it looks in Mosaic.)

```
<PRE>
            Diameter    Distance    Time to     Time to
            (miles)     from Sun    Orbit       Rotate
                        (millions
                        of miles)
          - - - - - - - - - - - - - - - - - - - - - - - - - - -
Mercury     3100          36        88 days     59 days
Venus       7700          67        225 days    244 days
Earth       7920          93        365 days    24 hrs
Mars        4200         141        687 days    24 hrs 24 mins
Jupiter     88640        483        11.9 years  9 hrs 50 mins
Saturn      74500        886        29.5 years  10 hrs 39 mins
Uranus      32000        1782       84 years    23 hrs
Neptune     31000        2793       165 days    15 hrs 48 mins
Pluto       1500         3670       248 years   6 days 7 hrs
</PRE>
```

Figure 5.18. *Tables in Mosaic.*

When creating text for the <PRE> tag, you can use link tags and character styles, but not element tags such as headings or paragraphs. Break your lines using a return, and try to keep your lines at 80 characters or less. (Some browsers may have limited horizontal space in which to display text, and since browsers cannot reformat preformatted text to fit that space, you should make sure you stay within the boundaries.)

The <PRE> tag is also excellent for converting files that were originally in some sort of text-only form, such as mail messages or Usenet news postings, to HTML quickly and easily. Just surround the entire content of the article within <PRE> tags:

```
<PRE>
To: lemay@netcom.com
From: jokes@lorelei.com
Subject: Tales of the Move From Hell, pt. 1
Date: Fri, 26 Aug 1994 14:13:38 +0800

I spent the day on the phone today with the entire household
services division of northern california, turning off services,
turning on services, transferring services and other such fun
things you have to do when you move.

It used to be you just called these people and got put on hold for
and interminable amount of time, maybe with some nice music, and
then you got a customer representative who was surly and hard of
hearing, but with some work you could actually get your phone
turned off.
</PRE>
```

```
            <PRE>
                     (  )
              "Moo"  (oo)
                    \/ — — — \
                     ||      |  \
                     ||  —W||    *
                     ||     ||
            </PRE>
```

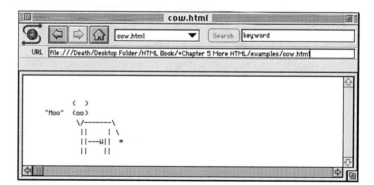

Figure 5.19. *The output in Mosaic.*

Figure 5.20. *The output in Lynx.*

Horizontal Rules

The `<HR>` tag, with no closing tag and no text associated with it, creates a horizontal line on the page. Rule lines are excellent for visually separating sections of the Web page; just before headings, for example, or to separate body text from a list of items. Figure 5.21 illustrates the effective use of rule lines.

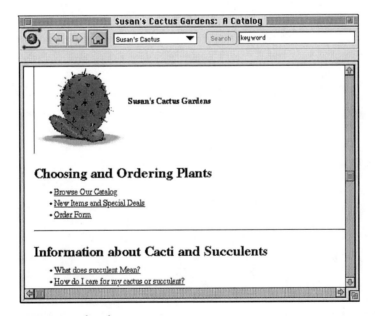

Figure 5.21. *Just enough rules.*

If one is good, more must be better, right? Not really. Be selective when you use rule lines; more than one together, or separating too many things on the page, makes a page look busy and distracts readers from the rest of its content—like the page in Figure 5.22.

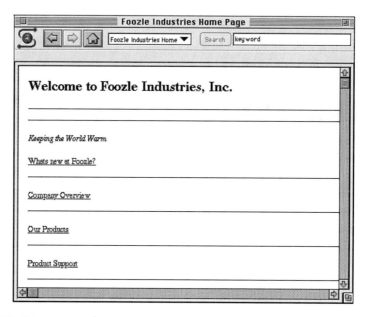

Figure 5.22. *Too many rules.*

Input

```
<HR>
<H2>To Do on Friday</H2>
<UL>
<LI>Do laundry
<LI>Send Fedex with pictures
<LI>Have lunch with Mollie
<LI>Read Email
<LI>Set up Ethernet
</UL>
<HR>
```

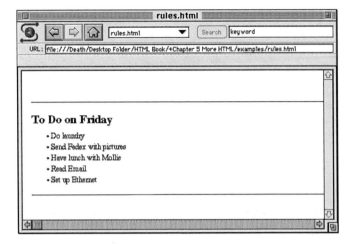

Figure 5.23. *The output in Mosaic.*

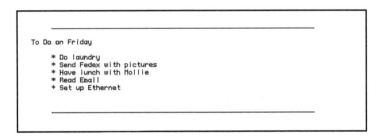

Figure 5.24. *The output in Lynx.*

Line Break

The <BR> tag, with no closing tag, when placed at the end of a line of text, breaks the line at that point. When a Web browser encounters a <BR> tag, it restarts the text after the tag at the left margin (whatever the current left margin happens to be for the current element). You can use <BR> within other tagged elements such as paragraphs or list items;
 will not add extra space above or below the new line or change the font or style of the current entity. All it does is restart the text at the next line.

```
<P>Tomorrow, and tomorrow, and tomorrow<BR>
Creeps in this petty pace from day to day<BR>
To the last syllable of recorded time;<BR>
And all our yesterdays have lighted fools<BR>
The way to dusty death. Out, out, brief candle!<BR>
Life's but a walking shadow, a poor player,<BR>
That struts and frets his hour upon the stage<BR>
And then is hear no more. It is a tale <BR>
Told by an idiot, full of sound and fury, <BR>
Signifying nothing.</P>
```

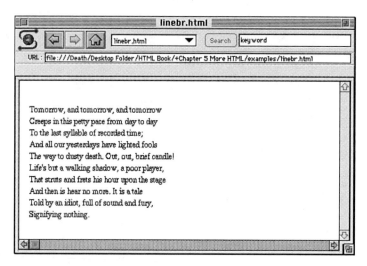

Figure 5.25. *The output in Mosaic.*

```
Tomorrow, and tomorrow, and tomorrow
Creeps in this petty pace from day to day
To the last syllable of recorded time;
And all our yesterdays have lighted fools
The way to dusty death. Out, out, brief candle!
Life's but a walking shadow, a poor player,
That struts and frets his hour upon the stage
And then is hear no more. It is a tale
Told by an idiot, full of sound and fury,
Signifying nothing.
```

Figure 5.26. *The output in Lynx.*

Addresses

The address tag <ADDRESS> is used for signature-like entities on Web pages. Address tags usually go at the bottom of each Web page and are used to indicate who wrote the Web

page, who to contact for more information, the date, any copyright notices or other warning, and anything else that seems appropriate. Addresses are often preceded with a rule line (`<HR>`), and the `<BR>` tag can be used to separate the lines, for example:

```
<HR>
<ADDRESS>
Laura Lemay lemay@netcom.com <BR>
A service of Laura Lemay, Incorporated <BR>
last revised September 30 1994 <BR>
Copyright Laura Lemay 1994 all rights reserved <BR>
Void where prohibited. Keep hands and feet inside the vehicle at all times.
</ADDRESS>
```

Without an address or some other method of "signing" your Web pages, it becomes close to impossible to find out who wrote it, or who to contact for more information. Signing each of your Web pages using the `<ADDRESS>` is an excellent way to make sure that if people want to get in touch with you, they can.

```
<HR>
<ADDRESS>
lemay@netcom.com Laura Lemay
</ADDRESS>
```

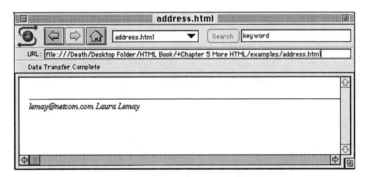

Figure 5.27. *The output in Mosaic.*

Figure 5.28. *The output in Lynx.*

5

Quotations

The `<BLOCKQUOTE>` tag is used to create a quotation. Quotations are generally set off from regular text by indentation or some other method. The Macbeth soliloquy I used in the example on line breaks would have worked better as a `BLOCKQUOTE` than as a simple paragraph.

```
<BLOCKQUOTE>
"During the whole of a dull, dark, and soundless day in the autumn of the year, when
the clouds hung oppressively low in the heavens, I had been passing alone, on horse-
back, through a singularly dreary trace of country, and at length found myself, as the
shades of evening grew on, within view of the melancholy House of Usher."—Edgar Allen
Poe
</BLOCKQUOTE>
```

As in paragraphs, you can separate lines in a `<BLOCKQUOTE>` using the line break tag `<BR>`.

```
<BLOCKQUOTE>
Guns aren't lawful, <BR>
nooses give.<BR>
gas smells awful.<BR>
You might as well live.<BR>
—Dorothy Parker
</BLOCKQUOTE>
```

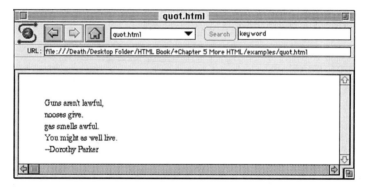

Figure 5.29. *The output in Mosaic.*

```
Guns aren't lawful,
nooses give.
gas smells awful.
You might as well live.
--Dorothy Parker
```

Figure 5.30. *The output in Lynx.*

Special Characters

As you know, HTML files are ASCII text and should contain no formatting or fancy characters. In fact, the only characters you should be putting in your HTML files are characters that are actually printed on your keyboard. If you have to hold down any key other than Shift, or type an arcane series of keys to produce a single character, you can't use that character in your HTML file. If your editor does things like smart quotes, turn them off when you're working on HTML files.

But wait a minute, I can hear you say. *If I can type a character, like a bullet or an accented "a" on my keyboard using a special key sequence, include it in an HTML file, and my browser can display it, what's the problem?*

The problem is that the internal encoding your computer does to produce that character (which allows it to show up properly in your HTML file and in your browser's display) most likely will not translate to other computers. Someone else on the Net reading your HTML file with that funny character in it may very well end up with some other character, or garbage. Or, depending on how your document gets shipped over the Net, the character may be lost before it ever gets to the computer the file is being viewed on.

> **Note:** In technical jargon, this means that the characters in HTML files must be from the standard (7-bit) ASCII character set, and cannot include any characters from "extended" (8-bit) ASCII, as every platform has a different definition of the characters that are included in the upper ASCII range. HTML browsers interpret codes from upper ASCII as characters in the ISO-Latin-1 (ISO-8859-1) character set, a superset of ASCII.

So what can you do? HTML provides a reasonable solution: It defines a special set of codes, called character entities. When interpreted by a browser, these character entities are displayed as the appropriate special characters for the given platform and font.

Character Entities for Special Characters

Character entities take one of two forms: named entities and numbered entities.

Named entities begin with an ampersand (&) and end with a semicolon (;). In between is the name of the character (or, more likely, a shorthand version of that name like agrave

for an a with a grave accent or reg for a registered sign). The names, unlike other HTML tags, must be in all lower case. Named entities look something like this:

```
&quot;
&laquo;
&copy;
```

The numbered entities also begin with an ampersand and end with a semicolon, but instead of a name, they have a hash sign and a number. The numbers correspond to character positions in the ISO-Latin-1 (ISO 8859-1) character set. Every character that you can type or use a named entity for also has a numbered entity. Numbered entities look like this:

```
&#130;
&#245;
```

You use either numbers and named entities in your HTML file by including them in the same place that the character they represent would go. So, to have the word "resumé" in your HTML file, you would use either:

```
resum&eacute;
```

or

```
resum&#233;
```

I've included a table in Appendix B that lists the named entities currently supported by HTML Levels 1 and 2. See that table for specific characters.

Note: Character entities seem to work better in theory than in practice. In a sampling of several browsers, I found only a few that could handle all the character entities defined in HTML Level One, and most couldn't handle anything other than accented characters. Be sure when you use character entities that you test the result in as many browsers as you can find to make sure that they will work, or avoid using special characters altogether.

Character Entities for Reserved Characters

For the most part, character entities exist so that you can include special characters that are not part of the standard ASCII character set. There are several exceptions, however, for the few characters that have special meaning in HTML itself. You must also use entities for these characters.

For example, say you wanted to include a line of code in an HTML file that looked something like this:

```
<P><CODE>if x < 0 do print i</CODE></P>
```

Doesn't look unusual, does it? Unfortunately, HTML cannot display this line as written. Why? The problem is with the < (less than) character. To an HTML browser, the less than character means "this is a start of a tag." Because in this context the less than character is not actually the start of a tag, the browser will get confused. You'll have the same problem with the greater than character (>) because it means the end of a tag in HTML, and with the ampersand (&), meaning the beginning of a character escape. So written correctly for HTML, that line of code would look like this:

```
<P><CODE>if x &lt; 0 do print i</CODE></P>
```

HTML provides named escape codes for each of these characters, and one for the double-quote, as well, as shown in Table 5.1.

Table 5.1. Escape codes for characters used by tags.

Tag	Result
&lt;	<
&gt;	>
&amp;	&
&quot;	"

The double-quote escape is the mysterious one. Technically, to produce correct HTML files, if you want to include a double-quote in text, you should be using the escape sequence and not typing the quote character. However, I have not noticed any browsers having problems displaying the double-quote character when it is typed literally in an HTML file, nor have I seen many HTML files that use it. For the most part, you are probably safe using plain old " in your HTML files rather than the escape code.

Exercise 5.2. Do a real HTML page.

Here's your chance to apply what you've learned and create a real live working Web page. No more disjointed or overly silly examples; the Web page you'll create in this section is a real one, suitable for use in the real world (or the real world of the Web, at least).

Your task for this example: to design and create a home page for a bookstore called The Bookworm, which specializes in old and rare books.

Plan the Page

In Chapter 2, "Getting Organized," I mention that planning your Web page before writing it usually makes things easier to build and to maintain. So first, consider the content you want to include on this page. Here are some ideas for topics for this page:

- ☐ The address and phone # of the bookstore
- ☐ A short description of what the bookstore is and why it is unique
- ☐ Recent titles and authors
- ☐ Upcoming events

Now, come up with some ideas for the content you're going to link to from this page. Each title in the list of recent titles seems like a logical candidate; you can link to more information about the book itself and about its author and publisher, its pricing, maybe even its availability.

The Upcoming Events section might also make a potential series of links, depending on how much you want to discuss each event. If you only have a sentence or two about each one, describing them on this page might make more sense than linking them to another page. Why make your reader wait for each new page to load for just a couple of lines of text?

Other interesting links may arise in the text itself, but for now, the basic link plan will be enough to start with.

Begin With a Framework

First, create the framework that all HTML files must include: the document structuring commands, a title, and an initial heading. Note that the title is descriptive but short; you can save the longer title for the <H1> element in the body of the text.

```
<HTML>
<HEAD>
<TITLE>The Bookworm Bookshop</TITLE>
</HEAD>
<BODY>
<H1>The Bookworm: A Better Book Store</H1>
</BODY></HTML>
```

Add Content

Now begin adding the content. Since this is a literary endeavor, a nice quote about old books to start the page will be a nice touch. Because it's a quote, you can use the <BLOCKQUOTE> tag to make it stand out as such. Also, the name of the poem is a citation, so use <CITE> there, too.

```
<BLOCKQUOTE>
"Old books are best—how tale and rhyme<BR>
Float with us down the stream of time!"<BR>
- Clarence Urmy, <CITE>Old Songs are Best</CITE>
</BLOCKQUOTE>
```

The address of the bookstore is a simple paragraph, with the lines separated by line breaks.

```
<P>The Bookworm Bookshop<BR>
1345 Applewood Dr<BR>
Springfield, CA 94325<BR>
(415) 555-0034
</P>
```

After the address comes the description of the bookstore itself. I've arranged the description to include a list of features, to make the features stand out from the text better:

```
<P>Since 1933, The Bookworm Bookshop has offered rare and hard-to-find titles for the
discerning reader. Unlike the bigger bookstore chains, the Bookworm offers:
<UL>
<LI>Friendly, knowledgeable, and courteous help.
<LI>Free coffee and juice for our customers
<LI>A well-lit reading room so you can "try before you buy."
<LI>Four friendly cats: Esmerelda, Catherine, Dulcinea and Beatrice
</UL>
```

Add one more note about the hours the store is open, and emphasize the actual numbers:

```
<P>Our hours are <STRONG>10am to 9pm</STRONG> weekdays,
<STRONG>noon to 7</STRONG> on weekends.
```

Add More Content

After the description come the other major topics of this home page: the recent titles and upcoming events sections. Since these are topic headings, we'll label them with second-level head tags:

```
<H2>Recent Titles (as of 9/25/94)</H2>
<H2>Upcoming Events</H2>
```

The Recent Titles section itself is a classic link menu. Here we'll put the list of titles in an unordered list, with the titles themselves as citations (the <CITE> tag).

```
<H2>Recent Titles (as of 9/25/94)</H2>
<UL>
<LI>Sandra Bellweather, <CITE>Belladonna</CITE>
<LI>Jonathan Tin, <CITE>20-Minute Meals for One</CITE>
<LI>Maxwell Burgess, <CITE>Legion of Thunder</CITE>
<LI>Alison Caine, <CITE>Banquo's Ghost</CITE>
</UL>
```

Now, add the anchor tags to create the links. How far should the link itself extend? Should it include the whole line (author and title), or just the title of the book? This is a matter of preference, but I like to link only as much as necessary to make sure the link

5

stands out from the text, rather than overwhelming the text. Here, I've linked only the titles of the books.

```
<UL>
<LI>Sandra Bellweather, <A HREF="belladonna.html">
    <CITE>Belladonna</CITE></A>
<LI>Johnathan Tin, <A HREF="20minmeals.html">
    <CITE>20-Minute Meals for One</CITE></A>
<LI>Maxwell Burgess, <A HREF="legion.html">
    <CITE>Legion of Thunder</CITE></A>
<LI>Alison Caine, <A HREF="banquo.html">
    <CITE>Banquo's Ghost</CITE></A>
</UL>
```

Note that I've put the `<CITE>` tag inside the link tag `<A>`. I could have just as easily put it outside the anchor tag; character style tags can go just about anywhere. But as I mentioned once before, be careful not to overlap tags, because your browser may not be able to understand what is going on. In other words, don't do this:

```
<A HREF="banquo.html"><CITE>Banquo's Ghost</A></CITE>
```

Next, let's move on to the Upcoming Events section. In the planning section we weren't sure if this would be another link menu, or if the content would work better solely on this page. Again, this is a matter of preference; here, because the amount of extra information is minimal, it doesn't make much sense to link people off elsewhere for just a couple of sentences. So for this section we'll create a menu list (using the MENU tag), which results in short paragraphs (bulleted in some browsers). I've made a few phrases near the beginning of each paragraph bold. Those phrases emphasize a summary of the event itself so that each paragraph can be scanned quickly and ignored if the reader isn't interested.

```
<H1>Upcoming Events</H1>
<MENU>
<LI><B>The Wednesday Evening Book Review</B> meets, appropriately, on Wednesday
evenings at PM for coffee and a round-table discussion. Call the Bookworm for informa-
tion on joining the group and this week's reading assignment.
<LI><B>The Children's Hour</B> happens every Saturday at 1pm and includes reading,
games, and other activities. Cookies and milk are served.
<LI><B>Carole Fenney</B> will be at the Bookworm on Friday, September 16, to read from
her book of poems <CITE>Spiders in the Web.</CITE>
<LI><B>The Bookworm will be closed</B> October 1 to remove a family
of bats that has nested in the tower. We like the company, but not
the mess they leave behind!
</MENU>
```

Review What You've Got

Here's the code for the page, so far:

```
<HTML>
<HEAD>
```

```
<TITLE>The Bookworm Bookshop</TITLE>
</HEAD>
<BODY>
<H1>The Bookworm: A Better Book Store</H1>
<BLOCKQUOTE>
"Old books are best—how tale and rhyme<BR>
Float with us down the stream of time!"<BR>
- Clarence Urmy, <CITE>Old Songs are Best</CITE>
</BLOCKQUOTE>
<P>The Bookworm Bookshop<BR>
1345 Applewood Dr<BR>
Springfield, CA 94325<BR>
(415) 555-0034
</P>
<P>Since 1933, The Bookworm Bookshop has offered rare and hard-to-find titles for the
discerning reader. Unlike the bigger bookstore chains,the Bookworm offers:
<UL>
<LI>Friendly, knowledgeable, and courteous help.
<LI>Free coffee and juice for our customers
<LI>A well-lit reading room so you can "try before you buy."
<LI>Four friendly cats: Esmerelda, Catherine, Dulcinea and Beatrice
</UL>
<P>Our hours are <STRONG>10am to 9pm</STRONG> weekdays,
<STRONG>noon to 7</STRONG> on weekends.
<H2>Recent Titles (as of 9/25/94)</H2>
<UL>
<LI>Sandra Bellweather, <A HREF="belladonna.html">
    <CITE>Belladonna</CITE></A>
<LI>Johnathan Tin, <A HREF="20minmeals.html">
    <CITE>20-Minute Meals for One</CITE></A>
<LI>Maxwell Burgess, <A HREF="legion.html">
    <CITE>Legion of Thunder</CITE></A>
<LI>Alison Caine, <A HREF="banquo.html">
    <CITE>Banquo's Ghost</CITE></A>
</UL>
<H2>Upcoming Events</H2>
<MENU>
<LI><B>The Wednesday Evening Book Review</B> meets, appropriately, on Wednesday
evenings at PM for coffee and a round-table discussion. Call the Bookworm for informa-
tion on joining the group and this week's reading assignment.
<LI><B>The Children's Hour</B> happens every Saturday at 1pm and includes reading,
games, and other activities. Cookies and milk are served.
<LI><B>Carole Fenney</B> will be at the Bookworm on Friday, September 16, to read from
her book of poems <CITE>Spiders in the Web.</CITE>
<LI><B>The Bookworm will be closed</B> October 1 to remove a family
of bats that has nested in the tower. We like the company, but not
the mess they leave behind!
</MENU>
</BODY></HTML>
```

So now we have some headings, some text, some topics, and some links. This is the basis for an excellent Web page. At this point, with most of the content in, consider what else you might want to create links for, or what other features you might want to add to this page.

5

For example, in the introductory section, a note was made of the four cats owned by the bookstore. Although you didn't plan for it in the original organization, you could easily create Web pages describing each cat (and showing pictures), and then link them back to this page, one link (and one page) per cat.

Is describing the cats important? As the designer of the page, that's up to you to decide. You could link to all kinds of things from this page if you had interesting reasons to link them (and something to link *to*). Link the bookstore's address to the local chamber of commerce. Link the quote to an online encyclopedia of quotes. Link the note about free coffee to the Coffee Home Page.

I'll say more about good things to link to (and how not to get carried away when you link) in the next chapter. My point for bringing this point up here is that once you have some content in place in your Web pages, opportunities for extending the pages and linking to other places may arise, opportunities that you didn't think of when you created your original plan. So when you're just about finished with a page, it's often a good idea to stop and review what you have, both in the plan and in what you already have down.

For the purposes of this example, we'll stop here and stick with the links we've got. We're close enough to being done that I don't want to make this chapter longer than it already is!

Sign the Page

You're finished; sign what you have so your readers know who did the work. Here I've separated the signature from the text with a rule line and included the most recent revision date, my name as the "Web Master" (cute Web jargon meaning the person in charge of a Web site), and a basic copyright (with a copyright symbol indicated by the numeric escape ©):

```
<HR>
<ADDRESS>
Last Updated: 9/25/94<BR>
WebMaster: Laura Lemay lemay@bookworm.com<BR>
&#169; copyright 1994 the Bookworm<BR>
</ADDRESS>
```

And that's it! Save the file as ASCII and open up your browser.

Test the Result

Now that all the code is in place, you can preview the results in a browser. Figure 5.31 shows how it looks in Mosaic. Actually, this is how it looks after you fix the spelling errors and forgotten closing tags and other strange bugs that always seem to creep into an HTML file the first time you create it. This always seems to happen no matter how good you get at it. If you use an HTML editor or some other help tool it will be easier, but there always seem to be mistakes. That's what previewing is for, so you can catch those problems before you actually make the document available to other people.

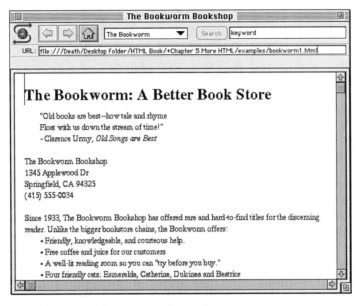

The Bookworm Bookshop

The Bookworm   Search   key word

URL: file:///Death/Desktop Folder/HTML Book/+Chapter 5 More HTML/examples/bookworm1.html

The Bookworm: A Better Book Store

"Old books are best--how tale and rhyme
Float with us down the stream of time!"
- Clarence Urmy, *Old Songs are Best*

The Bookworm Bookshop
1345 Applewood Dr
Springfield, CA 94325
(415) 555-0034

Since 1933, The Bookworm Bookshop has offered rare and hard-to-find titles for the discerning reader. Unlike the bigger bookstore chains, the Bookworm offers:

- Friendly, knowledgeable, and courteous help.
- Free coffee and juice for our customers
- A well-lit reading room so you can "try before you buy."
- Four friendly cats: Esmerelda, Catherine, Dulcinea and Beatrice

Figure 5.31. *The Bookworm home page, almost done.*

Looks good so far, but in the browsers I tested it in, the description of the store and the Recent Events sections tend to run together; there isn't enough distinction between them. (See Figure 5.32.)

You have two choices for making them more distinct:

☐ Add rule lines (<HR>) in between sections.

☐ Change the <H2> tags to <H1> for more emphasis of the individual sections.

With design issues like this, it comes down to a matter of preference and what looks the best in as many browsers as you can get your hands on. Either choice is equally correct, as both are visually interesting, and you haven't had to do strange things in HTML in order to get it to do what you want.

I settled on a single rule line between the description and the Recent Events section. Figure 5.33 shows how it came out.

5

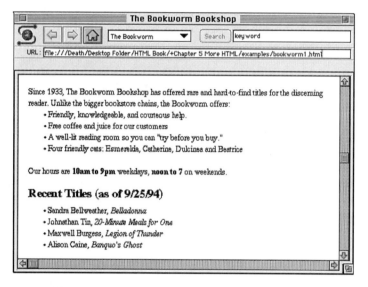

Figure 5.32. *A problem section.*

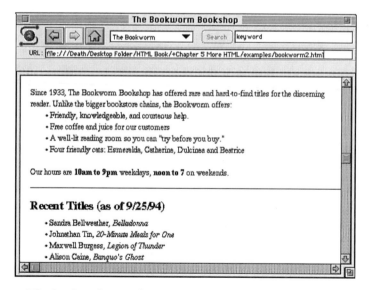

Figure 5.33. *The final Bookworm home page.*

Summary

Tags, tags, and more tags! After this chapter, you've learned about most of the remaining tags in the HTML language for presenting text, and put together a real-life HTML home page. You could stop now and create quite presentable Web pages. But there's more cool stuff to come, so don't put the book down yet.

Table 5.2 presents a quick summary of all the tags you've learned about in this chapter.

Table 5.2. HTML Tags from Chapter 5.

Tag	Use
`<OL>...</OL>`	An ordered (numbered) list. Items in the list each begin with `<LI>`.
`<UL>...</UL>`	An unordered (bulleted or otherwise marked) list. Items in the list each begin with `<LI>`.
`<MENU>...</MENU>`	A menu list (a list of short items or paragraphs).
`<DIR>...</DIR>`	A list of especially short (1-2 word) items. Directory lists are not often used in most HTML files.
`<LI>`	Individual list items in ordered, unordered, menu. or directory lists.
`<DL>...</DL>`	A glossary or definition list. Items in the list consist of pairs of elements: a term and its definition.
`<DT>`	The term part of an item in a glossary list.
`<DD>`	The definition part of an item in a glossary list.
`<EM>...</EM>`	Emphasized text.
`<STRONG>...</STRONG>`	Strongly emphasized text.
`<CODE>...</CODE>`	A code sample.
`<KBD>...</KBD>`	Text to be typed in by the user.
`<VAR>...</VAR>`	A variable name.
`<SAMP>...</SAMP>`	Sample text.
`<DFN>...</DFN>`	A definition, or a term about to be defined.
`<CITE>...</CITE>`	A citation.
`<B>...</B>`	Bold text.
`<I>...</I>`	Italic text.

continues

Table 5.2. continued.

Tag	Use
<TT>...</T>	Text in typewriter font (a monospaced font such as Courier).
<HR>	A horizontal rule line at the given position in the text.
 	A line break; start the next character on the next line (but do not create a new paragraph or list item).
<BLOCKQUOTE>	A quotation longer than a few words.
<ADDRESS>	A "signature" for each Web page; typically occurs near the bottom of each document and contains contact or copyright information.

Q&A

Q If there are line breaks in HTML (<BR>), what about page breaks?

A There is no page break tag in HTML. Consider what the term "page" means in a Web document. If each document on the Web is a single "page," then the only way to produce a page break is to split your HTML document into separate files and link between them.

Even within a single document, browsers have no concept of a page; each document simply scrolls by continuously. If you consider a single screen a page, you still cannot have what results in a page break in HTML because the screen size in each browser is different, and is based on not only the browser itself but the monitor on which it runs, the number of lines defined, and other factors that you cannot control from HTML.

When designing your Web pages, don't get too hung up on the concept of a "page" the way it exists in paper documents. Think in terms of small chunks of information and how they link together to form a complete presentation.

Q Is there any way to get real tables in HTML without using preformatted text?

A Not in the current state of HTML. HTML Level Three will contain more tags for handling better tables. In fact, some browsers are beginning to support table tags now, and the state of tables may have changed by the time you read this. Check with the people who made your browser.

If the Courier font doesn't bother you that much, there are packages that will convert tables written in HTML Level Three tags into preformatted text that works with HTML Levels One and Two. See Appendix A for a pointer to these packages.

Q My glossaries came out formatted really strangely! The terms are indented farther in than the definitions!

A Did you mix up the `<DD>` and `<DT>` tags? The `<DT>` tag is always used first (the definition term), and then the DD follows (the definition). I mix these up all the time. There are too many D tags in glossary lists.

Q I've seen HTML files out there that use `<LI>` outside of a list structure, alone on the page, like this:

```
<LI>And then the duck said, "put it on my bill"
```

A Although most browsers can figure out what you mean, and format a single `<LI>` as a paragraph, "good" HTML documents (those that follow the specification) will not do this. And, because we are all striving to write good HTML, you shouldn't do this either. Use `<P>` for paragraphs instead, and reserve `<LI>` for lists.

Q What about that pop quiz you threatened?

A OK, smarty. Without looking at Table 5.2, list all eight logical style tags and what they're used for. Explain why you should use the logical tags instead of the physical tags. Then create an HTML page that uses each one in a sentence, and test it in several browsers to get a feel for how it looks in each.

6

THREE

More About Links and URLs

Yesterday you learned about beginning HTML and beginning links. Earlier today in Chapter 5, "Still More HTML," you learned about more HTML, so it only makes sense that this chapter would include more about links.

This chapter explains

☐ How to use links and anchors to link to specific places within documents

☐ All about URLs: the various parts of the URL and the kinds of URLs you can use

Linking to Specific Places Within Documents

Yesterday, you learned how to use the link tag <A> to create links between documents, where each link pointed to another document, as Figure 6.1 shows.

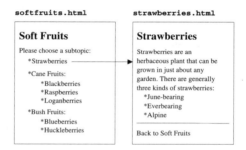

Figure 6.1. *Links to documents.*

But what if, instead of linking generally to the second document, you wanted to link to a specific place within that document; for example, to the fourth major section down?

You can do this in HTML by creating an *anchor* within the second document, and then creating a link in the first document that points to both the second document *and* that anchor. Then, when you follow the link with your browser, the browser will open the second document and scroll down to the location of the anchor (Figure 6.2).

You can also use links and anchors within the same document. Selecting a link in this instance doesn't load a new document; instead, it simply scrolls the document so that the part with the anchor is at the top of the window.

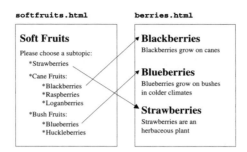

Figure 6.2. *Links and anchors.*

Creating Links and Anchors

You create an anchor in nearly the same way that you create a link, using the <A> tag. And, if you had wondered why the link tag uses an <A> name instead of an <L> name, now you know: A actually stands for Anchor.

When you specified links using <A>, there were two parts of the link: the HREF attribute in the opening <A> tag, and the text in between the opening and closing tags that served as a hot spot for the link.

Anchors are created in much the same way, except for instead of using the HREF attribute in the <A> tag, you use the NAME attribute. The NAME attribute takes a keyword (or words) that will be used to reference the anchor.

Anchors also require some amount of text between the opening and closing <A> tags. This text will be used by the browser when a link that is attached to this anchor is selected; the browser scrolls the document to the text within the anchor so that it is at the top of the screen and then highlights it.

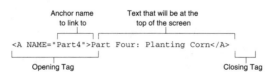

Figure 6.3. *The* <A> *tag and anchors.*

Unlike links, anchors do not show up in a different font or color in the final document. Anchors are invisible until you follow a link that points to them.

To reference an anchor in a link, you use the same form of link that you would to link to the document as a whole, with the file name or URL of the document in the HREF

attribute. After the name of the document itself, however, you include a hash sign (#) and the name of the anchor exactly as it appears in the NAME attribute of that anchor, like this:

```
<A HREF="../mybigdoc.html#Part4">Go to Part 4</A>
```

This link tells the browser to load the document mybigdoc.html, located one directory level up from the current document, and then to scroll down to the anchor name Part 4 such that the selected text is at the top of the screen.

Note that because NAME and HREF are different attributes, you can have both in the same <A> tag, referencing the same text. In this way, you can have a selection of text that is both an anchor and a link at the same time.

Exercise 6.1. Link sections between two documents.

Let's do an example with two documents. These two documents are part of an online reference to classical music, where each Web page contains all the references for a particular letter of the alphabet (A.html, B.html, and so on). Note that the reference could have organized such that each section was its own document, but that involves an awful lot of documents to manage, as well as an awful lot of documents the reader has to load if they are exploring the reference. It's more efficient in this case to bunch the related sections together under lettered groupings. (Chapter 9, "Writing and Designing Web Pages: Do's and Don'ts," goes into more detail about the trade-offs between short and long documents.)

The first document we'll look at is the one for "M," the first section of which looks like this in HTML:

Input

```
<HTML>
<HEAD>
<TITLE>Classical Music: M</TITLE>
</HEAD>
<BODY>
<H1>M</H1>
<H2>Madrigals</H2>
<UL>
<LI>William Byrd, <EM>This Sweet and Merry Month of May</EM>
<LI>William Byrd, <EM>Though Amaryllis Dance</EM>
<LI>Orlando Gibbons, <EM>The Silver Swan</EM>
<LI>Roland de Lassus, <EM>Mon Coeur se Recommande &agrave; vous</EM>
<LI>Claudio Monteverdi, <EM>Lamento d'Arianna</EM>
<LI>Thomas Morley, <EM>My Bonny Lass She Smileth</EM>
<LI>Thomas Weelkes, <EM>Thule, the Period of Cosmography</EM>
<LI>John Wilbye, <EM>Sweet Honey-Sucking Bees</EM>
</UL>
<P>Secular vocal music in four, five and six parts, usually a capella.
15th-16th centuries.</P>
```

```
<P><EM>See Also</EM>
Byrd, Gibbons, Lassus, Monteverdi, Morley, Weelkes, Wilbye</P>
</BODY>
</HTML>
```

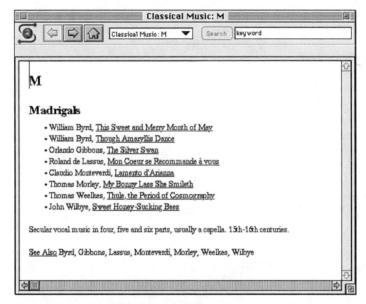

Figure 6.4. *Part M of the online music reference.*

In that last line (the See Alsos), it would be useful to link those composer names to their respective sections elsewhere in the reference. But if you used the procedure you learned in Chapter 4, "Putting the Hyper in Hypertext: All About Links," you'd create a link here around Byrd to the document B.html. When your reader selected the Byrd link, the browser would drop him or her at the top of the Bs. (See Figure 6.5.) That hapless reader would then have to scroll down through all the Bs (and there are lots of them: Bach, Beethoven, Brahms, Bruckner) to get to Byrd; a lot of work for a system that claims to link information so you can find what you want quickly and easily.

What you want is to be able to link the word Byrd in M.html directly to the section Byrd in B.html. Here's the relevant part of B.html. (I've deleted all the Bs before Byrd to make this file shorter for this example. Pretend they're still there.)

```
<HTML>
<HEAD>
<TITLE>Classical Music: B</TITLE>
</HEAD>
<BODY>
<H1>B</H1>
```

```
<!-- I've deleted all the Bs before Byrd to make things shorter -->
<H2>Byrd, William, 1543-1623</H2>
<UL>
<LI>Madrigals
     <UL>
     <LI><EM>This Sweet and Merry Month of May</EM>
     <LI><EM>Though Amaryllis Dance</EM>
     <LI><EM>Lullabye, My Sweet Little Baby</EM>
     </UL>
<LI>Masses
     <UL>
     <LI><EM>Mass for Five Voices</EM>
     <LI><EM>Mass for Four Voices</EM>
     <LI><EM>Mass for Three Voices</EM>
     </UL>
<LI>Motets
     <UL>
     <LI><EM>Ave verum corpus a 4</EM>
     </UL>
</UL>
<P><EM>See Also</EM>
Madrigals, Masses, Motets</P>
</BODY>
</HTML>
```

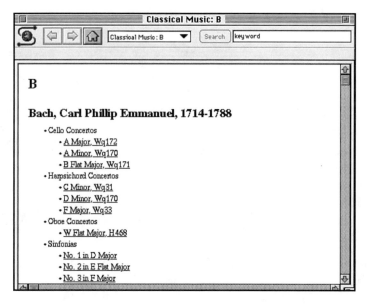

Figure 6.5. *Top of the Bs.*

What you'll need to do is to create an anchor at the section heading for Byrd. As described in the last section, you need two things for each anchor: an anchor name and the text that will be highlighted when this document is loaded at the tail end of a link. The latter is easy; the section heading itself makes excellent highlighted text.

For the anchor name, you can choose any name you want, but each anchor in the document must be unique. (If you had two or more anchors with the name "fred" in the same document, how would the browser know which one to point to when a link to that anchor is selected?) A good unique anchor name for this example would be simply "Byrd."

With the two parts decided on, you can create the anchor itself in your HTML file. Add the <A> tag to the William Byrd section heading, but be careful here. If this was normal text within a paragraph, you'd just surround the whole line with <A>. But when you're adding an anchor to a big section of text that is also contained within an element—like a heading, paragraph, address, quote, or so on—always put the anchor *inside* the element. In other words, do this:

```
<H2><A NAME="Byrd">Byrd, William, 1543-1623</A></H2>
```

But not this:

```
<A NAME="Byrd"><H2>Byrd, William, 1543-1623</H2></A>
```

The second example could confuse your browser. Is it an anchor, formatted just like the text before it, with mysteriously placed heading tags, or is it a heading that also happens to be an anchor? If you use the right code in your HTML file, with the anchor inside the heading, you solve the confusion.

It's easy to forget about this, especially if you're like me and you create text first and then add links and anchors. It makes sense to just surround everything with an <A> tag. Think of it this way: If you were linking to just one word, and not to the entire element, you'd put the <A> tag inside the <H2>. Working with the whole line of text isn't any different. Keep that rule in mind and you'll get less confused.

6

Note: If you're still confused, Appendix B has a summary of all the HTML tags and rules for which tags can and cannot go inside each one.

So you've added your anchor to the heading, and its name is "Byrd." Now go back to your M.html file, to the line with the See Alsos.

```
<P><EM>See Also</EM>
Byrd, Gibbons, Lassus, Monteverdi, Morley, Weelkes, Wilbye</P>
```

You're going to create your link here around the word Byrd, just like you would create any other link. But what's the URL? As you learned in the previous section, URLs to anchors look like this:

```
document#anchor_name
```

So the opening anchor tag to the document itself would be the following:

```
<A HREF="B.html">
```

And then once you added the anchor name, it would look like this:

```
<A HREF="B.html#Byrd">
```

Note the capital B. Anchor names and links are case sensitive; if you put #byrd in your HREF you might end up highlighting some other bit of text in the B document. Make sure that the anchor name you used in the NAME attribute and the anchor name in the link after the # are exactly the same.

So, with the new link to the new section, the See Also line looks like this:

```
<P><EM>See Also</EM>
<A HREF="B.html#Byrd">Byrd</A>,
Gibbons, Lassus, Monteverdi, Morley, Weelkes, Wilbye</P>
```

And, of course, you could go ahead and add anchors and links to the other parts of the reference for the remaining composers.

With all your links and anchors in place, test everything. Figure 6.6 shows the Madrigals section with the link to Byrd ready to be selected.

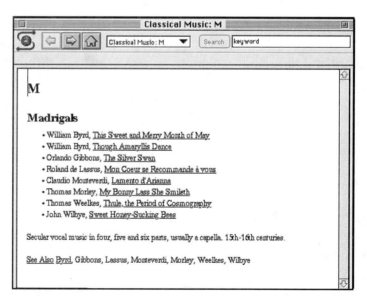

Figure 6.6. *The Madrigals section with link.*

Figure 6.7 shows what pops up when you select the Byrd link.

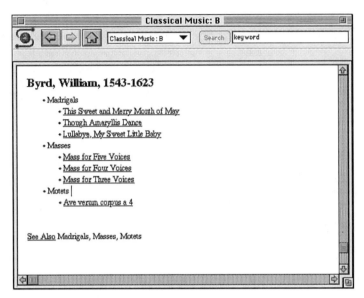

Figure 6.7. *The Byrd section.*

Anatomy of a URL

So far in this book you've encountered URLs twice—in Chapter 1, as part of the introduction to the Web; and in Chapter 3, when you created links to remote documents. And if you've ever done much exploring on the Web, you've encountered URLs as a matter of course. You couldn't start exploring without a URL.

As I mentioned in Chapter 1, "The World of the World Wide Web," URLs are Uniform Resource Locators. URLs are effectively street addresses for bits of information on the Internet. Most of the time, you can avoid trying to figure out your own URLs by simply navigating to the bit of information you want to point to with your browser, and then copying and pasting the long string of gobbledygook into your link. But it's often useful to understand what a URL is all about, and why it has to be so long and complex. Also, when you put your own information up on the Web, it'll be useful to know something about URLs so that you can tell people where your Web page is.

In this section, you'll learn what the bits of a URL are, and how you can use them to get to information on the Web. In the next section, you'll learn about the kinds of URLs you can use (HTTP, FTP, mailto, and so on).

> **Note:** URLs are one of several proposed methods of locating, managing, and identifying bits of information on the Web. Those methods include URIs (Universal Resource Identifiers), of which URLs are a subset, and URNs (Uniform Resource Names), which are unique identifiers for documents or other information. Appendix A has some pointers for further information about each of these methods.

Parts of URLs

Most URLs have (roughly) three parts: the protocol, the host name, and the directory. (See Figure 6.8.)

The *protocol* is the way in which the document is accessed; that is, the type of protocol or program your browser will use to get the file. If the browser is using HTTP to get to the file, the protocol part is `http`. If the browser, uses FTP, it's `ftp`. If you're using Gopher, it's `gopher`, and so on.

Figure 6.8. *URL parts.*

The *host name* is the system on the Internet on which the information is stored, such as `www.netcom.com`, `ftp.apple.com`, or `aol.com`. You can have the same host name but have different URLs with different protocols, like this:

```
http://mysystem.com
ftp://mysystem.com
gopher://mysystem.com
```

Same machine, three different information servers. As long as all three are installed on that system and available, there's not a problem.

The host name part of the URL may include a port number. The port number tells your browser to open a connection of the appropriate protocol on a specific network port other than the default port for each protocol. The only time you'll need a port number in a URL is if the server handling the information has been explicitly installed on that port. (This is covered in Chapter 11, "Putting It All Online.")

If a port number is necessary, it goes after the host name but before the directory, like this:

```
http://my-public-access-unix:1550/pub/file
```

Finally, the *directory* is the location of the file or other form of information on the host. The directory may be an actual directory and filename, or it may be another indicator that the protocol uses to refer to the location of that information. (For example, Gopher directories are not explicit directories.)

Special Characters in URLs

A "special character" in a URL is anything that is not an upper- or lower-case letter, a number (0–9), or the following symbols: dollar sign ($), dash (—), underscore (_), period (.), or (+). Any other characters must be specified using special URL escape codes to keep them from being interpreted as parts of the URL itself and for that URL to be recognized by as many browsers as possible.

URL escape codes are different from HTML character entities. URL escape codes are indicated by a percent sign (%) and a two-character hex symbol from the standard ASCII character set, for example %20 is a space, %3f is a question mark, and %2f is a slash.

For example, say you had a directory named All My Files, probably on a Macintosh, since there are spaces in the filename. Your first pass at a URL with that name in it might look like this:

```
http://myhost.com/harddrive/All My Files/www/file.html
```

If you put this URL in quotes in a link tag, it might very well work (but only if you put it in quotes). But because the spaces are considered special characters to the URL, some browsers may have problems with them and not recognize the path name. For full compatibility with all browsers, escape the spaces using %20:

```
http://myhost.com/harddrive/All%20My%20Files/www/file.html
```

Kinds of URLs

There are many kinds of URLs that are defined by the Uniform Resource Locator specification. (See Appendix A , "Sources for Further Information," for a pointer to the most recent version.) This section describes some of the more popular URLs and some things to look out for when using them.

HTTP

HTTP URLs are the most popular form of URL on the World Wide Web. HTTP stands for HyperText Transfer Protocol and is the protocol that World Wide Web servers use to send HTML documents over the Net.

HTTP URLs follow the basic URL form:

```
http://www.foo.com/home/foo/
```

If the URL ends in a slash, the last part of the URL is considered to be a directory name. The file that you get using a URL of this type is the "default" file for that directory as defined by the HTTP server, usually a file called `index.html`. (If the Web page you are designing is the top-level file for all the files in a directory, it's a good idea to call it `index.html`.)

You can also specify the filename directly in the URL. In this case, the file at the end of the URL is the one that is loaded.

```
http://www.foo.com/home/foo/index.html
http://www.foo.com/home/foo/homepage.html
```

Avoid using HTTP URLs like this, where `foo` is a directory:

```
http://www.foo.com/home/foo
```

Note that `foo` is a directory, but there is no slash at the end of the URL. Although most Web servers are smart enough to figure out that `foo` is a directory and not a file, some may have difficulties resolving this URL. Always make sure you are indicating either a file or a directory explicitly, and that if you are indicating a directory, a default file is available.

Anonymous FTP

FTP URLs are used to point to files located on FTP servers—and usually anonymous FTP servers; that is, those which you can log into using anonymous as the login ID and your e-mail address as the password. FTP URLs also follow the "standard" URL form.

```
ftp://ftp.foo.com/home/foo
ftp://ftp.foo.com/home/foo/homepage.html
```

Because you can retrieve either a file or a directory list with FTP, the restrictions on whether you need a trailing slash at the end of the URL are not the same. The first URL above retrieves a listing of the `foo` directory. The second URL retrieves and parses the file `homepage.html` in the `foo` directory:

Note that although your browser uses FTP to fetch the file, you can get an HTML file from that server just as if it were an HTTP server. Web browsers don't care *how* they get a hypertext file; as long as they can recognize it as HTML, either by the extension or by the `<HTML>` tag, depending on the browser, they will parse and display it as an HTML file. If they don't recognize it as an HTML file, it's not a big deal; the browser can either display it if it knows what kind of file it is, or just save it to disk.

> **Note:** Navigating FTP servers using a Web browser can often be much slower than navigating them using FTP itself, as the browser does not hold the connection open. Instead, it opens the connection, finds the file or directory listing, displays it, and then closes down the FTP connection. If you select a link to open a file or another directory in that listing, the browser will construct a new FTP URL from the items you selected, re-open the FTP connection using the new URL, get the next directory or file, and close it again. For this reason, FTP URLs are best when you know exactly which file you want to retrieve, rather than for browsing an archive.

Nonanonymous FTP

All of the FTP URLs in the previous section were used for anonymous FTP servers. You can also specify an FTP URL for named accounts on an FTP server, like this:

```
ftp://username:password@ftp.foo.com/home/foo/homepage.html
```

In this form of the URL, the username part is your login ID on the server, and password is that account's password. Note that no attempt is made to hide that password in the URL, so be very careful that no one is watching you when you are using URLs of this form—and don't put them into a link that someone else can find!

File

File URLs, which are only used in HTML files in limited instances, are intended to refer to files contained on the local disk; that is, files that are on the same system that the browser is running. For local files, file URLs take one of these two forms:

```
file:///dir1/dir2/file
file://localhost/dir1/dir2/file
```

Depending on the browser you are running, one or the other will usually work.

File URLs are very similar to FTP URLs, and in fact, if the host part of a file URL is not empty or localhost, your browser uses FTP to find the referenced file anyway. Both of the following URLs result in the same file being loaded in the same way:

```
file://somesystem.com/pub/dir/foo/file.html
ftp://somesystem.com/pub/dir/foo/file.html
```

Probably the best use of file URLs is in start-up pages for your browser (which are also called "home pages"). In this instance, since you will always be referring to a local file, a file URL makes sense.

The problem with file URLs is that they refer to local files, where local means on the same system that the browser pointing to the file is running on—*not* the same system that the document was retrieved from! If you use file URLs as links in your document, and then someone from elsewhere on the Net encounters your document and tries to follow those links, their browser will attempt to find the file on *their* local disk (and generally fail).

If your intention is to refer to files that are on the same file system or directory that the current document is in, use relative path names instead of file URLs. With relative path names for local files and other URLs for remote files, there's no reason why you should need to use a file URL at all.

> **Note:** One other reason to use file URLs would be in cases where you have a large central disk on a single host or network; for example, in large organizations with central file servers. In this case, since everyone who is using the links that contain the file URLs has access to those files, file URLs make more sense because the browser can open the file directly rather than loading it through a slower network connection such as FTP.

Mailto

The mailto URL is used to send electronic mail. If the browser supports mailto URLs, when a link that contains one is selected, the browser will prompt you for a subject and the body of the mail message and send that message to the appropriate address when you're done.

Many browsers, particularly those on the Macintosh and PC platforms, do not support mailto and produce an error if a link with a mailto URL is selected.

The mailto URL is different from the standard URL form. It looks like this:

```
mailto:internet_email_address
```

For example:

```
mailto:lemay@netcom.com
```

Note: If the e-mail address includes a percent sign (%), you'll have to use the escape character %25 instead.

Mailto URLs work especially well in the signature part of each document, that part enclosed in the <ADDRESS> tag. You can include your e-mail address in text and then make it into a link which uses a mailto URL in its HREF attribute, like this:

```
<ADDRESS>
Laura Lemay <A HREF="mailto:lemay@netcom.com">lemay@netcom.com</A>
</ADDRESS>
```

Note: Hopefully, by the time you read this, mailto URLs will be supported by more browsers.

Gopher

Gopher URLs use the standard URL file format up to and including the host name, and then they use special Gopher protocols to encode the path to the particular file. The directory in Gopher does not indicate a directory path name as HTTP and FTP URLs do and is too complex for this chapter; see the URL specification if you're really interested.

Most of the time you'll probably be using a Gopher URL just to point to a Gopher server, which is easy; a URL of this sort looks like this:

```
gopher://gopher.myhost.com/
```

If you really want to point directly to a specific file on a Gopher server, probably the best way to get the appropriate URL is not to try to build it yourself by hand, but instead to navigate to the appropriate file or collection using your browser and then copy and paste the appropriate URL into your HTML document.

Usenet

Usenet news URLs have one of two forms:

```
news:name_of_newsgroup
news:message-id
```

The first form is used to read an entire newsgroup, such as `comp.infosystems.www.providers` or `alt.gothic`. Your browser will provide you with a list of articles which you can then read individually.

The second form enables you to retrieve a specific news article. Each news article has a unique ID, called a message ID, which usually looks something like this:

```
<lemayCt76Jq.CwG@netcom.com>
```

To use a message ID in a URL, remove the angle brackets and include the `news:` part:

```
news:lemayCt76Jq.CwG@netcom.com
```

Note that news articles do not exist forever—they "expire" and are deleted—so a message ID that was valid at one point may become invalid several weeks later.

Both forms of URL assume that you are reading news from an NNTP server, and both can only be used if you have defined an NNTP server somewhere in an environment variable or preferences file for your browser. In this respect, news URLs are most useful simply for reading specific news articles locally, and not necessarily for using in links in documents.

Note: News URLs, like mailto URLs, may not be supported by all browsers.

Summary

This chapter shows how to use anchors to link to specific sections in documents and goes into more detail about URLs and how to use them.

Linking explicitly between documents, as you learned in Chapter 4, "Putting the Hyper in Hypertext," is fine if each document contains only one discrete piece of information. But if you have several bits of information in each document, linking between documents isn't specific enough. You need a method for linking to smaller bits of information within documents. That's where anchors come in. Anchors are a feature of the `<A>` tag that you can use to set a point to link to within a document, so that when the link is activated you

are taken directly to that bit of information within the new document—or even within the same document!

URLs (Uniform Resource Locators) are used to point to documents, files, and other information on the Internet. Depending on the type of information, URLs can contain several parts, but most generally contain a protocol type and location or address. URLs can be used to point to many kinds of information, but are most commonly used to point to Web documents (http), FTP directories or files (ftp), information on Gopher servers (gopher), electronic mail addresses (mailto), or Usenet news (news).

Q&A

Q You've only described two attributes of the `<A>` tag: HREF and NAME. Aren't there others?

A Yes; the `<A>` tag has several attributes including REL, REV, URN, METHODS, and TITLE. However, most of those attributes can only be used by tools that automatically generate links between documents, or by browsers that can manage links better than most of the browsers out there. Because 99 percent of you reading this book won't care about or ever use those links or browsers, I'm sticking to HREF and NAME and ignoring the other attributes.

If you're really interested, I've summarized them in Appendix B, and there are pointers to the various HTML specifications in Appendix A as well.

Q My links are not pointing to my anchors; when I follow a link, some other random bit of text is selected. What's going on here?

A Are you specifying the anchor name in the link after the hash sign exactly the same way that it appears in the anchor itself, with all the upper- and lower-case letters and spaces and other characters the same? Anchors are case sensitive, so if your browser cannot find an anchor name with an exact match, it may try to select something else in the document that is closer. This is dependent on browser behavior, of course, but if your links and anchors aren't working, it's usually because your anchor names and your anchors do not match.

Q Help! I can't keep my anchors and links straight! This is all really confusing. I need tools to manage all this.

A Some HTML editors help with building links and anchors by storing lists of anchors that you've built; when you create a link you can then just select from the list instead of trying to remember that anchor name. (There is a description of some HTML editors and tools in Chapter 14, "HTML Assistants: Editors and Converters.")

But real tools to manage links and anchors and the more general relationships between documents don't really exist yet. (Are you a programmer? Write some!) For now, having well-organized lists of anchors for files will go a long way to managing links and anchors across documents.

DAY

4

7

Including Images on Your Web Pages

Some people would argue that the sole reason the World Wide Web has become so popular is that formatted text and graphics can viewed together on the page. Text is fine, but there's nothing like a flashy color picture to really draw people's attention to your Web page.

This chapter explains almost everything you need to use images in Web pages:

- ☐ The kinds of images you can use
- ☐ How to include images on your Web page, either alone or alongside text
- ☐ How to use images as clickable links
- ☐ Providing alternatives for browsers that cannot view images
- ☐ Using images with transparent backgrounds
- ☐ How (and when) to use images in your Web page

Image Formats

There are two kinds of images that your Web browser can deal with: *inline* images and *external* images.

Inline images are images that appear directly on the Web page and are loaded when you load the page itself—assuming, of course, that you have a graphical browser, and that you have automatic image-loading turned on. Inline images, regardless of the system you're running on, should be in a format called GIF.

> **Note:** Some browsers can handle other formats for inline images, but GIF files are generally available on most platforms, so it's a good idea to stick with that format.

External images are images that are only downloaded at the request of your reader, usually on the other side of a link. Because browsers can be configured to handle different file types, you have more flexibility in the kind of image formats you can use for external images, for example JPEG or PCX or XBM. External images are covered in the next chapter.

> **Note:** So many acronyms! If you're not familiar with these formats, don't worry about it. Stick with GIF and you can't go wrong.

So how do you get images, and once you have them, how do you get them into GIF format?

You can get images by drawing them, scanning them, or buying them on a commercial clip art package. You can also find GIF images out on the Net, in the many image archives that are out there. But watch out for these images; many people scan and upload images without being aware of (or ignoring) the fact that those images may be copyrighted and owned by someone else who may not be pleased that you are using their work on the Web.

If you intend to use images on your home pages, your safest bet is to use images that you yourself create, to get explicit permission from the owner of the image to use those images online, or to take advantage of the market in CD-ROMs full of royalty-free clip art and stock photography (as I have in this book).

After you have an image in some kind of format, you'll need to convert it to GIF format to use it on your Web page. Many image editing programs such as Adobe Photoshop, Color It, Paint Shop Pro, or XV will read common input formats and output GIF files; look for an option called Compuserve GIF, or GIF87, or GIF89, or just plain GIF. There are also converter programs available (DeBabelizer on the Mac or the PBM filter package for UNIX) that do nothing except convert images to and from other formats.

Inline Images in HTML: The *<IMG>* Tag

After you have an image in GIF format, ready to go, you can put it in your Web page. Inline images are specified in HTML using the `<IMG>` tag. The `<IMG>` tag, like the `<HR>` and `<BR>` tags, has no closing tag. It does, however, have three attributes: `SRC`, `ALT`, and `ALIGN`. You'll learn about `ALT` and `ALIGN` later in this chapter; let's start here with `SRC`.

The `SRC` attribute indicates the filename of the image you want to include, in quotes. The path name to the file uses the same rules as path names in links to other documents. So, for a GIF file named `image.gif` in the same directory as this file, you can use the following tag:

```
<IMG SRC="image.gif">
```

For an image file one directory up from the current directory, use

```
<IMG SRC="../image.gif">
```

And so on, using the same rules as for document names in the `HREF` part of the `<A>` tag.

Note: For your GIF files to be recognized as such by a Web server or browser, make sure you name them with a .gif extension.

Note: If you use the same image several times in the same document, make an effort to use relative path names over full path names or URLs in the `<IMG>` tag. Using relative path names for each repeated image allows the browser to only download the image once, and then just redisplay it at each point on the page. If you specify the image using a full path name, the browser may repeatedly download it, slowing down the time it takes for your document to load.

Exercise 7.1. Try it!

Every year for Halloween, you've volunteered as a vampire for a local haunted house. This year, using all the excellent advice I've given you in the last six chapters, you've created a home page to advertise the "Halloween House of Terror," in `halloween.html`. Here's the HTML code for the top part of the file, and Figure 7.1 shows how it looks so far:

```
<HTML>
<HEAD>
<TITLE>Welcome to the Halloween House of Terror</TITLE>
<BODY>
<H1>Welcome to the Halloween House of Terror!!</H1>
<HR>
<P>Voted the most frightening haunted house three years in a row, the
<STRONG>Halloween House of Terror</STRONG> provides the ultimate in
Halloween thrills. Over <STRONG>20 rooms of thrills and excitement</STRONG>
to make your blood run cold and your hair stand on end!</P>
<P>The Halloween House of Terror is open from <EM>October 20 to November
1st</EM>, with a gala celebration on Halloween night. Our hours are:</P>
<UL>
<LI>Mon-Fri 5pm-midnight
<LI>Sat & Sun 5pm-3AM
<LI><STRONG>Halloween Night (10/31)</STRONG>: 3pm-???
</UL>
<P>The Halloween House of Terror is located at:<BR>
The Old Waterfall Shopping Center<BR>
1020 Mirabella Ave<BR>
Springfield, CA 94532<BR>
</P>
</BODY>
</HTML>
```

Figure 7.1. *The Halloween House home page.*

So far, so good, although it looks a little plain. Conveniently, you happen to have an image of a spider web kicking around in a clip art library (Figure 7.2) that would look excellent at the top of that Web page.

The image is called `web.gif`, and is in GIF format and in the same directory as the `halloween.html` page, so it's ready to go into the Web page. To include it, add the following line to the HTML file just before the initial heading:

```
<BODY>
<IMG SRC="web.gif">
<H1>Welcome to the Halloween House of Terror!!</H1>
```

And now, when you reload the `halloween.html` page, your browser should open and include the spider web image.

If the image doesn't load, first make sure you've specified the name of the file properly in the HTML file. Image filenames are case sensitive.

If that doesn't work, double-check the image file to make sure that it is indeed a GIF image.

Figure 7.2. *The spider web image.*

Finally, make sure that you have image loading turned on in your browser. (The option is called Auto-Load Images in Mosaic.)

Figure 7.3 shows the result with the spider web image included.

If one spider is good, two would be really good, right? Try adding another <IMG> tag next to the first one, and see what happens.

Note how this appears in your particular browser, and if you have multiple browsers available, try testing the file in each one. Different browsers will format adjacent images differently; some will format it as shown in Figure 7.4, whereas others will arrange the images on separate lines.

Figure 7.3. *The Halloween House home page, with spider.*

Figure 7.4. *Multiple images.*

Images and Text

The previous exercise showed how to put an inline image on a page on its own separate line, with text above or below the image. HTML also enables you to put an image next to (or inside) a line of text. (In fact, this is what the phrase "inline image" actually means.)

To include an image inline with text, simply include it in the text, inside the element tags (<H1>, <P>, <ADDRESS>, and so on). Figure 7.5 shows the difference putting the image inline with the text makes. (I've also shortened the title itself.)

```
<H1><IMG SRC="web.gif">The Halloween House of Terror!!</H1>
```

The image doesn't have to be large, and it doesn't have to be at the beginning of the text. You can include an image anywhere in a block of text:

```
<BLOCKQUOTE>
Love, from whom the world <IMG SRC="world.gif"> begun,<BR>
Hath the secret of the sun. <IMG SRC="sun.gif"> <BR>
Love can tell, and love alone,
Whence the million stars <IMG SRC="star.gif"> were strewn <BR>
Why each atom <IMG SRC="atom.gif"> knows its own. <BR>
—Robert Bridges
</BLOCKQUOTE>
```

Figure 7.6 shows how this looks.

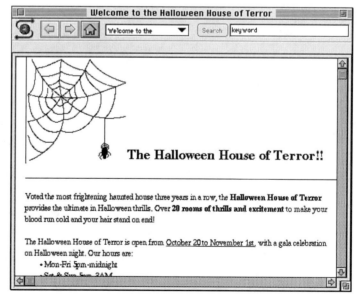

Figure 7.5. *The Halloween House page with image inside the heading.*

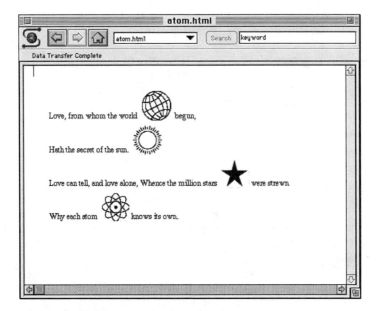

Figure 7.6. *Images can go anywhere in text.*

Text and Image Alignment

The ALIGN attribute of the <IMG> tag allows you to control how the text and the image are aligned. There are three possible values: ALIGN=TOP, ALIGN=MIDDLE, and ALIGN=BOTTOM. Figure 7.7 shows how each alignment attribute affects the appearance of the text and the image.

Note that all the alignment options in HTML affect only the single line of text in which the image occurs. Any other lines of text appear above or below that initial first line, as shown in Figure 7.8. In the current state of HTML, you cannot align an entire column of text next to an image, or wrap text around that image. HTML Level Three defines additional tags for better integrating text and graphics into the layout of a Web page.

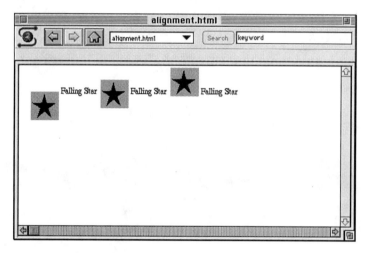

Figure 7.7. *Images and text alignment.*

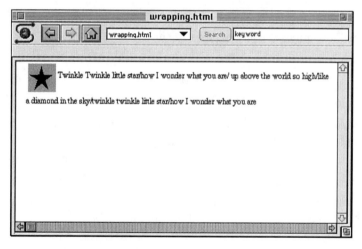

Figure 7.8. *Text does not wrap around images.*

Images and Links

If you include an `<IMG>` tag inside the opening and closing parts of a link tag (`<A>`), that image serves as a clickable hot spot for the link itself:

```
<A HREF="index.html"><IMG SRC="uparrow.gif"></A>
```

Images that are also hot spots for links appear with a border around them to distinguish them from ordinary nonclickable images, as Figure 7.9 shows.

Figure 7.9. *Images that are also links.*

If you include both an image and text in the anchor, both the image and the text itself become hot spots, pointing to the same document:

```
<A HREF="index.html"><IMG SRC="uparrow.gif">Up to Index</A>
```

Exercise 7.2. Navigation icons.

When you have a set of related Web pages between which the navigation takes place in a consistent way (for example, moving forward, or back, up, home, and so on), it makes sense to provide a menu of navigation options at the top or bottom of each page so that your readers know exactly how to find their way through your documents.

This example shows you how to create a set of icons that are used to navigate through a linear set of documents. You have three icons in GIF format: one for forward, one for back, and a third to enable the reader to jump to a global index of the entire document structure.

First, we'll write the HTML structure to support the icons. Here, the document itself isn't all that important, so I'll just include a shell document. Figure 7.10 shows how the document looks to begin with.

```
<HTML>
<HEAD>
<TITLE>Motorcycle Maintenance: Removing Spark Plugs</TITLE>
<H1>Removing Spark Plugs</H1>
<P>(include some info about spark plugs here)</P>
```

```
<HR>
</BODY>
</HTML>
```

 Output

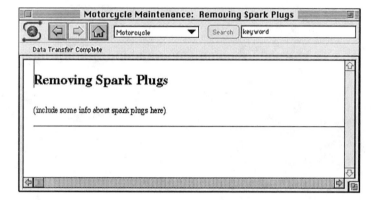

Figure 7.10. *The basic document, no icons.*

Now, at the bottom of the document, add your images using IMG tags:

 Input

```
<IMG SRC="arrowright.gif">
<IMG SRC="arrowleft.gif">
<IMG SRC="arrowup.gif">
```

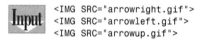 **Output**

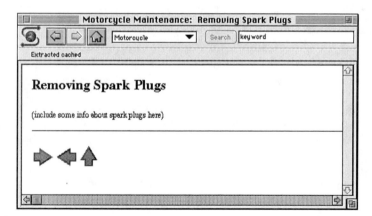

Figure 7.11. *The basic document with icons.*

Now, add the anchors to the images to activate them. Figure 7.12 shows the result.

```
<A HREF="replacing.html"><IMG SRC="arrowright.gif"></A>
<A HREF="ready.html"><IMG SRC="arrowleft.gif"></A>
<A HREF="index.html"><IMG SRC="arrowup.gif""></A>
```

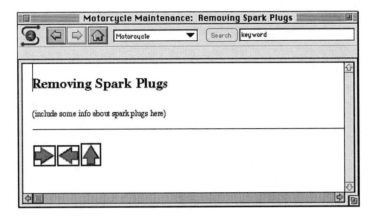

Figure 7.12. *The basic document with iconic links.*

Now when you click on the icons, the browser jumps to the document in the link just as it would have if you had used text links.

Speaking of text, are the icons usable enough as is? How about adding some text describing exactly what is on the other side of the link? You can add the text inside or outside the anchor, depending on whether you want the text to be a hot spot for the link as well. Here, we'll include it outside the link, so only the icon serves as the hot spot. We'll also align the bottoms of the text and the icons using the ALIGN attribute of the IMG tag. Finally, because the extra text causes the icons to move onto two lines, we'll arrange each one on its own line instead. See Figure 7.13 for the final menu.

```
<P>
<A HREF="replacing.html"><IMG SRC="arrowright.gif" ALIGN=BOTTOM></A>
On to "Gapping the New Plugs"<BR>
<A HREF="ready.html"><IMG SRC="arrowleft.gif" ALIGN=BOTTOM></A>
Back to "When You Should Replace your Spark Plugs"<BR>
<A HREF="index.html"><IMG SRC="arrowup.gif" ALIGN=BOTTOM></A>
Up To Index
</P>
```

Figure 7.13. *The basic document with iconic links and text.*

Providing Alternatives

Graphics can turn a simple text-only Web page into a glorious visual feast. But what happens if someone is reading your Web page from a text-only browser, or what if he or she has image-loading turned off, so all your careful graphics appear as simple envelope icons? All of a sudden that glorious visual feast isn't looking as nice. And, worse, if you haven't taken these possibilities into consideration while designing your Web page, your work could be unreadable and unusable by that portion of your audience.

There is a simple solution to one of these problems: the ALT attribute of the IMG tag, which enables you to substitute something meaningful in place of the image on browsers that cannot display that image.

Usually, in a text-only browser such as Lynx, graphics that are specified using the <IMG> tag in the original file are "displayed" as the word [IMAGE]. (An example is shown in Figure 7.14.) If the image itself was a link to something else, that link is preserved.

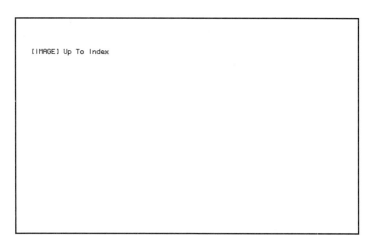

Figure 7.14. *"Images" in Lynx.*

The ALT attribute in the <IMG> tag enables you to provide a more meaningful text alternative to the blank [IMAGE] for your readers who are using text-only Web browsers. The ALT attribute contains a string with the text you want to substitute for the graphic:

```
<IMG SRC="myimage.gif" ALT="[a picture of a cat]">
```

Note that most browsers will interpret the string you include in the ALT attribute as a literal string; that is, if you include any HTML tags in that string they will be printed as typed instead of being parsed and displayed as HTML code. Try to limit the use of ALT to a simple string.

For example, in the example you did in Exercise 7.2, with the arrow icons for navigation, you could provide text alternatives for the icons, or just include an empty string (" ") to "hide" the image in the text version. Here are two ideas:

1. Use text-only markers (Figure 7.15). Here's the code:

    ```
    <P>
    <A HREF="replacing.html"><IMG SRC="arrowright.gif" ALIGN=BOTTOM
    ALT="[NEXT]"></A>On to "Gapping the New Plugs"<BR>
    <A HREF="ready.html"><IMG SRC="arrowleft.gif" ALIGN=BOTTOM
    ALT="[PREVIOUS]"></A> Back to "When You Should Replace your Spark
    Plugs"<BR>
    <A HREF="index.html"><IMG SRC="arrowup.gif" ALIGN=BOTTOM ALT="[UP]"></
    A>Up To Index
    </P>
    ```

7

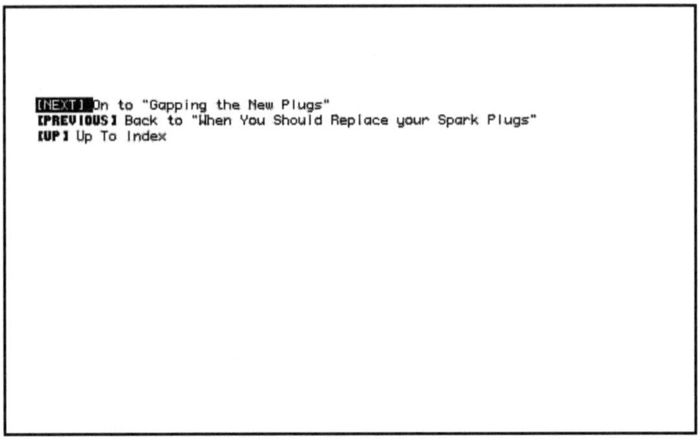

```
[NEXT] On to "Gapping the New Plugs"
[PREVIOUS] Back to "When You Should Replace your Spark Plugs"
[UP] Up To Index
```

Figure 7.15. *Text markers to replace images.*

2. Hide the images altogether and make the text the anchor instead (shown in Figure 7.16). Enter

```
<P>
<A HREF="replacing.html"><IMG SRC="arrowright.gif" ALIGN=BOTTOM
ALT="">On to "Gapping the New Plugs"<BR></A>
<A HREF="ready.html"><IMG SRC="arrowleft.gif" ALIGN=BOTTOM ALT="">
Back to "When You Should Replace your Spark Plugs"</A><BR>
<A HREF="index.html"><IMG SRC="arrowup.gif" ALIGN=BOTTOM ALT="">Up To
Index</A>
</P>
```

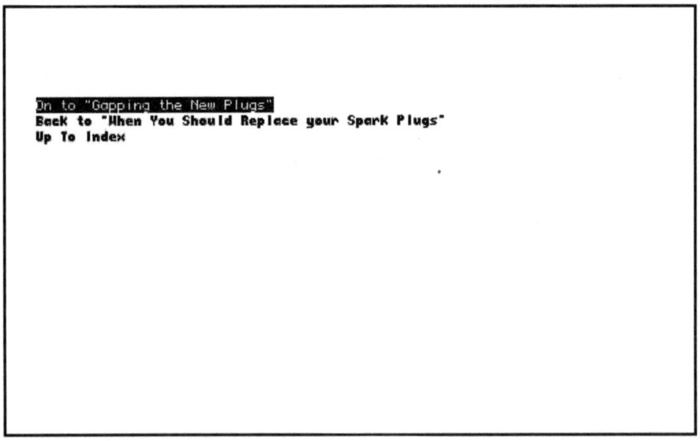

```
On to "Gapping the New Plugs"
Back to "When You Should Replace your Spark Plugs"
Up To Index
```

Figure 7.16. *Hide the images.*

Tip: A sneaky trick I've seen used for the ALT attribute is to include an ASCII art picture (a picture made up of characters, like the cow in Chapter 5, "Still More HTML") in the ALT tag, which then serves as the "picture" in text-only browsers. To accomplish this trick, you'll need the ASCII art prepared ahead of time. Then, in your HTML code, include the entire `<IMG>` tag inside `<PRE>`...`</PRE>` tags, and the ASCII art inside the ALT attribute, like this:

```
<PRE>
<IMG SRC="cow.gif" ALT="
          (  )
   Moo    (oo)
          \/ — — — \
            | |       | \
            | | —W| |   *
            | |       | |
            | |       | |
">
</PRE>
```

In this code, the original image (`cow.gif`) will be replaced by the text version, neatly formatted, in text-only browsers. Note that because the `<PRE>` tags are outside the `<IMG>` tag itself (to get around the fact that you can't put HTML inside the ALT attribute), this trick works best when the image is alone on a line; that is, there is no text on the line before or after it.

Images with Transparent Backgrounds

A recent innovation on the Web has been support for images with transparent backgrounds; that is, images whose backgrounds are opaque so the GIF appears to "float" on the background of the page. Figure 7.17 illustrates the difference between normal and transparent GIFs.

Most current GIF files are in a format called GIF87, which doesn't allow a transparent background. To create an image with a transparent background, you need a tool that can convert the image to GIF89 format. The giftrans program on UNIX and DOS and Transparency on the Macintosh are readily available tools for creating images with transparent backgrounds.

Figure 7.17. *Normal and transparent backgrounds.*

Before you can convert the image, however, you need an image with an appropriate background. The easiest images to convert to have transparent backgrounds are icons or other simple art in which the image and the background are distinct. (See Figure 7.18.) Although you can have photographs with transparent backgrounds, the results might not be as nice if the defining line between the image and the background is not clear.

Figure 7.18. *Good and bad images for transparent backgrounds.*

The goal is to make sure that your background is all one single color. If that background is made up of several colors that are sort of close to each other (as they might be in a photograph), then only one of those colors will be transparent.

You can isolate the background of your image using any image-editing program. Simply edit the pixels around the image so they are all one color. Also, be careful that the color you're using for the background isn't also used extensively in the image itself because the color will become transparent there, too, when you convert the image to GIF89 format.

Although the actual color you choose for the background isn't overly important, it's a good idea to choose a light gray (RGB values of somewhere around 200, 200, 200). Many browsers do not support transparent GIFs yet, but most of them use that light gray color for their backgrounds; so if you make the background of your GIF light gray, you'll still get kind of a transparency effect even if the browser doesn't support transparent GIFs.

After you've made sure that the image has an appropriate background, you'll need to convert it. The next couple of sections describe how to convert the GIF file on different platforms.

Note: These sections describe the current popular tools for converting to the GIF89. By the time you read this there may be more and better tools for accomplishing the same thing. Don't feel that you have to use these tools if there are better ones available.

Convert the Image: UNIX and DOS/Windows

To convert your image to GIF89, you can use a program called giftrans. You can FTP the source for this program from:

```
ftp://ftp.rz.uni-karlsruhe.de/pub/net/www/tools/giftrans.c
```

In that same directory is a binary file for DOS-based systems. If you don't have a C compiler (or don't feel like compiling it), you can find the file at

```
ftp://ftp.rz.uni-karlsruhe.de/pub/net/www/tools/giftrans.exe
```

Once you have giftrans compiled and ready to go, you'll need to know the index of the color you want to make transparent in the color map (sometimes called the color table) for this image.

Many image-editing programs allow you to view a palette of the colors used in the image's color map. In Photoshop, the Color Table command shows the palette; in xv for X11, the Color Editing window does the same thing. Select the color in the image that you want to use as the background color. This will highlight a color in the palette. (See Figure 7.19 for an example of how it works in xv.) To find out the index of this color, count the colors in the palette across from left to right, row by row, until you get to the color you are using as the background. That's the index number.

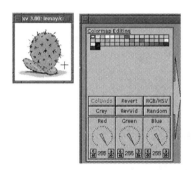

Figure 7.19. *Index numbers in xv.*

With the color index and a compiled version of giftrans you can convert the image, like this:

```
giftrans -t index -o newfile.gif imagefile.gif
```

where index is the *index* number of the transparent color, imagefile.gif is the original GIF file, and newfile.gif is the name of the file you want to create.

> **Note:** Instead of the index of the color in the palette, giftrans can also accept the RGB value of the color you want to make transparent. This is often easier to figure out in many image-editing programs. The catch is that you have to convert the usual 0 to 255 RGB values into hexadecimal numbers. For example, the color white, which is 255 255 255 in normal RGB values, would be #FFFFFF, and it's this value that you would give to giftrans instead of the index number.

Convert the Image: Macintosh

Transparency, by Aaron Giles, is a wonderful program for converting GIF files to GIF89 and making any color in the file transparent. You should be able to get Transparency from most Macintosh FTP archives. To use Transparency, do the following:

1. Open the GIF file you want to convert.
2. With the mouse, click and hold the color in the GIF you want to be transparent. A pop-up window of the colors available in the GIF will be displayed. (See Figure 7.20.)

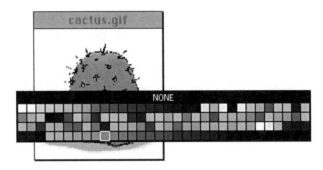

Figure 7.20. *Color maps in Transparency.*

3. Choose the appropriate color, or NONE if you want no transparent colors in your GIF file.
4. Save the file as a GIF89 file.

Using the Image in Your Web Page

Once you have an image with a transparent background, you don't need to do anything special in HTML; use the `<IMG>` tag just as you always would to include the image inline on your Web page.

> **Note:** Even if you have a GIF image in the proper format with a transparent background, some browsers that do not understand GIF89 format may not be able to display that image or may not display it with an opaque background. Transparent GIFs are still a new phenomenon, and full support for them in browsers has not yet become commonplace.

Hints for Better Use of Images

The use of images in Web pages is one of the bigger arguments among users and providers of Web pages today. For everyone who wants to design Web page with more, bigger, brighter images to take full advantage of the graphical capabilities of the Web, there is someone on a slow network connection who is begging for fewer images so that his or her browser does not take three hours to load a page.

As a designer of Web pages, you should take both of these points of view under consideration. Balance the fun of creating a highly visual, colorful Web page with the need to get your information to everyone you want to get it—and that includes people who may not have access to your images at all.

This section offers some hints and compromises you can make in the design of your Web pages so that you can make everyone happy (or everyone unhappy, depending on how you look at it).

Do You Really Need This Image?

For each image you put inline on your Web page, consider why you are putting it there. What does that image add to the design? Does it provide information that could be presented in the text instead? Is it just there because you like how it looks?

Try not to clutter your Web page with pretty but otherwise unnecessary images. A simple Web page with only a few iconic images is often more effective than one that leaps out at you with fancy 3-D buttons and big photographs and drop-shadow bullets.

Keep Your Images Small

A smaller image takes less time to transfer over the Net; therefore, using smaller images makes your Web page load faster and causes less frustration for people trying to read it over a slow link.

Smaller images can mean smaller in actual physical dimensions on the screen, but you can also create smaller images by reducing the number of colors you have in the image. Your goal is to reduce the file size of the image so that it transfers faster, but a 4-inch by 4-inch black-and-white image (two colors) may be smaller in file size than a 1/2-inch by 1/2-inch 8-bit color photographic image. With most image-processing programs, you can reduce the number of colors and touch up the result so it looks good even with fewer colors.

A good rule to follow is that you should try to keep your inline images somewhere under 20K. That may seem small, but a single 20K file takes nearly that many seconds to download over a 14.4K baud SLIP connection. Multiply that time by the number of images on your Web page, and it may take a substantial amount of time for that page to load. Will someone care about what you have in your Web page if they have had to go off and have lunch while it was loading?

> **Note:** The small icons that I used for the arrows in the navigation examples are less than 1K apiece. The spider web image in the Halloween example is 17K.

Provide Alternatives to Images

If you're not using the ALT attribute in your images, you should be. The ALT attribute is extremely useful for making your Web page readable by text-only browsers. But what about people who turn off images in their browser because they have a slow link to the Internet? Most browsers do not use the value of ALT in this case (although they should). And sometimes ALT isn't enough; because you can only specify text inside an ALT string, you can't substitute HTML code for the image.

To get around all these problems while still keeping your nifty graphical Web page, consider creating additional text-only versions of your Web pages and putting links to them on the full-graphics versions of that same Web page, like this:

```
<P>A <A HREF="TextVersion.html">text-only</A> version of this page is
available.</P>
```

The link to the text-only page only takes up one small paragraph on the "real" Web page, but makes the information you have to offer much more accessible to your readers. It's a courtesy that those readers will thank you for, while still allowing you to load up your "main" Web page with as many graphics as you like for those with fast connections.

Watch Out for Display Assumptions

Many people create problems for their readers by making a couple of careless assumptions about other people's hardware. When developing Web pages, be kind and remember these two guidelines:

☐ **Don't assume everyone has screen dimensions or resolutions the same as yours.**

I've seen quite a few Web pages recently that have long images across the top of the page, and some text centered within that image (probably an attempt to get around the fact that HTML won't center text). The problem is that the author centered the text in the image based on the width of the display in his or her own browser—probably XMosaic, which uses a great deal of screen real estate.

But when I view that page in my browser on the Macintosh, I can only see the left side of the image. The centered text is off the right edge of the screen, and I have to scroll over to see it. (If I had a bigger screen I could resize the window, but I'm stuck with the screen I've got.)

My browser could format the rest of the text in the page to fit my screen, but it couldn't do anything about that image. Because of the assumption that page's author made about their audience and their screen dimensions, I am not getting the information I need from that Web page without some work.

☐ **Don't assume everyone has full color**.

Test your images in resolutions other than full color. You may be surprised at the results: Colors drop out or dither strangely in gray scale or black and white, and the affect may not be what you had intended. Keep in mind that people with gray-scale or black-and-white monitors may be reading your Web pages.

Make sure your images are visible at all resolutions, or provide alternatives for high- and low-resolution images on the page itself.

Summary

One of the major features that makes the World Wide Web stand out from other forms of Internet information is that documents on the Web can contain full-color graphics. It was arguably the existence of those graphics that allowed the Web to catch on so quickly and to become so popular in so short an amount of time.

To place images on your Web pages, those images must be in GIF format and small enough that they can be quickly downloaded over a potentially slow link. The HTML tag `<IMG>` allows you to put an image on the Web page, either inline with text or on a line by itself. The `IMG` tag has three attributes:

☐ `SRC`: the location and filename of the image to include

☐ `ALIGN`: how to align the image vertically with its surrounding text. `ALIGN` can have one of three values: `TOP`, `MIDDLE`, or `BOTTOM`.

☐ `ALT`: A text string to substitute for the image in text-only browsers.

You can include images inside a link tag (`<A>`) and have those images serve as hot spots for the links, same as text.

Q&A

Q How can I create thumbnails of my images?

A You'll have to do that with some kind of image-editing program; the Web won't do it for you. Just open up the image and scale it down to the right size.

Q Can I put HTML tags in the string for the ALT attribute?

A That would be nice, wouldn't it? Unfortunately, you can't. All you can do is put an ordinary string in there. Keep it simple and you should be fine.

Q I've seen some Web pages where you can click on different places in an image and get different link results, like a map of the United States where each state has a different page. How do you do this in HTML?

A That's called an *image map*, and it's an advanced form of Web page development. It involves writing code on the server side to interpret the mouse clicks and send back the right result. I describe image maps in Chapter 13, "Forms and Image Maps."

8

Using External Media: Images, Sound, and Video

As the last chapter explains, inline images are images that can be displayed directly on the page along with text. The World Wide Web also supports other media, including images, sound, and video that can be retrieved on demand and loaded in windows separate from the browser window itself. These forms of media on the Web are called external media because they are stored externally from your Web files themselves.

In this chapter, you learn about

☐ What "external media" means

☐ How different browsers handle different forms of external media

☐ Specifying external media in your HTML file

☐ Using sound

☐ Using video

What's External Media?

In its most general form, external media are any files that are not directly loadable by a Web browser, which can include everything from non-inline GIF files to MPEG video to PostScript to some other random format. You can create a link in an HTML file to an external media file in exactly the same way that you link to another document: using the <A> tag.

When a server sends a browser a file, it also includes information about what kind of file it is, using a special code. If the browser cannot itself display that kind of file, it matches the file type to an additional list of "helper" applications (sometimes called "viewers") for that platform. If the file type can be recognized and a helper application is listed, the browser starts the helper application and feeds it the file. The helper application in turn displays or runs or plays the external media file that the browser could not read.

Browsers also can execute helper applications for files that it loads from the local disk, except that it uses the extension of the file (.gif, .jpeg, and so on) to find out the type of the file, and to execute the appropriate helper application. This is why your HTML and GIF files must have extensions of .html and .gif, respectively, so that the browser can figure out what they are.

This system works especially well as it keeps the browser itself small (no need to include viewers or players for every strange media type out there), and it's also configurable for new file types and new and better helper applications as they are written. Each browser has a list that maps file extensions to file types, and another list that maps file types to applications. You should be able to configure your browser to use the helper applications you want to use, as well as be able to add new file extensions to the list of file types.

8

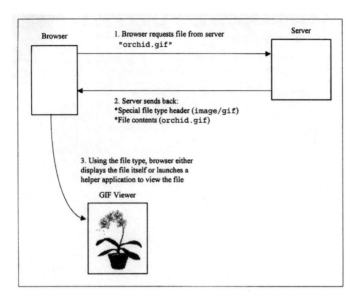

Figure 8.1. *Browsers and other files.*

Note: The list of file types that browsers use in their helper application lists are drawn from a standard called MIME, which was originally intended for encoding media in electronic mail messages. You won't need to know this now, but it may be important once you start dealing with servers in Day Six.

Specifying External Media in HTML

To specify an external media file in HTML, you link to it just as you would another document using the `<A>` tag and the HREF attribute. The path to the external file is a path name or URL just as you would use if the file were another HTML document:

```
<A HREF="some_external_file">A media file.</A>
```

If you're going to make use of links to external media files, it is helpful if you include in the body of the link (or somewhere nearby) some information about the format of the media, such as what kind of file format it is and its file size.

Knowing the format of the file ahead of time is useful so that readers know if they can read it or not. They're not going to want to retrieve a file if they can't do anything with it once it's been downloaded.

Telling them how big the file is allows your readers to decide before selecting the link whether they have the time (or the inclination) to sit and wait for the download to take place.

A simple sentence as part of the link satisfies both these suggestions:

```
<A HREF="bigsnail.jpeg">A 59K JPEG Image of a snail</A>
<A HREF="tacoma.mov">The Fall of the Tacoma Narrows Bridge </A>
(a200K QuickTime File)
```

Using External Images

If you're using images inline on your Web page, the one format that all graphical browsers can read is GIF. Linking to external images, however, gives you slightly more flexibility in the image formats you can use.

Some popular image formats for external media include the following:

☐ **GIF**

Even though GIF files can be read inline, it often makes sense, particularly in the case of larger files, to link to external GIF files.

☐ **JPEG**

JPEG files are nearly as popular as GIF files. In comparison to GIFs, JPEG file sizes are significantly smaller and therefore faster to download, but for many images the quality is not as good. Providing optional JPEG files in addition to GIFs is a great help to your readers who have installed JPEG viewers.

☐ **XBM**

XBM files are X Window System Bitmaps.

☐ **PICT**

PICT files are a common graphics format for the Macintosh.

Image processing programs such as Adobe Photoshop, xv for X, the pbm conversion programs for UNIX, and deBabelizer for Macintosh and Windows should be able to convert between each of these formats given an existing file.

Once you have a converted file, you must name it with the appropriate extension so that your browser can recognize it. Extensions for graphics files are shown in Table 8.1.

Table 8.1. Image formats and extensions.

Format	Extension
GIF	.gif
JPEG	.jpg, .jpeg
XBM	.xbm
PICT	.PICT

Exercise 8.1 uses external image files.

Exercise 8.1: Linking to external GIF and JPEG files.

A common practice in Web pages is to provide a very small GIF image (a "thumbnail") inline on the page itself, and then link that image to its larger counterpart. This has two major advantages over including the entire image inline:

☐ It keeps the size of the Web page small, so that page can be downloaded quickly.

☐ It gives your reader a "taste" of the image before downloading the entire thing.

In this simple example, you'll set up a link between a small image and the external, larger version of that same image. The large image is a photograph of some penguins in GIF format, called `penguinsbig.gif` (shown in Figure 8.2).

First, create a "thumbnail" version of the penguins photograph in your favorite image editor. The thumbnail can be a scaled version of the original file, a clip of that file (say, one penguin out of the group), or anything else you want to indicate the larger image.

Here, I've created a picture of one penguin in the group to serve as the inline image. (I've called it `penguinslittle.gif`.) Unlike the large version of the file, which is 100K, the small picture is only 3K. Using the `<IMG>` tag, I'll put that image directly on a nearly content-free Web page:

```
<HTML>
<HEAD>
<TITLE>Penguins</TITLE>
</HEAD></BODY>
<H1>Penguins</H1>
<IMG SRC="penguinslittle.gif">
</BODY></HTML>
```

Figure 8.2. *Penguins.*

Now, using a link tag, you can link the small icon to the bigger picture by enclosing the
<IMG> tag inside an <A> tag:

```
<A HREF="penguinsbig.gif"><IMG SRC="penguinslittle.gif"></A>
```

The final result of the page is shown in Figure 8.3. Now, if you click on the small penguin
image, the big image will be downloaded and viewed by the helper application defined
for GIF files for that browser.

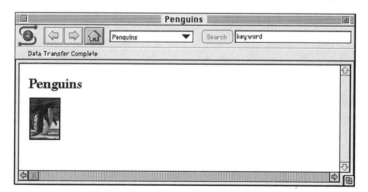

Figure 8.3. *The Penguin home page with link.*

An alternative to linking the small image directly to the large image is to provide the external image in several different formats, and provide descriptive links for each one (as in the hint in the previous section). In this part of the example, I'll link to a JPEG version of that same penguins file.

To create the JPEG version of the penguin photograph, you need to use your image editor or converter again to convert the original photograph. Here, I've called it penguinsbig.jpg.

> **Note:** JPEG files should always be named with a .jpg or .jpeg extension so the browser and server can figure out what kind of files they are.

To provide both GIF and JPEG forms of the penguin photo, we'll convert the link on the image into a simple link menu to the GIF and JPEG files, providing some information about file size:

```
<IMG SRC="penguinslittle.gif">
<UL>
<LI>Penguins (<A HREF="pengiunsbig.gif">100K GIF file</A>)
<LI>Penguins (<A HREF="pengiunsbig.jpg">25K JPEG file</A>)
</UL>
```

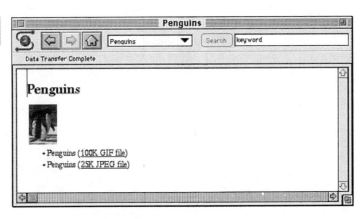

Figure 8.4. *The Penguins link menu.*

Using Sound

Including sound files on your Web page can provide optional annotations to existing text, welcome messages from you or someone important in your organization, or extra information that words and pictures cannot convey. If you're musically inclined, you can provide sound clips of your work on the Web or create archives of clips from your favorite bands—be sure to get their permission first!

To include a link to an external sound on your Web page, you must have that sound sample in the right format, just as you would for an image. Currently, the only fully cross-platform sound file format for the Web is Sun Microsystems's AU format. AU allows several different kinds of sound sample encoding, but the most popular one is 8-bit μ-law. For this reason, AU files are often called simply μ-law files. AU files are of only barely acceptable quality, as the 8-bit sampling causes them to sound a bit like they are being transmitted over a telephone.

You can use other better quality sound formats for specific platforms. The most popular are AIFF for the Macintosh and WAV for Windows. Note, however, that if you use one of these formats (or any other unusual formats), those sounds will probably not be playable cross-platform; therefore, you should be sure to indicate the format of the sound file in the link that points to it.

A recent addition to the already mind-boggling array of sound formats is MPEG audio. MPEG is generally better known as a video standard, but the audio portion of the standard allows for very high-quality sound, and players exist for many platforms. At the time that I'm writing this, no browsers support MPEG audio out of the box (all require some sort of special configuration), but the popularity for this form of sound file seems to be growing, and this situation may have changed by the time you read this.

So how does one get or create a sound file, and once you have it, how do you use it? Read on.

Getting Sound Files

Where can you get sound files? From a variety of sources:

- [ ] Many systems allow you to record and digitize sounds or voice using a microphone that came with your system or with inexpensive add-on equipment. For PC-compatible systems, your soundboard may have come with some sort of recording capabilities. For simple sound or music, this is the easiest and cheapest way to get sound into your Web page. The quality will not be wonderful, but it'll work.

Doing higher-quality recording and production, however, requires specialized (and expensive) equipment. Recording high-quality sound samples is beyond the scope of this book.

☐ Some platforms with CD-ROM drives may allow you to record digital sounds directly off a standard audio CD; you'll need a CD-ROM drive that supports this, of course. Keep in mind if you go this route that most published audio material is copyrighted, and its owners may not appreciate your making their songs or sounds available for free on the Internet.

☐ Many Internet archives have collections of small, digitized samples in the appropriate format for the platform they emphasize (for example, SND format files for Macintosh archives, WAV format for Windows, AU for Sun's UNIX, and so on).

Note: Keep in mind that, like images, sounds you find on the Net may be owned by someone who won't like your using them. Use caution when using "found" sounds.

☐ Commercial "clip sound" products are available, again, in appropriate formats for your platform. These sounds have the advantage of usually being public domain or royalty-free, meaning that you can use them anywhere without needing to get permission or pay a fee.

Converting Sound Files

Once you have a sound file, it may not be in the right format—that is, the format you want it to be in. The programs introduced in this section can read and convert many popular sound formats.

For UNIX and PC-compatible systems, a program called SOX by Lance Norskog can convert between many sound formats (AU, WAV, AIFF, Macintosh SND) and perform some rudimentary processing including filtering, changing the sample rate, and reversing the sample.

On DOS, WAVany by Bill Neisius converts most common sound formats (including AU and Macintosh SND) to WAV format.

Waveform Hold and Modify (WHAM), for Windows, is an excellent sound player, editor, and converter that also works really well as a helper application for your browser.

For the Macintosh, the freeware SoundApp by Norman Franke reads and plays most sound formats, and converts to WAV, Macintosh SND, AIFF, and NeXT sound formats (but mysteriously, not Sun AU). The freeware μ-law will convert Macintosh sounds (SND) to AU format.

FTP sources for each of these programs are listed in Appendix A, "Sources for Further Information."

Including Sound Files on Web Pages

In order for a browser to recognize your sound file, it must have the appropriate extension for its file type. Common formats and their extensions are listed in Table 8.2.

Table 8.2. Sound formats and extensions.

Format	Extension
AU/μ-law	.au
AIFF/AIFC	.aiff
WAV	.wav
MPEG Audio	.mp2

After you have a file in the right format and with the right extension, you can go ahead and link to it from your Web page like any other external file:

```
Laurence Olivier's "To Be or Not To Be" soliloquy from the film of the play
Hamlet (<A HREF="olivier_hamlet.au">AIFF format, 357K)</A>
```

Two further hints for using sound files in your Web page:

☐ *Always* tell your readers that your link is to a sound, and also be sure to note what format that sound file is in. This is especially important if you use a format other than AU; otherwise, your readers will have to download it to find out if they can handle it or not.

☐ Sound files tend to be quite large, so consider creating sound files of lesser quality for people on slower connections. In particular, mono sound files generally are smaller than stereo, and 8-bit files are smaller than 16-bit.

☐ If you use multiple sound files on your Web page, consider providing an explanatory note at the top of the page, and then using a small inline GIF icon (such as the one shown in Figure 8.5) as the link to the sound file itself.

(Include the size of the file in the link as well.) Using a sound file icon provides an elegant way to show that a sound lurks on the other side of the link without needing to explain it in text all the time.

Figure 8.5. *A sound file icon.*

Using Video

"Video" refers to any digitally encoded motion video, which can include both animation as well as "real" video files.

For video files that can be read across platforms, the current standard on the Web is MPEG, but Apple's QuickTime format has been gaining ground as players become more available for platforms other than the Macintosh. QuickTime also has the advantage of being able to include an audio track with the video; although MPEG video files can have audio tracks, few existing players can play it.

Unfortunately, most browsers still do not support QuickTime files without some configuration, but as players become more available this should change.

Getting and Converting Video Files

Just as with images and sound, you can get video clips by making them yourself, downloading them from the Net, or purchasing royalty-free clips that you can read on your platform.

Making video files yourself is generally expensive and difficult unless you have a computer specifically designed for it (Macintosh "AV" systems such as the Power Macintosh 7100/66AV and SGI workstations being the most obvious examples). Whole books have been written on how to digitize video; I'll leave it up to them to explain it.

The best way to get video is to find it. Once again, the best place to get short video clips is through the use of royalty-free video libraries on CD-ROM or through sources over the Internet.

Converting files is much easier than creating them.

To convert video on the Macintosh, use the freeware program Sparkle. Sparkle can read and play both MPEG and QuickTime files, and convert between them. In addition, the program AVI->Quick can convert AVI (Video for Windows) files to QuickTime format.

On DOS/Windows systems, a commercial program called XingCD enables you to convert AVI files to MPEG. AVI to QuickTime converters are also available; one is a program called SoundCap, intended to read Indeo files (files created by Intel Smart Video Recorder). To use AVI files, you'll need the Video for Windows package, available from Microsoft. To use QuickTime movies, you'll need the QuickTime for Windows package, available from Apple. You'll need both to convert from one format to the other.

On UNIX systems, there are several tools for creating MPEG files from tape or from individual frames, but none to convert from other popular formats such as QuickTime or AVI. The best source for updated information on MPEG tools for UNIX is in the MPEG FAQ.

FTP locations and other information for these programs are in Appendix A.

Including Video Files on Web Pages

Once you have a video file, you must do two things:

☐ Name the file appropriately. MPEG files should have an extension of .mpg or .mpeg; QuickTime movies have a .mov extension.

☐ Link to the file using the <A> tag just as you did with external images and sounds.

In addition, if you want a QuickTime movie to be read on a platform other than the Macintosh, you will need to "flatten" that movie. On the Macintosh, files contain resource and data forks for different bits of the file. Flattening a QuickTime file involves moving all the data in the QuickTime file into the data fork so other platforms can read it.

A small freeware program called FastPlayer will flatten QuickTime movies on the Mac; on Windows try a program called Qflat. FTP locations are in Appendix A.

As with all external media files, you should be sure to tell your readers the type and size of file they are linking to; this is especially important for video files, since the sizes are often frighteningly large. As I noted with sound files, linking to an icon on the Web page itself is often a nice design touch. (See Figure 8.6.)

Figure 8.6. *A video file icon.*

Exercise 8.2: Creating a media archive.

One of the uses of Web pages I have only vaguely mentioned up to this point is that of creating a media archive: a Web page that serves no purpose other than to provide quick access to image or other media files for viewing and downloading.

Previously on the Net, media was stored in FTP or Gopher archives. The text-only nature of these sorts of archives makes it difficult for people to find what they're looking for in images, sounds, or video simply because the filename is often the only description they have of the content of the file. And even reasonably descriptive file names such as `red-bird-in-green-tree.gif` or `verdi-aria.aiff` aren't all that useful when you're talking about images or sounds; it's only through actually downloading the file itself that people can really decide whether they want it or not.

Through the use of inline images, icons, and splitting up sound and video files into small clips and larger files, you can create a media archive on the Web that is far more usable than any of the text-only archives.

> **Note:** Keep in mind that this sort of archive, in its heavy use of inline graphics and large media files, is only optimally useful in graphical browsers attached to fast networks. However, the Web does provide advantages in this respect even for text-only browsers, simply because there is more room available. Rather than having only the filename to describe the file, you can use as many words as you need. For example:
>
> A `<A HREF="orangefish.jpeg">34K JPEG file</A>` of an orange fish with a bright yellow eye, swimming in front of some very pink coral.

In this exercise, you'll create a simple example of a media archive with several GIF images, AU sounds, and MPEG video.

First, start with the framework for the archive, which includes some introductory text, some inline images explaining the kind of files, and headings for each file type:

Input

```
<HTML>
<HEAD>
<TITLE>Laura's Way Cool Image Archive</TITLE>
<H1>Laura's Way Cool Image Archive</H1>
<P>Select an image to download the appropriate file.</P>
<P><IMG SRC="penguinslittle.gif">Picture icons indicate GIF images</P>
<P><IMG SRC="earicon.gif">This icon indicates an AU Sound file</P>
<P><IMG SRC="film.gif">This icon indicates an MPEG Video File</P>
<HR>
<H2>Images</H2>
<H2>Sound Files</H2>
<H2>Video Files</H2>
```

Figure 8.7 shows how it looks so far.

Output

Figure 8.7. *The framework for the media archive.*

For the archive, we have four large GIF images:

- ☐ A drawing of a pink orchid
- ☐ A photograph full of jelly beans
- ☐ The cougar from the Palo Alto Zoo home page
- ☐ A biohazard symbol

Using your favorite image editor, you can create thumbnails of each of these pictures to serve as the inline icons, and insert `<IMG>` links in the appropriate spots in your archive file:

```
<H2>Images</H2>
<IMG SRC="orchidsmall.gif" ALT="a drawing of a pink orchid">
<IMG SRC="jellybeansmall.gif" ALT="a photograph of some jellybeans">
<IMG SRC="cougarsmall.gif" ALT="a photograph of a cougar">
<IMG SRC="biohazardsmall.gif" ALT="a biohazard symbol">
```

Note that I did include values for the `ALT` attribute to the `<IMG>` tag, which will be substituted for the images in browsers that cannot view those images. Even though you may not intend for your Web page to be seen by nongraphical browsers, it's polite to at least offer a clue to people who stumble onto it. This way, everyone can access the media files you are offering on this page.

Now, link the thumbnails of the files to the actual images:

```
<A HREF="orchid.gif"><IMG SRC="orchidsmall.gif" ALT="a drawing of a pink
orchid"></A>
<A HREF="jellybean.gif"><IMG SRC="jellybeansmall.gif" ALT="a photograph of
some -jellybeans"> </A>
<A HREF="cougar.gif"><IMG SRC="cougarsmall.gif" ALT="a photograph of a
cougar"> </A>
<A HREF="biohazard.gif"><IMG SRC="biohazardsmall.gif" ALT="a biohazard
symbol"> </A>
```

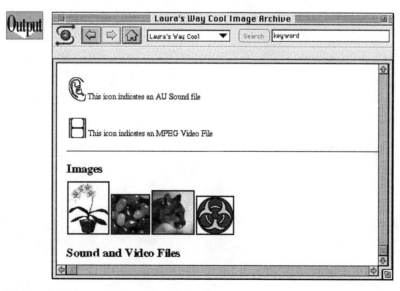

Figure 8.8. *Image links to larger images.*

If I leave the archive like this, it does look nice, but I'm breaking one of my own rules: I haven't noted how large the files themselves are. Here, you have several choices for formatting. You could just put the size of the file inline with the image and let the images wrap on the page however they want, as illustrated in Figure 8.9, as follows:

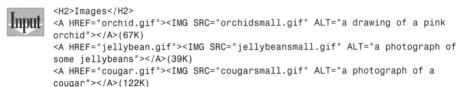

```
<H2>Images</H2>
<A HREF="orchid.gif"><IMG SRC="orchidsmall.gif" ALT="a drawing of a pink
orchid"></A>(67K)
<A HREF="jellybean.gif"><IMG SRC="jellybeansmall.gif" ALT="a photograph of
some jellybeans"></A>(39K)
<A HREF="cougar.gif"><IMG SRC="cougarsmall.gif" ALT="a photograph of a
cougar"></A>(122K)
<A HREF="biohazard.gif"><IMG SRC="biohazardsmall.gif" ALT="a biohazard
symbol"></A>(35K)
```

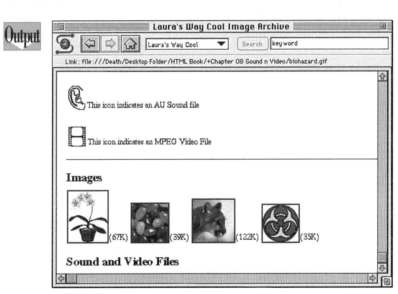

Figure 8.9. *Images with text.*

Or you could put in line breaks after each image to make sure they line up along the left edge of the page. I prefer the first method, as it allows a more compact layout of images.

Now, moving on to the sound and video files. You have three sound files and two videos. Because these files can't be reduced to a simple thumbnail image, we'll describe them in the text in the archive itself (including the huge sizes of the files):

```
<H2>Sound and Video Files</H2>
<P>A five-part a capella renaissance madrigal called "Flora Gave me Fairest
Flowers" (650K)</P>
<P>Some lovely wind-chime sounds (79K) </P>
```

```
<P>Chicken noises (112K)</P>
<P>The famous Tacoma Narrows bridge accident (where the bridge twisted and
fell down in the wind)(13Meg)</P>
<P>A three-dimensional computer animation of a flying airplane over a
landscape (2.3Meg)</P>
```

Now, add the icon images to each of the descriptions—the ear icon to the sounds and the filmstrip icon to the videos. Here we'll also include a value for the ALT attribute to the <IMG> tag, this time providing a simple description that will serve as placeholder for the link itself in text-only browsers.

And finally, just as you did in the image part of the example, link the icons to the external files. Here is the HTML code for the final list:

Input
```
<H2>Sound and Video Files</H2>
<P><A HREF="flora.au"><IMG SRC="earicon.gif" ALT="[madrigal sound]"> A five-
part a capella renaissance madrigal called "Flora Gave me Fairest Flowers"
(650K)</A></P>
<P><A HREF="windchime.au"><IMG SRC="earicon.gif" ALT="[windchime sound]">
Some lovely wind-chime sounds (79K)</A></P>
<P><A HREF="bawkbawk.au"><IMG SRC="earicon.gif" ALT="[chicken sound]">
Chicken noises (112K)</A></P>
<P><A HREF="tacoma.mpeg"><IMG SRC="film.gif" ALT="[tacoma video]">
The famous Tacoma Narrows bridge accident (where the bridge twisted and fell
down in the wind) (13Meg)</A></P>
<P><A HREF="airplane.mpeg"><IMG SRC="film.gif" ALT="[3D airplane]">A three-
dimensional computer animation of a flying airplane over a landscape (2.3Meg)
</A></P>
```

Output

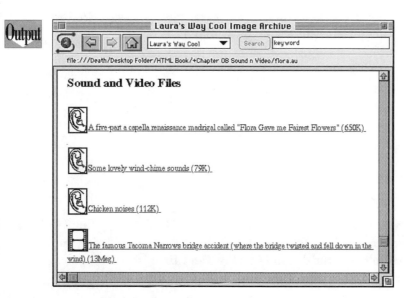

Figure 8.10. *Sound and video files.*

Et voilà, your media archive. It's simple with the combination of inline and external images. And, with the use of the ALT attribute, you can even use it reasonably well in text-only browsers. Figure 8.11 shows how it came out!

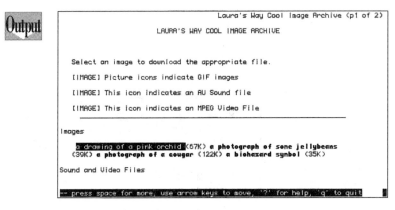

Output

```
                                    Laura's Way Cool Image Archive (p1 of 2)
                       LAURA'S WAY COOL IMAGE ARCHIVE

    Select an image to download the appropriate file.

    [IMAGE] Picture icons indicate GIF images

    [IMAGE] This icon indicates an AU Sound file

    [IMAGE] This icon indicates an MPEG Video File
    _____
  Images

          a drawing of a pink orchid (67K) a photograph of some jellybeans
          (39K) a photograph of a cougar (122K) a biohazard symbol (35K)

  Sound and Video Files

  _____
  -- press space for more, use arrow keys to move, '?' for help, 'q' to quit
```

Figure 8.11. *The media archive in Lynx.*

Summary

External media files are files that cannot be read directly by your Web browser. Instead, if you link to an external file, your browser starts up a "helper" application to view or play those files.

Non-inline images, sound, and video are the most popular external media files used on Web pages. In this chapter, you've learned about the popular formats for each of these kinds of media and how to obtain samples of them, as well as other information regarding converting between formats and naming the files appropriately so that they can be recognized by Web browsers.

Q&A

Q My browser has a helper application for JPEG images listed in my helper applications list. But when I downloaded a JPEG file, it complained that it couldn't read the document. How can I fix this?

A Just because an application is listed in the helper application list (or initialization file) doesn't mean that you have that application available on your system.

Browsers are generally shipped with a default listing of helper applications that are most commonly used for the common external file formats available on the Web. But you have to locate and install each of those helper applications before your browser can use them. The fact that an application is listed isn't enough.

Q If JPEG files are so much smaller than GIF files, with some slight image degradation that is forgivable, why do browsers use only GIF files for inline images?

A At the time that image support was put into Mosaic (the first browser to use inline images), GIF was a much more popular format than JPEG, there were many more viewers across platforms for GIF than JPEG, and the size issue was not as important. Now that JPEG has caught on more, some browsers (such as Netscape) are beginning to accept inline JPEG images in addition to GIFs.

Q I've been using AU files for my sound samples, but there's an awful hiss during the quiet parts. What can I do?

A Some sound editing programs can help remove some of the hiss in AU files, but because of the nature of AU encoding, you'll usually have some amount of noise. If sound quality is that important to you, consider using AIFF or, if you have the converters, MPEG audio.

Q Why don't my MPEG files have sound?

A Maybe they do! The MPEG standard allows for both video and audio tracks, but few players can handle the audio track at this time. You have two choices, if you must have sound for your MPEG movies: wait for better players (or bribe a programmer to write one), or convert your movies to QuickTime and show your readers how to install and use QuickTime players.

DAY

5

DAY

FIVE

9

Writing and Designing Web Pages: Do's and Don'ts

You won't learn about any tags in this chapter, or how to convert files from one strange file format to another. You're done with the HTML part of Web page design; next come the intangibles, the things that separate your documents from those of someone who just knows the tags and can spread text and graphics around and call it a presentation.

Armed with the information from the last four days, you could put this book down now and go off and merrily create Web pages to your heart's content. However, armed with both that information and what you'll learn today, you can create *better* Web pages. Do you need any more incentive to continue reading?

This chapter includes hints for creating well-written and well-designed Web pages, and highlights do's and don'ts concerning

- [ ] How to write your Web documents so that they can be easily scanned and read
- [ ] Issues concerning design and layout of your Web pages
- [ ] When and why you should create links
- [ ] Other miscellaneous tidbits and hints

Writing for Online

Writing on the Web is no different from writing in the real world. Even though the writing you do on the Web is not sealed in hardcopy, it is still "published," and still a reflection of you and your work. In fact, because it is online, and therefore more transient to your reader, you'll have to follow the rules of good writing that much more closely because your readers will be less forgiving.

Because of the vast quantities of information available on the Web, your readers are not going to have much patience with your Web page if it is full of spelling errors or organized poorly. They are much more likely to give up after the first couple of sentences and move on to someone else's page. After all, there are several million pages out there. There isn't time to waste on bad pages.

This doesn't mean that you have to go out and become a professional writer in order to create a good Web page. But a few hints to keep in mind as you write will go a long way towards making your Web page easier to read and to understand.

Write Clearly and Be Brief

Unless you are writing the Great American Web Novel, your readers are not going to visit your page to linger lovingly over your words. One of the best ways you can make the writing in your Web documents effective is to write as clearly and concisely as you possibly can, present your points, and then stop. Obscuring what you want to say with extra words just makes it more difficult for your reader to figure out what your point is.

If you don't have a copy of Strunk and White's *The Elements of Style*, put this book down right now and go buy it and read it. And then re-read it, memorize it, inhale it, sleep with it under your pillow, show it to all your friends, quote it at parties, make it your life. There is no better guide to the art of good, clear writing than that book.

Organize Your Documents for Quick Scanning

Even if you write the clearest, briefest, most scintillating prose ever seen on the Web, chances are good your readers will not start at the top of your Web page and carefully read every word down to the bottom.

Scanning, in this context, is the first quick look your readers give to each page to get the general gist of the content. Depending on what your users want out of your documents, they may scan the parts that jump out that them (headings, links, other emphasized words), perhaps read a few contextual paragraphs, and then move on. By writing and organizing your documents for easy "scannability," you can help your readers get the information they need as fast as possible.

To improve the scannability of your Web documents:

- ☐ Use headings to summarize topics. Note how this book has headings and subheadings, so that you could flip through quickly and find the portions you're interested in. The same thing applies to Web pages.

- ☐ Use lists. Lists are wonderful for summarizing related items. Every time you find yourself saying something like "each widget has four elements," or "use the following steps to do this," the content after that phrase should be an ordered or unordered list.

☐ Don't forget link menus. As a form of list, link menus have all the advantages of lists for scannability and double as excellent navigation tools.

☐ Don't bury important information in text. If you have a point to make, make it close to the top of the page or at the beginning of a paragraph. Long paragraphs are harder to read and more difficult to glean information from, and the further into the paragraph you put your point, the less likely it is to be read.

Figure 9.1 shows the sort of writing technique that you should avoid.

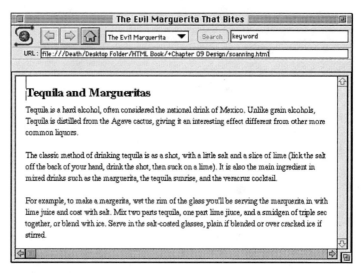

Figure 9.1. *A Web page that is difficult to scan.*

Because all the information on this page is in paragraph form, your readers have to read all three paragraphs in order to find out what they want and where they want to go next.

How would you improve this example? Try rewriting this section so that the main points can be better picked out from the text. Consider that:

☐ There are actually two discrete topics in those three paragraphs.

☐ The four ingredients of the drink would make an excellent list.

Figure 9.2 shows what an improvement might look like.

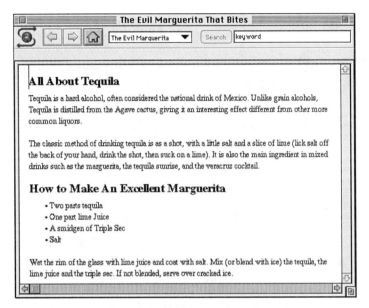

Figure 9.2. *An improvement to the difficult Web page.*

Make Each Page Stand on Its Own

Keep in mind as you write that your reader could jump into any of your Web pages from anywhere. Although you may have structured things such that section four distinctly follows section three and has no other links to it, someone you don't even know might create a link to the page starting section four, and a reader could very well find himself or herself on section four without even being aware that section three exists.

Be careful to write each page so that it stands on its own. These guidelines will help:

☐ Use descriptive titles, as I mention in Chapter 3, "Begin with the Basics." The title should provide not only the direct subject of this page, but its relationship to the rest of the pages in the presentation of which it is a part.

☐ If a document depends on the one before it, provide a navigational link back to the document before it (and preferably also one up to the top level as well).

☐ Avoid initial sentences like: "You can get around these problems by..." "After you're done with that, do..." and "The advantages to this method arc...." The information referred to by "these," "that," and "this" are off on some other page. If those sentences are the first thing your reader sees, he or she is going to be confused.

Be Careful with Emphasis

Use emphasis sparingly in your text. Paragraphs with a whole lot of **boldface** and *italic* or words in ALL CAPS are hard to read, both if you use all three several times in a paragraph or if you emphasize long strings of text. The best emphasis is used only with small words such as and, this, or, but, and so on.

Link text is also a form of emphasis. Use single words or short phrases as link text. Do not use entire passages or paragraphs as links.

Figure 9.3 illustrates a particularly bad example of too much emphasis obscuring the rest of the text.

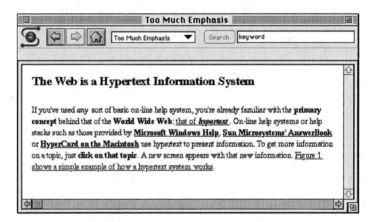

Figure 9.3. *Too much emphasis.*

By removing some of the boldface and using less text for your links, you can considerably reduce the amount of distraction in the paragraph. (See Figure 9.4.)

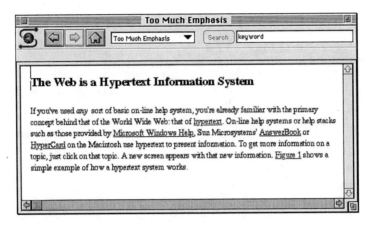

Figure 9.4. *Less emphasis.*

Don't Use Browser-Specific Terminology

Avoid references in your text to specific features of specific browsers. For example, don't use wording like:

- *Click Here.* What if your reader is using a browser without a mouse? A more generic phrase is "select this link." (Of course, you should be avoiding the "here" syndrome in the first place, which neatly gets around this problem as well.)

- *To save this document, pull down the File menu and select Save.* Each browser has a different set of menus and different ways of accomplishing the same action. If at all possible, do not refer to specifics of browser operation in your Web pages.

- *Use the Back button to return to the previous page.* As in the previous note, each browser has a different set of buttons and different methods for going "back." If you want your readers to have the ability to go back to a previous page, or to any specific page, then link them explicitly there.

211

Spell Check and Proofread Your Documents

Spell checking and proofreading may seem like obvious suggestions, but given the number of documents I have seen on the Web that have obviously not had either, it bears mentioning.

Designing a set of Web pages and making them available on the Web is like publishing a book, producing a magazine, or releasing a product. It is, of course, considerably easier to publish Web pages than it is books, magazines, or other products, but just because it is easy does not mean it can be sloppy.

Potentially thousands of people may be reading and exploring the content you provide. Spelling errors and bad grammar reflect badly on your work, on you, and on the content you are describing. Poor writing may be irritating enough that your reader won't bother to delve any deeper than your home page, even if the subject you're writing about is fascinating.

Proofread and spell check each of your Web documents. If possible, have someone else read them—other people can often pick up errors that you, the writer, can't see. Even a simple edit can greatly improve many documents and make them easier to read and navigate.

Design and Page Layout

Design? What design? I've been noting throughout this book that the Web is not a good place to experiment wildly with visual design, and that you shouldn't take design into consideration when you write your Web pages. Have I changed my mind?

No, not really. Although the design capabilities of HTML and the Web are quite limited in terms of graphic design, there's still a lot you can work with, and still quite a few opportunities for people without a sense of design to create something that looks simply awful.

Probably the best rule to follow at all times as far as laying out each Web page is this: Keep the design as simple as possible. Reduce the number of elements (images, headings, rule lines), and make sure that the eye is drawn to the most important parts of the page first.

Keep that cardinal rule in mind as you read the next sections, which offer some other suggestions for basic design and layout of Web pages.

Don't Overuse Images

Be careful about including lots of images on your Web page. Besides the fact that each image slows down the time it takes to load the document, including too many images on the same page can make your document look busy and cluttered and distract from the point you are trying to get across. (See Figure 9.5.)

Figure 9.5. *Too many images.*

Remember the hints I gave you in Chapter 7, "Including Images on Your Web Pages." Consider why you need to use each image before you put it on the page, and if it doesn't directly contribute to the content, consider leaving it off.

Use Alternatives to Images

And of course, as soon as I mention images, I have to also mention that not all browsers can view those images. To make your documents accessible to the widest possible audience, you're going to have to take the text-only browsers into account when you design your Web pages. Two possible solutions that can help:

☐ Use the ALT attribute of the <IMG> tag to automatically substitute appropriate text strings for the graphics in text-only browsers. Use either a descriptive label to substitute for the default [image] that appears in the place of each inline image, or use an empty string (" ") to ignore the image altogether.

☐ If providing a single-source page for both graphical and text-only browsers becomes too much work and the result is not turning out to be acceptable, consider creating separate pages for each one: a page designed for the full-color full-graphical browsers, and a page designed for the text-only browsers. Then provide the option of choosing one or the other from your home page.

Use Headings as Headings

Headings are often rendered in graphical browsers in a larger or bolder font. Because of this, it's often tempting to use a heading tag to provide some sort of warning, note, or emphasis in regular text, as shown in Figure 9.6.

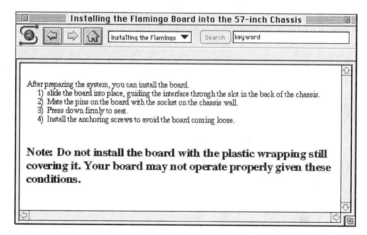

Figure 9.6. *The wrong way to use headings.*

Headings work best when they're used as headings, because they stand out from the text and signal the start of a new topic. If you really want to emphasize a particular section of text, consider using rule lines and a small icon, instead. Figure 9.7 shows an example of the same text in Figure 9.6 with a different kind of visual emphasis.

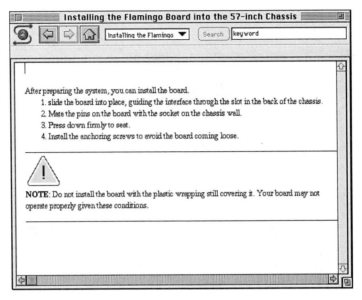

Figure 9.7. *An alternative to the wrong way to use headings.*

Group Related Information Visually

Grouping related information within a page is a task for both writing and design. By grouping related information under headings, as I suggested in the writing hints section, you improve the scannability of that information. Visually separating each section from another helps to make each section distinct and emphasizes the relatedness of the information.

If a Web page contains several sections of information, find a way to visually separate those sections; for example, with a heading or with a rule line <HR>. (See Figure 9.8.)

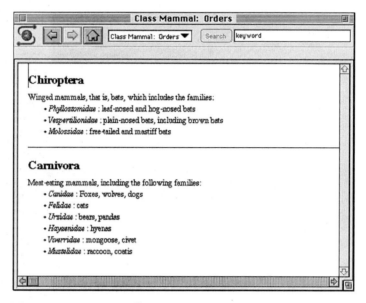

Figure 9.8. *Separate sections visually.*

Use a Consistent Layout

When you're reading a book or a magazine, each page, each section, usually has the same layout. The page numbers are where you expect them, and the first word on each page starts in the same place.

The same sort of consistent layout works equally well in Web pages. A single "look and feel" for each page in your Web presentation is comforting to your readers. After two or three pages, they will know what the elements of each page are and where to find them. With a consistent design, your readers can find the information they need and navigate through your pages without having to stop at every page and try to find where things are.

Consistent layout can include:

☐ Consistent page elements. If you use second-level headings (<H2>) on one page to indicate major topics, then use level two headings for major topics on all your pages. If you have a heading and a rule line at the top of your page, then use that same layout on all your pages.

☐ Consistent forms of navigation. Put your navigation menus in the same place on every page (usually the top or the bottom of the page), and use the same number of them. If you're going to use navigation icons, make sure you use the same icons in the same order for every page.

To Link or Not to Link

Just as with graphics, every time you create a link, consider why you are linking two documents or two sections together. Is the link useful for your readers? Will it give them more information or take them closer to their goal? Is the link relevant in some way to the current content?

Each link should serve a purpose. Link for relevant reasons. Just because you mention the word "coffee" deep in a page about some other topic, you don't have to link that word to the coffee home page. It may seem cute, but if a link has no relevance to the current content, it just confuses your reader.

This section describes some of the categories of links that are useful in Web documents. If your links do not fall into one of these categories, consider why you are including them in your document.

Note: Thanks to Nathan Torkington for his "Taxonomy of Tags," published on the www-talk mailing list, which inspired this section.

Explicit navigation links are links that indicate the specific paths one can take through your Web documents: forward, back, up, home. These links are often indicated by navigation icons (Figure 9.9).

Implicit navigation links (Figure 9.10) are different from explicit navigation links in that the link text implies, but does not directly indicate, navigation between documents. Link menus are the best example of this; it is apparent from the highlighting of the link text that you will get more information on this topic by selecting the link, but the text itself does not necessarily say that. Note that the major difference between explicit and implicit navigation links are that if you print out a page with both on it, you should no longer be able to pick out the implicit links.

Implicit navigation links can also include table-of-contents-like structures or other overviews made up entirely of links.

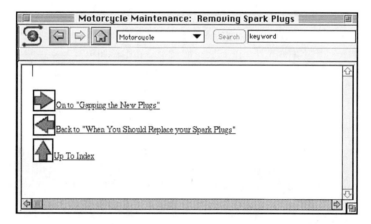

Figure 9.9. *Explicit navigation links.*

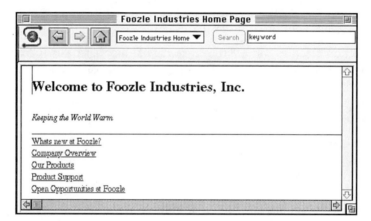

Figure 9.10. *Implicit navigation links.*

Word or *concept definitions* make excellent links, particularly if you are creating large networks of documents that include glossaries. By linking the first instance of a word in a document to its definition elsewhere, you can explain the meaning of that word to your readers who don't know what it means while not distracting your readers who do (Figure 9.11).

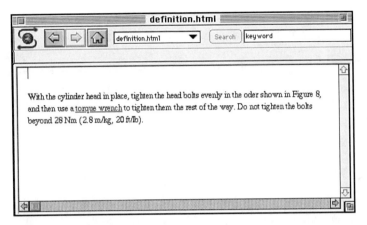

Figure 9.11. *Definition links.*

Finally, links to *tangents* and *related information* are valuable when the text content would distract from the main purpose of the document. Think of tangent links as footnotes or end notes in printed text; they can refer to citations to other works, or to additional information that is interesting but not necessarily directly relevant to the point you're trying to make on the Web page itself.

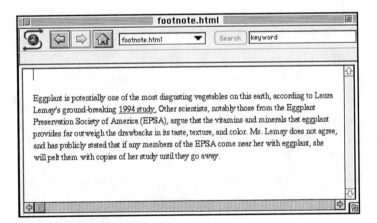

Figure 9.12. *Footnote links.*

Be careful that you don't get carried away with definitions and tangent links. Link to only the *first* instance of a definition or tangent, and resist the urge to link every time you possibly can—for example, linking every instance of the letters "WWW" on your page to the WWW project home page in Switzerland. If you are linking twice or more to the same location on one page using the same or similar link text, consider removing most of the extra links. Your readers can make the effort to select one of the other links if they are interested in the information.

Other Good Habits and Hints

In this section, I've gathered several other miscellaneous hints and advice about good habits to get into when working with groups of Web pages, including notes on how big to make each document in your presentation and how to sign your documents.

Link Back to Home

Consider including a link on every single page in your presentation that takes your reader back to the top level or home page. Providing this link allows readers a quick escape from the depths of your content, if they suddenly discover that they've followed a few links too far or found themselves "lost." Using a home link is much easier for your readers than trying to navigate back up through a hierarchy that they may not understand, or worse, to use the "back" facility of their browser to retrace their steps.

Don't Split Topics Across Pages

Each Web document works best if it covers a single topic in its entirety. Don't split topics up across pages; even if you link across them, the transition can be confusing. And it will be even more confusing if someone jumps in on the second or third page covering that topic and wonders what is going on.

If you think that one topic is becoming too large for a single document, then rather than breaking up that document at arbitrary points, consider reorganizing the content so that you can break that topic up into subtopics. This works especially well in hierarchical organizations as it allows you to determine exactly to what level of detail each "level" of the hierarchy should go into, and exactly how big and complete each page should be.

Don't Create Too Many or Too Few Documents

There are no rules for how many pages you must have in your Web presentation, or rules for how large each page should be. You can have one single page or several thousand, depending on the amount of content you have to cover and how you have organized it.

With this in mind, you may decide to go to one extreme or to another, each of which has advantages and disadvantages. For example, say you put all your content in one big document, and create links to sections within that document (as illustrated in Figure 9.13).

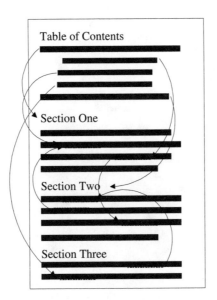

Figure 9.13. *One big document.*

Advantages:

- ☐ One file is easier to maintain, and links within that file won't ever break if you move things around or rename files.
- ☐ Mirrors real-world document structure; if you are distributing documents both in hard-copy and online, then having a single document for both makes producing both easier.

Disadvantages:

☐ A large file takes a very long time to download, particularly over slow network connections and especially if the document includes lots of graphics.

☐ Readers must scroll a lot to find what they want. Accessing particular bits of information can become tedious. Navigating at points other than at the top or bottom becomes close to impossible.

☐ The structure is overly rigid. A single document is inherently linear. Although you can skip around within sections in the document, the structure still mirrors that of the printed page and doesn't take advantage of the flexibility of smaller documents linked together in a non-linear fashion.

Or, on the other extreme, you could create a whole bunch of little documents with links between them (illustrated in Figure 9.14).

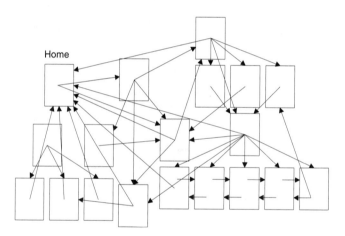

Figure 9.14. *Lots of little documents.*

Advantages:

☐ Smaller documents load very quickly.

☐ You can often fit the entire page on one screen, so the information in that document can be scanned very easily by your reader.

Disadvantages:

☐ Maintaining all those links will be a nightmare. Just adding some sort of navigational structure to that many documents may create thousands of links.

- [ ] If you have too many jumps between documents, the jumps may seem jarring. Continuity is difficult when your reader spends more time jumping than actually reading.

So what is the solution? Often the content you're describing will determine the size and number of documents that you need, especially if you follow the one-topic-per-page suggestion. Often, testing your Web pages on a variety of platforms and network speeds (as I discuss tomorrow) will let you know if a single document is too large. If you spend a lot of time scrolling around in it or if it takes more time to load than you expected, for example, it may be too large.

Sign Your Documents

Each document should contain some sort of information at the bottom of the page that acts as the "signature" for the document. I mention this briefly in Chapter 5, "Still More HTML," as part of the description of the <ADDRESS> tag; that particular tag was intended for just this purpose.

Here is a list of some useful information to consider putting in the ADDRESS tag on each page:

- [ ] Contact information for the person who created this Web page or the person responsible for it, colloquially known as the "web master." This should include at least his or her name and preferably an e-mail address.
- [ ] The status of the document. Is it complete? Is it a work-in-progress? Is it intentionally left blank?
- [ ] When this document was last revised. This is particularly important for documents that change a lot. Include a date on each document so that people know how old it is.
- [ ] Copyright or trademark information, if it applies.
- [ ] The URL of this document. Including a printed URL of a document that is found at that same URL may seem a bit like overkill, but what happens if someone prints out the page and loses it in a stack of documents on a desk? Where did it come from? (I've done this many times and often wished for a URL to be typed on the document itself.)

Figure 9.15 shows a nice example of an address block.

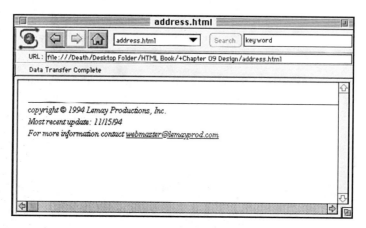

Figure 9.15. *An example address.*

A nice touch to include on your Web page is to link a mailto URL to the text containing the e-mail address of the web master, like this:

```
<ADDRESS>
Laura Lemay <A HREF="mailto:lemay@netcom.com">lemay@netcom.com</A>
</ADDRESS>
```

This enables the readers of the document who have browsers that support the mailto URL to simply select the link and send mail to the relevant person responsible for the page without having to retype the address into their mail programs.

Note: This will only work in browsers that support mailto URLs. But even in browsers that don't accept it, the link text will appear as usual, so there's no harm in including the link regardless.

Finally, if you don't want to clutter each page with a lot of personal contact or boilerplate copyright information, a simple solution is to create a separate page for the extra information, and then link the signature to that page, like this:

```
<ADDRESS>
<A HREF="copyright.html">Copyright</A> and
<A HREF="webmaster.html">contact</A> information is available.
</ADDRESS>
```

Provide Non-Hypertext Versions of HyperText Documents

Even though the Web provides a way to create documents in new and exciting ways, some readers still like to read many things offline, on the bus, or at the breakfast table. These kinds of readers have real problems with hypertext documents, because once you start using hypertext to organize a document it becomes difficult to be able to say "print the whole thing." It would be nice if you could just point your browser to the top level of a Web presentation and say "go get every page that this page is linked to, and every page that those pages are linked to, and so on." But where would the browser stop downloading linked-to documents (Figure 9.16)? You could very well end up downloading the entire Web with a process like that.

Figure 9.16. *Where does it stop?*

If you are using the Web to publish documents such as books, FAQs, journal articles, or anything that might be readable and usable outside the Web, and you have designed the presentation so that it spans several Web pages and links, consider creating a single text or PostScript file for your Web documents and making it available as an external document for downloading. This enables your readers both to browse the document online and, if they want to, also to print it out for reading offline. You can even link the location of hard-copy document to the start of the hypertext version, like this:

```
A <A HREF="ftp://myhome.com/pub/mydir/myfile.ps">PostScript version</A> of
this document is available via ftp at myhome.com in the directory /pub/mydir/
myfile.ps.
```

And, of course, a handy cross-reference for the hardcopy version would be to provide the URL for the hypertext version:

> "This document is also available on hypertext form on the World Wide Web at the URL: `http://myhome.com/pub/mydir/myfile.index.html`."

Summary

The main do's and don'ts for Web page design from this chapter are as follows:

- ☐ DO write your documents clearly and concisely.
- ☐ DO organize the text of your document so that your readers can scan for important information.
- ☐ DON'T write Web pages that are dependent on pages before or after them in the structure. DO write context-independent pages.
- ☐ DON'T overuse emphasis (boldface, italic, all caps, link text). DO use emphasis sparingly and only when absolutely necessary.
- ☐ DON'T use terminology specific to any one browser (click here, use the back button, and so on).
- ☐ DO spell check and proofread your documents.
- ☐ DO keep your layout simple.
- ☐ DON'T clutter the page with lots of pretty but unnecessary images.
- ☐ DO provide alternatives to images for text-only browsers.
- ☐ DON'T use heading tags to provide emphasis.
- ☐ DO group related information both semantically (through the organization of the content) and visually (through the use of headings or by separating sections with rule lines).
- ☐ DO use a consistent layout across all your pages.
- ☐ DO have good reasons for using links. DON'T link to irrelevant material.
- ☐ DON'T link repeatedly to the same site on the same page.
- ☐ DO always provide a link back to your home page.
- ☐ DO match topics with pages.
- ☐ DON'T split individual topics across pages.
- ☐ DO provide a signature block or link to contact information at the bottom of each page.
- ☐ DO provide single-document, non-hypertext versions of linear documents.

Q&A

Q **I'm converting existing documents into Web pages. These documents are very text-heavy and are intended to be read from start to finish instead of being quickly scanned. I can't restructure or redesign the content to better follow the guidelines you've suggested in this chapter—that's not my job. What can I do?**

A Some content is going to be like this, particularly when you're converting a document written for paper to online. Ideally, you would be able to rewrite and restructure for online presentation, but realistically you often won't be able to do anything with the content other than throw it online.

All is not lost, however. You can still improve the overall presentation of these documents by providing reasonable indexes to the content (summaries, tables of contents pages, subject indexes, and so on), and by including standard navigation links back out of the text-heavy pages. In other words, you can create an easily navigable framework around the documents themselves, which can go a long way towards improving content that is otherwise difficult to read online.

Q **I have a standard signature block that contains my name and e-mail address, revision information for the document, and a couple lines of copyright information that my company's lawyers insisted on. It's a little imposing, particularly on small pages, where the signature is bigger than the page itself!**

A If your company's lawyers agree, consider putting all your contact and copyright information on a separate page, and then linking it on every page instead of duplicating it every time. This way your pages won't be overwhelmed by the legal stuff, and if the signature changes, you won't have to change it on every single page.

10

Producing HTML Documents for Business and Fun: Some Examples

In this chapter, you'll explore some examples of pages that you might find out on the Web. (Actually, you *won't* find them out on the Web; I developed these examples specifically for this chapter.) Each of these Web presentations is either typical of the kind of information being provided on the Web today, or shows some unique method for solving problems. In particular, you'll explore the following Web presentations:

☐ A company profile for the Foozle Sweater Company

☐ An encyclopedia of motorcycles, with images, sounds, and other media clips

☐ The catalog for a small nursery, in which you can both browse and order cacti and succulents

☐ A Web-based book about making bread

In each example, I note some of the interesting features of the page as well as some of the issues that you should take into account if you use a topic or a format similar to it.

Example One: A Company Profile

Foozle Industries, Inc., makes a wide variety of sweaters for all occasions. (They were responsible for the demon sweater mentioned in Chapter 3, "Begin with the Basics.") In a burst of strangeness from their marketing department, they decided to be the first sweater manufacturer to provide a company profile on the Web.

If you pointed your browser at the Foozle Industries Web server, you would be presented with the Foozle Industries Home Page (Figure 10.1).

From this nicely laid out home page, you have several choices, arranged in a link menu. You won't visit all of them in this section, just a few that provide interesting features.

Figure 10.1. *Foozle Industries home page.*

What's New at Foozle?

The first obvious link to check out from the Foozle home page is the What's New page. The link to this page has been time stamped, noting the last time it changed.

Selecting the What's New link takes you, appropriately, to the What's New page.

Organized in chronological order, the What's New page contains information about interesting things going on at Foozle Industries. The topmost item in the list of new things is the existence of a paper on how Alpaca wool is treated. Since that item has a link, let's follow it. The result is shown in Figure 10.3.

Alpaca wool is fascinating, but now what? The links at the top of the page indicate you can go to the Technical Papers Overview, or up to the home page. Since you haven't seen the technical papers page yet, let's go there.

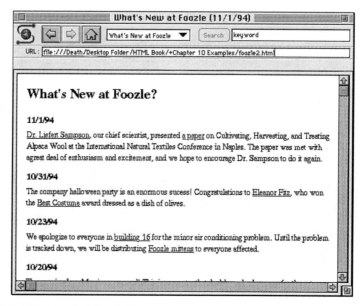

Figure 10.2. *The Foozle What's New page.*

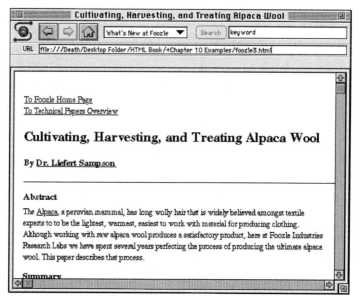

Figure 10.3. *All About Foozle Alpaca wool.*

Technical Papers

The Technical Papers section provides a simple list of the available papers describing technical issues surrounding the making of sweaters. (Didn't know there were any, did you?)

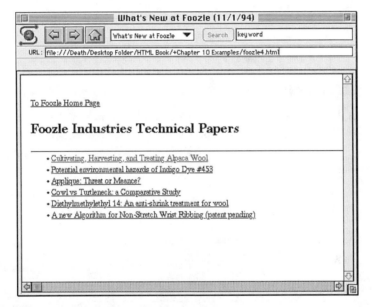

Figure 10.4. *The Technical Papers section.*

Each link in the list takes you to the paper it describes. (Note in the figure that the link to the paper on Alpaca wool indicates that you've already visited it—in the previous paragraph.)

From here, you could visit any of the papers, or go back up to the overview page. Going back up to the overview page would enable you to explore the other features of this Web page you haven't visited: the company overview, the product descriptions, or the listing of open opportunities.

Features and Issues for Development

The company profile page is quite straightforward in terms of design; the structure is a simple hierarchy, with link menus for navigation to the appropriate pages. Extending it is a simple matter of adding additional "limbs" to the hierarchy by adding new links to the top-level page.

Complications arise when you link between the levels of the hierarchy, as you noted when you followed the link from What's New to the paper on Alpaca wool. All of a sudden you're out of the What's New branch, and into the Technical Papers branch. Lateral movement within the hierarchy can sometimes be confusing; make sure in similar situations that you provide good hints in the navigation links so that your reader can get back to a known position.

Example Two: A Multimedia Encyclopedia

The Multimedia Encyclopedia of Motorcycles is a set of Web pages that provides extensive information about motorcycles and their makers. It is the largest collection of motorcycle information on the Web and includes photographs, sounds (engine noises!), and video for many of the motorcycles listed, making it a multimedia encyclopedia.

The Overview Page

The overview page is the main entry point into the encyclopedia (Figure 10.5).

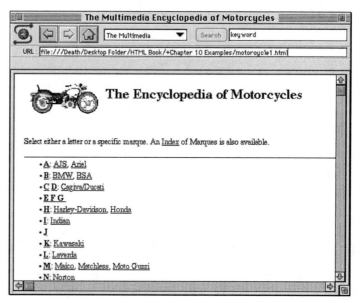

Figure 10.5. *The Motorcycle Encyclopedia overview page.*

This page provides two main ways to get into the encyclopedia: by selecting the letter of the manufacturer you are interested in, or by selecting a link for one of the manufacturers mentioned in the list itself.

So, for example, if you wanted to find out information about the Norton motorcycle company, you could select N, for Norton, and then scroll down to the appropriate entry. But since Norton is one of the major manufacturers listed next to the N link, you could select that link instead, and go straight to the entry for Norton.

The Entry for Norton

After loading the N document, the browser would scroll down to the entry for Norton (shown in Figure 10.6), which contains information about the manufacturer and the various motorcycles they have produced over the years.

Figure 10.6. *Entry for Norton.*

So where are the pictures? This was supposed to be a multimedia encyclopedia, wasn't it? In addition to the text describing Norton itself, the entry includes a list of external media files: images of various motorcycles, sound clips of what they sound like, and film of famous riders on their Nortons (Figure 10.7).

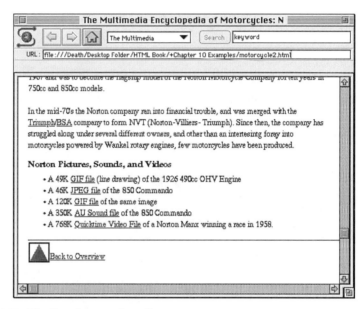

Figure 10.7. *The list of external media.*

Each media file is described in text, and contains links to those files so you can download them if you want to. For example, selecting the 850 Commando Link accesses a JPEG image of the 850 commando (Figure 10.8).

Figure 10.8. *The Norton 850 Commando.*

Note also that in each point in the text where another manufacturer is mentioned, that manufacturer is linked to its own entry. For example, selecting the word BSA in the last paragraph takes you to the entry for BSA (Figure 10.9).

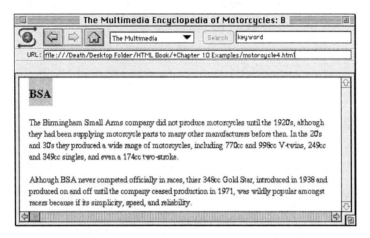

Figure 10.9. *Entry for BSA.*

Once you were done browsing, you would select the Back to Overview link to get back out of the encyclopedia. Note that each entry in each file contains this link, meaning that you would never have to scroll far in order to get out again.

The Index of Marques

Back on the main page, there is also a link to an Index of Marques, a listing of all the manufacturers of motorcycles mentioned in the encyclopedia (Figure 10.10).

Note: A *marque* is a fancy term used by motorcycle and sports car fanatics to refer to manufacturers of each vehicle.

Each name in the index is, as you might expect, a link to the entry for that manufacturer in the encyclopedia itself, allowing you yet another way to quickly navigate into the alphabetic listings.

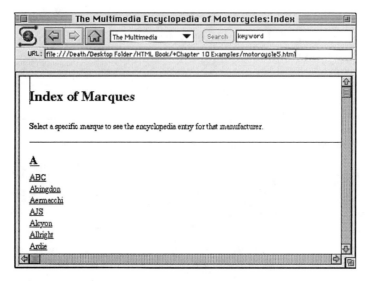

Figure 10.10. *The Index of Marques.*

Features and Issues for Development

Probably the best feature of the design of this encyclopedia is the overview page. In many cases, an online encyclopedia of this sort would provide links to each letter in the alphabet, and leave it at that. If you wanted to check out Norton motorcycles, you would select N and then scroll down to Norton. By providing links to some of the more popular motorcycle makers on the overview page itself, the author of this Web page provides a simple quick-reference that shortens the scrolling time and takes its readers directly to where they want to be.

The addition of the Index of Marques is also a nice touch, as it enables readers to jump directly to the entry of a particular manufacturer's name—again, to reduce the amount of scrolling required to find the entry they want.

The encyclopedia itself is structured in a loosely based Web pattern, making it possible for readers to jump in just about anywhere and then follow cross-references and graze through the available information until they get bored and go somewhere else. Also, by providing all the extra media externally, the author of this Web presentation not only allows the encyclopedia to be used equally well by graphical and text-only browsers, but also keeps the size of the individual files for each letter small so they can be quickly loaded over the Net.

Finally, note that every listing in each letter has a link back to the overview page. If there were more than a single link, they would clutter the page and look ugly. But because the

only explicit navigation choice is up, including a single link enables readers to quickly and easily get back out of the encyclopedia, rather than having to scroll to the top of the bottom of the document in a more conventional organization.

The biggest issue with developing a Web presentation of this kind is in setup and maintenance. Depending on the amount of material you have to put online, the task of arranging it all (Do you use exactly 26 files, one for each letter of the alphabet? Or more? Or less?) and creating the links for all the cross-references and all the external media can be daunting indeed. Fortunately, a presentation of this sort does not have to be updated very often, so after the initial work is done, the maintenance is not all that difficult. To add new information, you simply put it in the appropriate spot, create new links to and from the new information, and there you are.

Example Three:
A Shopping Catalog

Susan's Cactus Gardens is a commercial nursery specializing in growing and shipping cacti and succulents. They offer over 120 species of cacti and succulents as well as books and other cactus-related items. Figure 10.11 shows the home page for Susan's Cactus Gardens.

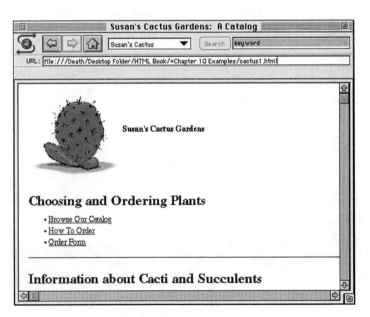

Figure 10.11. *Susan's Cactus Gardens home page.*

From here, customers could read some background about the nursery itself, get information about specials and new plants, browse the catalog, get information about ordering, and actually order the cacti or succulents they have chosen.

Browsing the Catalog

Selecting the Browse the Catalog link takes customers to another menu page, where they have several choices for *how* they want to browse the catalog (Figure 10.12).

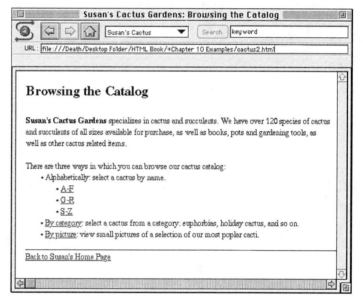

Figure 10.12. *How to browse the catalog.*

By providing several different views of the catalog, the author is serving many different kinds of customers: those who know about cacti and succulents and just want to look up a specific variety, in which case the alphabetic index is most appropriate; those who know they would like, say, an Easter Cactus with pink flowers, but are not sure which particular variety they want (the listing by category); as well as those who don't really know or care about the names but would like something that looks nice (the photo gallery).

The alphabetical links (A-F, G-R, S-Z) take customers to an alphabetical listing of the plants available for purchase. Figure 10.13 shows a sample listing from the alphabetical catalog.

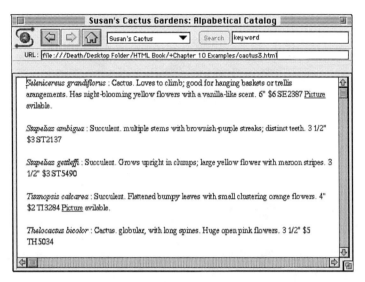

Figure 10.13. *The Cactus Catalog, alphabetical.*

Each item indicates the Latin or scientific name of the cactus; a common name, if any; a simple description; size; order number; and price. If a photograph of this cactus is available in the photo gallery section of the catalog, a link is provided to that photograph, so readers can see what this cactus looks like before they buy it.

The catalog is also cross-referenced by each cactus's common name, if any. The link from the common name takes you back to the primary entry for the cactus. So if you really wanted a plant called Crown of Thorns, selecting that entry would take you to the true entry for that plant, *Euphorbia Milii.*

Each section of the alphabetical catalog also includes navigation buttons both at the top and the bottom of the page, so that you can go back up to the list of catalog views (Browsing the Catalog), or go straight up to the home page. Here the navigation buttons are placed both at the top and at the bottom of each page so that customers won't have to scroll all the way up or all the way down to get to them; they can just go to the nearest set.

Now, if they returned to Browsing the Catalog, they could take a look at the category view. Selecting the category view would take them to another page of menus, listing the available categories (Figure 10.14).

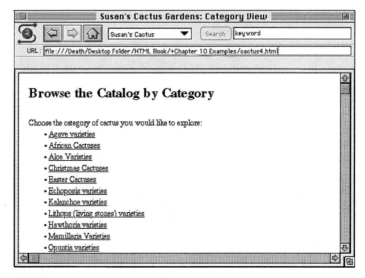

Figure 10.14. *The category view.*

Selecting a particular category—for example, Orchid Cacti—would take customers to a listing of the available plants in that category. Each element in the category listing should look familiar; they're the same elements as in the alphabetical listing, sorted in a different order (Figure 10.15).

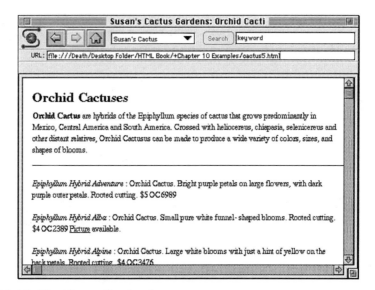

Figure 10.15. *The Cactus Catalog, by category.*

From the category index, customers can go back to the category list, or back to the list of catalog views. Here, we'll go back up to the list of views so that you can take a look at the last item in the list: the photo gallery.

The photo gallery enables customers to browse many of the cacti available at the nursery by looking at pictures of them, rather than having to know their scientific names. This feature is obviously only available to graphical browsers, but provides an excellent way to browse for interesting cacti.

The photo gallery page (shown in Figure 10.16) is organized as a series of icons, with each small picture of the cactus linked to a larger JPEG equivalent. The text description of each picture also takes you back to the appropriate entry in the main catalog.

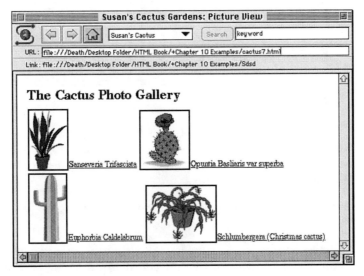

Figure 10.16. *The Cactus Catalog, photo gallery.*

Ordering

After customers finished browsing the catalog, and had an idea of the cacti they wanted to order, they could jump back up to the home page for Susan's Cactus Gardens and find out how to order. (It's the second bullet in the list shown previously in Figure 10.11.)

The page for ordering is just some simple text (Figure 10.17): information about where to call or send checks, tables for shipping costs, notes on when they will ship plants, and so on.

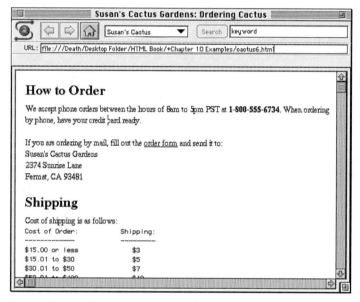

Figure 10.17. *Ordering plants.*

In the section on ordering by mail, there is a link to an order form. The form itself is a PostScript file that customers would download, print out, and then fill out and send to the nursery. (It's an external file, specified in the HREF attribute to a link tag just as you would specify an external media file.)

After reading the information about ordering or downloading the order form, you could return to the home page using a link at the bottom of the page.

The third bullet on this page is another link to the order form file; it's provided here so repeat customers won't have to take the added step of going back to the Ordering, Shipping, and Payment page again.

Features and Issues for Development

In any online shopping service, the goals are to allow the reader to browse the items for sale, and then to order those items. Within the browsing goal, there are several subgoals: What if the reader wants a particular item? Can it be found quickly and easily? What if someone just wants to look through the items for sale until he or she finds something interesting?

These two goals for browsing the online inventory may seem conflicting, but in this particular example it's been handled especially well through the use of the multiple views on the content of the catalog. The multiple views do provide a level of indirection (an extra menu between the top-level page and the contents of the catalog itself), but that small step provides a branching that helps each different type of customer accomplish his or her goals.

Probably the hardest part of building and maintaining a set of Web pages of this sort is maintaining the catalog itself, particularly if items need to be added or removed, or if prices change on a frequent basis. If the nursery only had one catalog view (the alphabetical one), this would not be so bad, as you could make changes directly to the catalog files. The additional view, however, with the list of items sorted by category, means that maintenance of the catalog becomes twice as difficult.

This sort of arrangement would probably be easiest to maintain if the catalog were actually stored in some sort of database external to the Web pages themselves, and then the whole thing were converted to HTML on a regular basis. The primary difficulty with that solution, of course, is how much work it would take to do the conversion each time while still preserving the cross-references to the other pages. Could the process be automated, and how much setup and daily maintenance would that involve? These are the sorts of questions you may have to solve given a Web presentation of this sort.

Having a database back end on the Web pages could also allow you to search the database for a given cactus from the browser side. Web servers do provide mechanisms for allowing this sort of interaction between browsers and back-end tools; you'll learn about this tomorrow when you install and use a Web server.

Example Four: An Online Book

Bread and Circuses was a small volume, self-published, in which the author expounded at length about the theory of breadmaking and offered some of his best recipes for various kinds of popular breads. After the sales of the book itself faded out, the author decided to put the content of the book on the Web and spread his ideas even further than the printed page would allow him to do. The Bread and Circuses home page is the start of that online book.

Table of Contents

The home page for *Bread & Circuses* is, appropriately, a table of contents, just as it might be in a real book. Organized as lists within lists, this table of contents is essentially a large link menu, with pointers to the various sections in the book. (See Figure 10.18.)

245

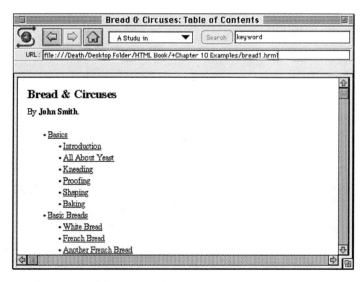

Figure 10.18. *The Bread & Circuses table of contents.*

Readers who were interested in all the content the book had to offer could simply select the link for Basics and read all the way through. But, to be different, why not jump in at the middle of the first chapter, Proofing.

Proofing

The link for Proofing takes the reader to the file for Chapter One and then scrolls down to the appropriate section in that file (shown in Figure 10.19).

The reader can read all about proofing and reach the end of the section. Following it is the next section, "Kneading and Proofing Again." And following it is the remainder of the chapter. Finally, at the end of the chapter, there are navigation links back to the table of contents, or on to the next chapter (Figure 10.20).

From here, the reader would go on to the next chapter, and once again the only navigation links are at the end of the file. It's easy to get into the content using the table of contents, but difficult to get out again without scrolling all the way down to the end of the chapter or using the back command in the browser.

From this point, it is possible to jump back to the table of contents. At the bottom of the list is an entry for the index, which might very well be interesting.

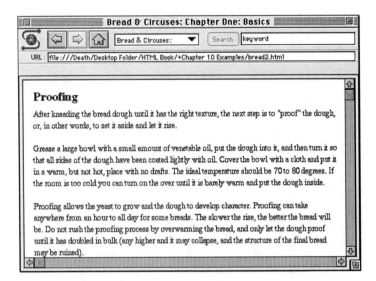

Figure 10.19. *The section on proofing.*

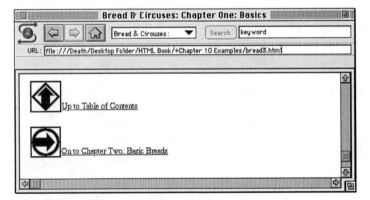

Figure 10.20. *Navigation links.*

The Index

The index is similar to the table of contents in that it provides an overview of the content and links into specific places within the book itself. Like a paper index, the online version contains an alphabetical list of major topics and words, each one linked to the spot in the text where it is mentioned (Figure 10.21).

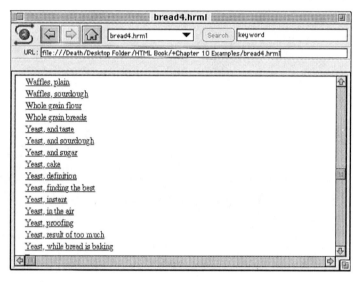

Figure 10.21. *The index.*

Yeast is mentioned multiple times in the book. Because online books do not have page numbers (generally; I've seen quite a few that do, mysteriously enough), linking index entries to multiple locations becomes more of a chore, as the author has to describe some context for each entry rather than just linking blindly to that element.

So is this index useful? Like the table of contents, it does help readers jump to a specific place within the content. But also like the table of contents, it's harder for readers to get back out again once they're in the book—even more so for the index, since the author did not provide a navigation link at the end of the chapter directly back to the index. This makes the index useful only in limited circumstances.

Features and Issues For Development

The biggest problem with putting books or other linear material online is that the material is more difficult to navigate online than it was on paper. Online, readers can't flip through the pages as quickly and easily as they can on paper. For this reason, it is crucial to include overview pages, such as the table of contents in this example, to enable readers to jump in and out of the content and to find what they want. In this book, the table of contents made it possible to jump into the content, but jumping back out again was less easy because there were few navigation links except at the end of the chapter. But would you want to jump back out again, or would you start from that section and read

through to the end? The authors' assumptions about how readers would be using the content form their decisions about how often to provide navigation hints.

Major considerations involved in putting books and papers online include

☐ The book in this example had a table of contents and a set of chapters. You might also want to include an index, in which the words in the index link back to the place they appear. Complications arise with multiple citations, however. In a hard-copy book the index indicates the different citations using page numbers—without page numbers, how do you note the different instances of a single word?

☐ In this example, each chapter is a single document with multiple sections. The author could have broken it down further so that each section is a separate page as well. How you split up the material depends on how much content you have, of course, but is mostly a design choice you'll have to make before you start converting the text to HTML.

☐ You should probably always link back to the table of contents. But should you also link to the index? If you've divided the content into separate pages for the sections, should you also link back to the beginning of each chapter as well?

☐ How many nonnavigational links do you want to make, if any?

Because a book's structure is essentially linear, links between different sections because of related material may create confusion for readers.

Limited forms of nonnavigational links can work well, however—for example, an explicit reference to another section of the book in the text such as, "For more information about yeast, see 'yeast' in Chapter One."

Summary

I've only presented a couple ideas for using and structuring Web pages here; the variations on these themes are unlimited for the Web pages you will design.

Probably the best way to find examples of the sort of Web pages you might want to design and how to organize them is to go out on the Web and browse what's out there. While you're browsing, in addition to examining the layout and design of individual pages and the content they describe, keep an eye out for the structures people have used to organize their pages, and try to guess why they might have chosen that organization. ("They didn't think about it" is a common reason for many poorly organized Web pages, unfortunately.) Critique other people's Web pages with an eye for structure: Is it easy to navigate them? Did you get lost? Can you easily get back to a known page from any other location in their presentation?

Learning from other people's mistakes and seeing how other people have solved difficult problems can help you make your own Web pages better.

Q&A

Q These Web presentations are really cool. What are their URLs?

A As I noted at the beginning of this chapter, the Web presentations I've described here are mockups of potential Web presentations that *could* exist. Although many of the designs and organizations that I have created here were inspired by existing Web pages (the company profile and tutorial Web pages, in particular), these pages do not actually exist on the Web.

Q Three out of the four examples here used some sort of hierarchical organization. Are hierarchies that common and do I have to use them? Can't I do something different?

A Hierarchies are extremely common on the Web, but that doesn't mean that they're bad. Hierarchies are an excellent way of organizing your content, especially when the information you're presenting lends itself to a hierarchical organization.

You can certainly do something different to organize your presentation. But the simplicity of hierarchies allows them to be easily structured, easily navigated, and easy maintained. Why make more trouble for yourself and for your reader by trying to force a complicated structure on otherwise simple information?

Q You mentioned earlier in this book that the Web can do interactive forms. Why wasn't the form in the cactus example an interactive form?

A Mostly because you haven't learned how to do forms yet, and I didn't want to jump ahead.

Ideally, yes, the ordering form would be an interactive Web page that allowed you to fill out your name and address, the items you were interested in, and your credit card information. If this were really an ideal situation, you'd also be able to mark items that you were interested in when you were browsing the catalog, and then review and order your selections when you were done. Although the Web does have facilities for developing online forms (you'll learn about this on Day 7), it is not quite robust enough for total online ordering,

and sending credit card numbers over the Net unencrypted is a bad idea. However, the word is future servers and browsers under development will have capabilities for handling transactions of this sort.

Also, some Web page designers may not have the server capabilities for handling forms (only UNIX servers currently provide full flexibility in forms processing), and even if they do, the designer may not have the programming ability. Creating forms and processing the results is no small task.

10

DAY

6

11

Putting It All Online

The day of reckoning. You've put together a Web presentation with a well-organized structure, included meaningful images (and specified values for the ALT attributes), written your text with wit and care, used only relative links, and tested it extensively on your own system.

It's finally time to put it all online and link your documents into the real Web. In this chapter, you learn nearly everything you need to get started publishing the work you've done:

☐ Where you can find a Web server on which to put your presentation

☐ Some hints for administering your own server

☐ How to install your Web presentation

☐ How to find out your URL

☐ How to test your Web pages

☐ Methods for advertising your presentation

What Does a Web Server Do?

A Web server is a program that sits on a machine on the Net, waiting for a Web browser to connect to it and make a request, usually for a file. Once a request comes over the wire, the server locates and sends the file. It's as easy as that.

Servers and browsers communicate using the HyperText Transfer Protocol (HTTP), a special "language" created specifically for transferring hypertext documents over the Web. Because of this, Web servers are often called HTTPD servers.

Note: The "D" stands for "daemon." A daemon is a UNIX term for a program that sits in the background and waits for requests. When it receives a request, it wakes up, processes that request, and then goes back to sleep. You don't have to be on UNIX for a program to act like a daemon, so Web servers on any platform are still called HTTPDs. Most of the time I call them Web servers.

When a server sends a file to a browser, it also includes some information about what kind of file it is sending (for example, a GIF file or a Quicktime movie), so the browser can

figure out whether it can read it itself or if it needs to start up a helper application. You can also extend the behavior of your server to include files that may not be part of the default set.

Finally, Web servers can also be set up to run scripts and programs based on information that your readers provide from their browsers. For example, you could set up a Web page that asks your reader for a search string. When the browser sends back the string to search for (as entered by the reader, using the browser), the server passes that string to a program on the server side; the program does the search and passes the result to the server, which in turn hands it back to the browser (whew!).

These special programs are called gateway programs or gateway scripts and are the basis for creating interactive forms and clickable image maps (images that contain several "hot spots" and do different operations based on the location within the image that has been selected). You'll learn a little about these scripts in the next chapter, and about forms and image maps tomorrow.

Finding a Server to Use

Before you can put your Web presentation on the Web, you'll need to find a Web server.

Using a Web Server Provided by Your School, Work, or Network Provider

Ideally, you'll be able to publish your Web pages using the same organization that gives you access to the Internet. Many schools and organizations allow their users to publish Web pages, and some even provide help. If you get access to the Internet through a commercial provider, that organization may offer Web space that you can use as well. Ask the administrator of your system if they offer Web server access.

Using a Commercial Web Service

In the last few months, organizations that allow you to "rent" Web space for your presentation have been popping up all over the country. You are provided with some method for transferring your files on their site, and they provide the disk space and the network connection. Generally you are charged a flat monthly rate, with some additional cost if you use a large amount of disk space. Some services even allow gateway

scripts for forms and image maps and will provide consulting to help you set them up. These features can make commercial Web sites an especially attractive option.

Appendix A, "Sources for Further Information," includes pointers to lists of these sites that are updated when a new service appears.

Using Anonymous FTP or Gopher

You don't need a real Web server to serve simple HTML documents with links and graphics. Anything that will send a file over the Net can be used to serve Web documents; for example, FTP or Gopher. Since these kinds of information services are quite commonly available on public access Internet providers, and software to enable your system to handle these protocols is freely available, this may be an excellent low-cost option if you do not have Web access through your normal Internet provider.

Using FTP or Gopher to serve your HTML documents, you can do everything you've learned up to this point in the book: create hypertext-linked HTML files with graphics and specify external media as well. Note, however, that if you want to write gateway scripts, perform searches, or handle forms and clickable images, you will have to use a true Web server.

Setting Up Your Own Server

If none of the previous options are available to you, you might have to resort to setting up your own server. If you have the equipment and the connection, this may not be a problem; if you don't, you might want to seriously consider looking into an alternative option.

To set up your own server, you'll not only need access to a system to run it on, but more importantly, you'll need a fast full-time connection to the Internet. A part-time 14.4 SLIP connection may be fine for browsing other people's Web pages, but if you are publishing information yourself, you'll want your server available all the time, and you'll want the fastest connection you can possibly afford.

In addition, you'll need the technical background to be able to administer the server. For Macintosh and PC systems this may not be that great of a problem, but for UNIX systems you'll have to know something about UNIX and network administration as well as how to set up and administer the server itself.

Between the system you'll need to serve documents, the fees for the Internet connection, the amount of knowledge you need, and the time you'll need to spend administering it, setting up your own server may not be a cost-effective method of publishing Web documents. But it does provide the most flexibility and power of all these solutions because you could configure everything the way you want it to be and be able to install and use gateway scripts for interactivity and forms.

Installing Server Software

If you do decide to install your own server on your own system, you can choose from several servers for each platform. This section describes the most popular servers and their major features.

Servers for UNIX Systems

The Web began on UNIX systems, and even today new features are being introduced on UNIX systems first. In many ways, UNIX systems make the best Web servers because of this advantage they have in Web technology—more tools and hints and publicly available software exist for managing Web servers on UNIX than on any other platform.

Many Web servers are publicly available for UNIX, but the two most widely used are CERN's HTTPD and NCSA's HTTPD. Both are freeware, and both serve Web files equally well. They have the following features:

- They can serve Web documents from a central repository or from individual users' home directories.
- They can be set up to run gateway scripts that handle forms, clickable images, and so on.

In addition, CERN's HTTPD can be run as a proxy; that is, it can be set up to handle outgoing Web connections from inside an Internet firewall. Some organizations set up their networks so that the majority of the machines are on an internal network, with only one machine actually talking to the Internet at large, to prevent (or minimize) unauthorized access on the internal network. That one machine is called a firewall, and with CERN's HTTPD running on it, it can pass Web information back and forth between the internal network and the Web at large.

CERN servers running as proxies also have a facility for *caching*—storing frequently retrieved documents on the firewall system instead of retrieving them from the Web every time they are requested. This can significantly speed up the time it takes to access a particular document through a firewall.

With NCSA's HTTPD, on the other hand, documents can be user- and password-protected; only browsers that support user-authentication can use this feature. In addition, NCSA's HTTPD supports server-side include files, which allow documents to include other documents and be customized at the time a reader requests them.

Which server you use is mostly a matter of personal choice, depending on which particular features you need.

At the time that I'm writing this book, the most current versions of the CERN and NCSA Web servers are 3.0 and 1.3, respectively. FTP locations for both CERN's and NCSA's servers are listed in Appendix A.

Note: To install either CERN's or NCSA's server to run most effectively in its default configuration, you should have root access on the system that you are running on. But you can run a Web server even if you don't have root access by installing it on a port number above 1024. (See the documentation for your server for instructions on doing this.) If you decide to go this route, be sure to check with your system administrator first. Web servers can be a significant draw on system resources, and the providers of your system may not want you running a Web server at all, in which case you'll have to look for an alternate solution to serving your files.

Servers for Microsoft Windows and Macintosh

NCSA's popular freeware HTTPD has been ported to Windows systems by Bob Denny, and is colloquially called WinHTTPD. Its current version as of this writing is 1.3Pre (pre-release), and it has many of the features of UNIX, plus many extra features specific to operation under Microsoft Windows.

MacHTTP is a mostly freeware HTTP server for the Macintosh (there are some licensing restrictions for commercial use), whose current version is 1.3, although a new version with user-authentication and caching is expected to be released by the time this book is published. You can get MacHTTP from most of the common Macintosh archives.

Appendix A lists some pointers to locations for these servers.

Hints for Good Server Administration

If you've set up your own Web server, there are several simple things you can do to make that server run effectively and well. If you're not a Web server administrator, skip to "Organizing and Installing Your HTML Files," later in this chapter.

Alias Your Hostname to *www.yoursystem.com*

A common convention on the Web is that the system that serves Web pages to the Network has the name that begins with www. Typically, your network administrator or your network provider will create a hostname alias, called a CNAME, that points to the actual machine on the Network serving Web files. You don't have to follow this convention, of course, but it is helpful for several reasons:

☐ It's easier to remember than some other host name, and is a common convention for finding the Web server for any given site. So, if your primary system is mysystem.com and I want to get to your Web pages, www.mysystem.com would be the appropriate place for me to look first.

☐ If you change the machine on your network that is serving Web pages, you can simply reassign the alias. If you don't use an alias, all the links that point to your server will break.

Create a Webmaster Mail Alias

If the system you're using has the ability to send and receive mail, create a globally available mail alias for "webmaster" which points to your e-mail address, so that if someone sends mail to webmaster@yoursite.com, that mail is sent to you. Like other

administrative mail aliases such as root (for general problems), postmaster (for e-mail problems), and usenet (for news), the webmaster alias provides a standard contact address for problems or complaints about your Web server. (You may not want to hear about problems or complaints, but it is the polite thing to do.)

Create a Server Home Page

Your server may be home to several different Web presentations, especially if you are serving many different users (for example, if you've set up a Web "storefront.") In cases such as this, you should provide a site-wide home page, typically http://www.yoursite.com /index.html, that provides some general information about your site, legal notices, and perhaps an overview of the contents of your site—with links to the home pages for each presentation, of course.

The configuration file for your server software should have an entry for a site-specific home page.

Create Site-Wide Administrative and Design Guidelines

If you are the Web master for a large organization, it may be helpful for you and for your organization to define who is responsible for the Web server: who is the contact for day-to-day complaints or problems, who is the person to set up access control for users, and who can answer questions about policy concerning what can appear in a public Web page on this site.

In addition, your organization may want to have some kind of creative control over the Web pages it publishes on the Web. You can use many of the hints and guidelines in this book to create suggestions for Web page style and create sample pages that your users can use as a basis for their own Web pages.

Organizing and Installing Your HTML Files

Once you have access to a Web server of some sort, you can install the Web presentation you've labored so hard to create. But before you actually move it into place, it's best to

have your files organized and a good idea of what goes where so you don't lose files or so your links don't break.

Probably the best way to organize each of your presentations is to include all the files for that presentation in a single directory. If you have lots of extra files—for your images, for example—you can put those in a subdirectory to that main directory. Your goal is to contain all your files in a single place rather than scattering them around on your disk. Once you have your files contained, you can set all your links in your files to be relative to that directory. If you follow these hints, you stand the best chance of being able to move that directory around to different servers without breaking the links.

Your home page or top-level index for each presentation should be called index.html (or index.htm for DOS). This is the file that is most often loaded by default if your reader loads a URL that does not include an explicit home page—for example, http://myserver/www/ rather than http://myserver/www/homepage.html.

Note: The name of the "default" home page for each directory is configurable in each server. I've picked index.html here because it's the file name supported by most servers.

Each file should also have an appropriate extension indicating what kind of file it is so the server can map it to the appropriate file type. Table 11.1 shows a list of the common file extensions you should be using for your files and media.

Table 11.1. File types and extensions.

Format	Extension
HTML	.html, .htm
ASCII Text	.txt
PostScript	.ps
GIF	.gif
JPEG	.jpg, .jpeg
AU Audio	.au
MPEG Video	.mpeg, .mpg

Installing Your Files

With your files in a single directory, all you have to do is put them in the appropriate spot on the server.

If you're using a server someone else has installed, you'll have to find out from them where to put your documents. For many servers, this may be as easy as creating a subdirectory with a particular name (usually `public_html`) in your home directory for your files and putting them there. Other services may have you copy or ftp your files to the appropriate spots.

If you've installed your own server, of course, you'll know where to put your files.

Some Gotchas About Moving Files Between Systems

If you're using a Web server that has been set up by someone else, you'll probably have to move your Web files from your system to theirs using FTP, Zmodem transfer, or some other method. Although the HTML markup within your files is completely portable, moving the actual files from platform to platform has its gotchas. In particular, be careful to do the following:

☐ **Convert binary files as binary.**

Watch out for your images and other media; make sure you send them in binary mode when you transfer them or they may not work on the other end.

Watch out for Macintosh media; in particular, that you transfer them as regular binary and not MacBinary. MacBinary files cannot be read on other platforms.

☐ **Observe filename restrictions.**

If you're moving your files to or from DOS systems, you'll have to watch out for the dreaded 8.3—the DOS rule that says filenames must be only 8 characters long with 3-character extensions.

When you move files from a DOS system to a system such as UNIX, you should rename all your files to have a .html rather than an .htm extension. (Most UNIX-based servers don't recognize the .htm extension to be an HTML file.)

And, if you're moving to a DOS system, you'll have to make sure you shorten your filenames appropriately before moving them.

Also, watch out if you're moving files from a Macintosh to other systems that your filenames do not have spaces or other funny characters in them. Keep your filenames as short as possible and use only letters and numbers and you'll be fine.

☐ **Be aware of carriage returns and line feeds.**

Different systems use different methods for ending a line; the Macintosh uses carriage returns, UNIX uses line feeds, and DOS uses both. When you move files from one system to another, most of the time the end-of-line characters will be converted appropriately, but sometimes they are not. This can result in your file coming out double-spaced or all on one single line on the system that it was moved to.

Most of the time it does not matter, as browsers ignore spurious returns or line feeds in your HTML files. The existence or absence of either one is not terribly important. Where it may be an issue is in sections of text you've marked up with <PRE>; you may find that your well-formatted text that worked so well on one platform doesn't come out well-formatted after it's been moved.

Note: This is only an issue when you move files between platforms, not when you use a browser on one platform to view a file being served from another platform. The Web server and browser know enough to convert the end-of-line conventions properly.

If you do have end-of-line problems, this information may help:

☐ Many text editors allow you to save ASCII files in a format for another platform. If you know what platform you're moving to, you can prepare your files for that platform before moving them.

☐ If you're moving to a UNIX system, small filters for converting line feeds called dos2unix and unix2dos may exist on the UNIX or DOS systems.

☐ Macintosh files can be converted to UNIX-style files using the following command line on UNIX:

```
tr '\015' '\012' < oldfile.html > newfile.html
```

where oldfile.html is the original file with end-of-line problems, and newfile.html is the name of the new file.

What's My URL?

At this point you have a server, your Web pages are installed and ready to go, and all that is left is to set the world loose on your presentation. All you need now is a URL so that the world can find your presentation.

If you're using a commercial Web server, or a server that someone else administers, you may be able to easily find out what your URL is by asking the administrator. Otherwise, you'll have to figure it out yourself. Luckily, this isn't that hard.

As I note in Chapter 6, "More About Links and URLs," URLs are made of three parts: the protocol, the host name, and the path to the file. To determine each of these parts, use the following questions:

☐ **What are you using to serve the files?**

If you're using a real Web server, your protocol is http. If you're using FTP or Gopher, the protocol is ftp and gopher, respectively. (Isn't this easy?)

☐ **What's the name of your server?**

This is the network name of the machine your Web server is located on, typically beginning with www; for example, www.mysite.com or www.netcom.com. If it doesn't start with www, don't worry about it; that doesn't affect whether or not people can get to your files.

With some SLIP or PPP connections, you may not even have a network name, just a number—something like 192.123.45.67. You can use that as the network name.

If the server has been installed on a port other than 80, you'll need to know that number, too.

☐ **What's the path to my home page?**

The path to your home page most often begins at the root of the directory Web pages are stored in (part of your server configuration), which may or may not be the top level of your file system.

If your Web server has been set up so that you can use your home directory to store Web pages, you can use the UNIX convention of the tilde (~) to refer to the Web pages in your home directory. You don't have to include the name of the directory you created in the URL itself. So, for example, if the Web page home.html is in a directory called public_html in your home directory, the path to that file in your URL would be:

```
/~lemay/home.html
```

> **Tip:** Most browsers can recognize the tilde to mean a home directory, but some may not be able to. All browsers will be able to recognize it if you specify the tilde as a URL escape character, like this: `/%Elemay/home.html.`

Once you know these three things, you can construct a URL. You'll probably remember from Chapter 6 that a URL looks like this:

```
protocol://machinename.com:port/path
```

You should be able to plug your values for each of those elements into the appropriate places in the URL structure. For example

```
http://mymachine.com/www/tutorials/index.html
ftp://ftp.netcom.com/pub/lemay/index.html
http://commercialweb.com:8080/~lemay/index.html
```

> **Note:** Many HTTP servers are set up in the default to use `index.html` as the default document to load for a directory (which is why I suggested you use that name for your home page). If your server has been configured to do this, you can leave off the name of the file in your URL, making it slightly shorter to type:
>
> ```
> http://mymachine.com/www/tutorials/
> ```
>
> The Web server will append the name of the file to the end of the URL.

11

Test, Test, and Test Again

Now that your Web pages are available on the Net, you can take the opportunity to test them on as many platforms using as many browsers as you possibly can. It is only when you've seen how your documents look on different platforms that you'll realize how important it is to design documents that can look good on as many platforms and browsers as possible.

Try it and see...you might be surprised at the results.

Registering and Advertising Your Web Pages

There is no central repository of Web pages or authority to register with when you create a new Web page. Instead, there are common ways you can publicize your new Web page once its up on the Net and working:

- [ ] Send mail to `whats-new@ncsa.uiuc.edu`. This is the listing that appears off a link from the NCSA Mosaic home page at periodic intervals.

- [ ] If you have published your Web presentation on a commercial Web site or one provided by your Internet provider, there may be a local "What's New" page to which you can add your presentation. Check with your administrator.

- [ ] Post it to the appropriate `comp.infosystems` newsgroup. Currently, `comp.infosystems.announce` is the appropriate group, but a proposal is in the works for creating the group `comp.infosystems.www.announce`. If this group is available by the time you read this, use it for announcements instead.

   If you must post to the `comp.infosystems.www` series of groups, post only to `comp.infosystems.www.misc`, and include the word ANNOUNCE in your subject line.

- [ ] Send e-mail to the www announcement mailing list: `www-announce@info.cern.ch`

- [ ] Register with CERN's Virtual Library at `http://info.cern.ch/hypertext/DataSources/WWW/Geographical_generation/new-servers.html`

- [ ] Register with the ALIWEB (an Archie-like index of Web pages). For more information, see `http://web.nexor.co.uk/aliweb/doc/aliweb.html`.

Summary

In this chapter, you've reached the final point in creating a Web presentation: releasing your work to the World Wide Web at large through the use of a Web server, either installed by you or available from a Network provider.

From here on, everything you learn is icing on an already-substantial cake. You'll simply be adding more features (interactivity, forms) to the presentation you already have available on the Web.

Q&A

Q I really don't understand all this network stuff. CNAMEs? protocols? ports? hostnames? Help!!

A You don't have to know any of this if you can get access to a Web server through the people who provide your usual Net access, or if you rent space on a commercial Web site. You can let someone else do all the network stuff; all you'll have to do is make sure your documents have relative path names and can be moved as a group onto the server. And once they're there, you're done.

Q How can I set up a server to do access control (to only let certain sites in), or to run as a proxy across a firewall?

A If this were a book all about setting up Web servers, I'd have written whole chapters on these subjects. As it is, the documentation for your server should tell you how to do each of these things (and the documentation for all four servers I've mentioned in this chapter is excellent, so with a little poking around you should be able to find what you need).

Q I really like the concept of HTML being so simple and cross-platform, but I don't want to distribute documents over the Net; I want to distribute them via CD-ROM. Can I do this?

A With the current state of browsers on the Web, it's possible, but not easy.

First of all, note that most browsers are freeware only for personal use; if you want to ship a browser with your CD, you'll usually have to license it for business use, and the cost may be prohibitive. Contact the author of your favorite browser to see what their licensing restrictions are.

Secondly, most of the browsers assume they will be run with a network connection, and may complain if one doesn't exist. The "complaint" may only be a simple dialog saying "You can only use local documents," but it's difficult to get rid of that dialog. For Windows systems, you will need to ship and install what is called a null winsock before many Windows browsers will work.

With those caveats in mind, there is nothing any more special about distributing HTML documents on CD-ROM than there is about distributing documents using a Web server. A link is a link is a link, whether it is over the Net or on the local file system. Simply provide the URL (usually the file URL) of the home page on the CD as a starting point, and if all the links in your presentation are relative to that one (as they should be), your reader should have no

Putting It All Online

problem viewing and navigating your presentation locally. If you can license a browser that doesn't complain about the lack of a network, you can set up that browser on the CD so that its default home page is your home page—and then loading the browser will load your presentation.

Discussion about using HTML and the Web offline happens quite often on the `comp.infosystems.www` series of newsgroups.

12

An Introduction to Gateway Scripts

Gateway scripts are an extremely powerful feature of Web browser and server interaction that can completely change how you think of a Web presentation. Gateway scripts enable your reader to interact with your Web pages—to search for an item in a database, to offer comments on what you've written, or to select several items from a form and get a customized reply in return. If you've ever come across a fill-in form or a search dialog on the Web, you've used a gateway script. You may not have realized it at the time because most of the work happens on the Web server, behind the scenes. You only see the result.

As a Web author, you create all the sides of the gateway: the side the reader sees, the programming on the server side to deal with the reader's input, and the result given back to the reader. This does require some amount of programming, and depending on what you want to do, this may be beyond your abilities.

This chapter explains

- [ ] What a gateway script is and how they work
- [ ] When you should use a gateway script
- [ ] What the output of a gateway script looks like
- [ ] How to create simple scripts that execute programs
- [ ] How to create scripts that prompt the reader for a small reply
- [ ] How to create scripts that return special responses

Once you have learned the basics of creating gateway scripts, you can use them to create all kinds of customized Web pages. Also, gateways are the starting point from which you can create fill-out forms and clickable image maps, which you'll learn about tomorrow.

What Is a Gateway Script?

A gateway script, most simply, is a program that is run on a Web server, triggered by input from a browser. The gateway script is usually a link between the server and some other program running on the system; for example, a database.

Gateway scripts do not have to be actual scripts—depending on what your Web server supports, they can be compiled programs or batch files or any other executable entity. For the sake of a simple term for this chapter, however, I'll call them gateway scripts.

Gateway scripts are often also called CGI scripts, after the term Common Gateway Interface. CGI is the method the CERN and NCSA Web servers on UNIX use to allow interaction between servers and programs (and specifically, between forms and programs); again, UNIX was first, so UNIX sets the standard. Other servers on other

platforms may provide similar gateway capabilities, but they don't necessarily use the Common Gateway Interface to do so. Again, for the sake of simplicity, I'll simply call them gateway scripts rather than using the term CGI.

What Programming Language Should I Use to Write Gateway Scripts?

You can use just about any programming language you are familiar with to write gateway scripts. Some servers, however, may only support programs written in a particular language. For example, MacHTTP uses AppleScript for its gateway scripts.

For the examples in this chapter, I use the UNIX bourne shell script language (sh), which has a simple syntax and is commonly available on UNIX systems. Given some basic programming background, you should be able to figure out the equivalent commands in the language you're using. (I explain what I'm doing in each example so you'll know what's going on.)

How Do Gateway Scripts Work?

Gateway scripts are called by the server based on information from the browser. Figure 12.1 shows the path of how things work between the browser, the server, and the script.

Here's a short version of what's actually going on:

1. A URL points to a gateway script the same way that it points to any other document on a server. The browser requests that URL from a server just as it would any other document.

2. The server receives the request, notes that the URL points to a script (based on the location of the file or based on its extension, depending on the server), and executes that script.

3. The script performs some action based on the input, if any, from the browser. The action may include querying a database, calculating a value, or simply calling some other program on the system.

4. The script formats its result in a manner that the Web server can understand.

5. The Web server receives the result from the script and passes it back to the browser, which formats and displays it for the reader.

Got it? No? Don't be worried; it can be a confusing process. Read on, it'll become clearer with a couple of examples.

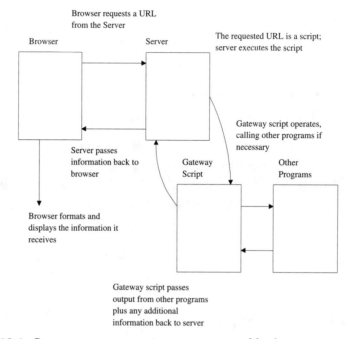

Figure 12.1. *Browser to server to script to program and back again.*

A Simple Example

Here's a simple example, with a step-by-step explanation of what's happening on all sides of the process. In your browser, you encounter a page that looks like the page shown in Figure 12.2.

The link to Display the Date is a link to a gateway script, embedded in the HTML code for the page just like any other link. If you were to look at the HTML code for that page, that link might look like this:

```
<A HREF="http://somesite.com/cgi-bin/getdate">Display the Date</A>
```

The fact that there's a `cgi-bin` in the path name is a strong hint that this is a gateway script, since in many servers (the CERN and NCSA servers, in particular) that's the only place that gateway scripts can be kept.

When you select the link, your browser requests that URL from the server at the site `somesite.com`, a UNIX system running the CERN httpd. The server receives the request

and figures out from its configuration that the URL it's been given is a script called getdate, so it executes that script.

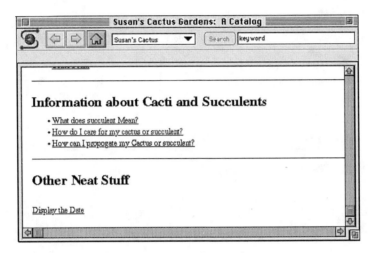

Figure 12.2. *A page with a script link.*

The getdate script, in this case a shell script to be executed on a UNIX system, looks something like this:

```
#!/bin/sh

echo Content-type: text/plain
echo

/bin/date
```

This script does two things: It outputs the line Content-type: text/plain, followed by a blank line, and it calls the UNIX date program. So the complete output of the script looks something like this:

```
Content-type: text/plain

Tue Oct 25 16:15:57 EDT 1994
```

What's that Content-type thing? That's a special code that the Web server passes on to the browser to tell it what kind of document this is. The browser then uses that code to figure out if it can display the document or not, or if it needs to load an external viewer. You'll learn specifics about this line later in this chapter.

So after the script is finished executing, the server gets the result and passes it back to the browser. And when the browser gets it, it simply displays the date in a new window (Figure 12.3).

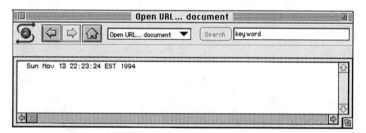

Figure 12.3. *The result of the date script.*

That's the basic idea; although things can get much more complicated, it's this interaction between browser and server and script that is at the heart of how gateway scripts work.

Can I Use Gateway Scripts?

Often, whether or not you can use gateway scripts as part of your Web presentation depends on whether the administrator of your Web server will allow you to. Many network services do not allow gateway scripts because of security concerns. Of course, if you are your own Web administrator, this is not a problem. You'll have to make the decision yourself. But keep in mind the following issues that gateway scripts bring up:

☐ Each script is a program, and it runs on your system when the browser requests it, using CPU time and memory during its execution. What happens to the system if dozens or hundreds of these scripts are running at the same time? Your system may not be able to handle the load, or it may make your system unusable.

☐ Unless you are very careful with the gateway scripts you write, you can potentially open yourself up to someone breaking into or damaging your system by passing arguments to your gateway script that are different from those it expects.

If you do decide to work with gateway scripts, you may have to configure your server to accept script requests and to tell it where you'll be storing scripts. Consult your server documentation for information on configuring your server as well as specific information on how that server handles gateway scripts.

Gateway Script Output

Because you're programming the gateway script yourself, you can have it accomplish any operation you want based on the input you get from the browser. But in order for the output of your script to be recognized by the server and, eventually, by the browser, you must format it in a specific way. Particularly, your output generally has two main parts: the header and the data.

The Output Header

Each script has a special header that gives the server, and eventually the browser, information about the output you're sending it. The header isn't actually part of the document; it's never displayed anywhere. Web servers and browsers actually send information like this back and forth all the time; you just never see it.

There are three types of headers that you can output from scripts: Content-type, Location, and Status. Content-type is the most popular, so I'll explain it here; you'll learn about Location and Status later in this chapter.

A Content-type header has the words "Content-type," a special code for describing the kind of file you're sending, and a blank line, like this:

```
Content-type: text/html
```

In this example, the contents of the data to follow are of the type text/html; in other words, it's an HTML file. Each file format you work with when you're creating Web presentations has a corresponding content-type, so you should match the format of the output of your script to the appropriate one. Table 12.1 shows some common formats and their equivalent content-types.

Table 12.1. Common formats and content-types.

Format	Content-Type
HTML	text/html
Text	text/plain
GIF	image/gif
JPEG	image/jpeg
PostScript	application/postscript
MPEG	video/mpeg

> **Note:** The content-types are derived from MIME content-types. MIME is a method for sending included files in e-mail messages. There are a lot more content-types available than I've listed here. In fact, if you're using the NCSA server, the file `conf/mime-types` has a whole list of the content-types that the server can accept. As long as a file type is in that list, you can send that content of the file as output to your script.

Note that the content-type line MUST be followed by a blank line. The server will not be able to figure out where the header ends if you don't include the blank line.

The Output Data

The remainder of your script is the actual data that you want to send on to the browser. The content you output in this part should match the content type you told the server you were giving it; that is, if you use a content-type of text/html then the rest of the output should be in HTML. If you use a content-type of image/gif, the remainder of the output should be a binary GIF file, and so on for all the content-types.

Exercise 12.1: Try it.

This exercise is similar to the simple example from earlier in this chapter, the one that printed out the date, except this time, let's modify the script so that it outputs an HTML document, which will then be parsed and formatted by the browser.

First, determine the content-type you'll be outputting. Since this will be an HTML document, the content-type is text/html. So the first part of your script simply prints out a line containing the content-type, and a blank line after that:

```
#!/bin/sh

echo Content-type: text/html
echo
```

Now, add the remainder of the script: the body of the HTML document, which you had to construct yourself from inside the script. Basically what you're going to do here is

- [ ] Print out the tags that make up the first part of the HTML document
- [ ] Call the date program to add the text
- [ ] Print out the last bit of HTML tags to finish up the document

Start with the first bit of the HTML. The following commands will do this in the UNIX shell:

```
cat << EOF
<HTML><HEAD>
<TITLE>Date</TITLE>
</HEAD></BODY>
<P>The current date is: <B>
EOF
```

> **Note:** Just to explain; the `cat << EOF` part is essentially saying "echo everything up to the EOF." I could have done this with individual "echo" statements, but brackets (<>) are special characters to the UNIX show and that was more work and less easy to explain. So I did it this way. You get the idea.

So now you've printed the HTML structuring commands, a nice sentence explaining the output, and you've turned on boldface. Now call the date program to output the date itself:

```
/bin/date
```

And, finally, do another block to print out the last of the HTML document:

```
cat << EOF
</B></BODY></HTML>
EOF
```

And that's it. If you run the program by itself, you'll get a result something like this:

```
Content-type: text/html

<HTML><HEAD>
<TITLE>Date</TITLE>
</HEAD></BODY>
<P>The current date is: <B>
Tue Oct 25 17:11:12 EDT 1994
</B></P></BODY></HTML>
```

Looks like your basic HTML document, doesn't it?

Now, install this script. This step will vary depending on the platform you're on and the server you're using; since I've used UNIX up to this point, I might as well continue with UNIX. In CERN's httpd, gateway scripts go into a `cgi-bin` directory, which is usually contained at the root of the central repository for Web documents. I'll put this script (which I've called `prettydate`) in that directory.

> **Warning:** On UNIX, make sure your scripts are executable. If you can't run them from a command line, the server won't be able to run them either.

Now that you've got a script ready to go, you can call it from a browser. Let's assume, for the purposes of this example, that you've installed the script into a cgi-bin directory on a machine called ostrich.com. The URL to the script would then be

```
http://ostrich.com/cgi-bin/prettydate
```

Figure 12.4 shows the result of running the script.

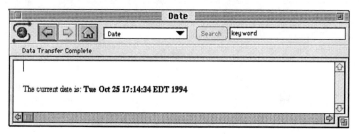

Figure 12.4. *The result of the* prettydate *script.*

Just for reference, here's what the final script looks like:

```
#!/bin/sh

echo Content-type: text/html
echo

cat << EOF
<HTML><HEAD>
<TITLE>Date</TITLE>
<HEAD></BODY>
<P>The current date is: <B>
EOF
/bin/date
cat << EOF
</B></BODY></HTML>
EOF
```

Creating an Interactive Search

Writing a gateway script is easy if you just want to do one thing on the server and get a single result back. But what if you want to do something more complicated, like prompt your reader for a string, search for that string in a file, and then return that result as a nice formatted page?

In this case, things get considerably more complicated. For this, you'll have to actually write a single script that produces one of two HTML documents: one that prompts for the search, and one that returns the formatted result.

So how will your script know which one to output at what point? And how will it get the search key back from the browser? Be patient; all will be revealed.

Gateway scripts can get their information from browsers in one of two ways: through a document-based query or through a form-based query. You'll learn more about forms tomorrow; this section explains more about the document-based query.

Document-based queries were designed to get search keys from a browser and use them to make queries to databases or search in files. For this reason, document queries are good for getting small bits of information (like single words or phrases) back from the reader.

Document-based queries work through the interaction of three things: the use of an HTML tag called ISINDEX, a special form of URL a browser generates, and a set of arguments to your script.

Here's what's going on at each step of the query:

1. When a reader first requests your gateway script through a URL, your script is called with no arguments. In your script, you test for the existence of arguments, and since there are none, you output a default page that prompts for the search.

   In the HTML code for the default page, you include the special `<ISINDEX>` HTML tag inside the `<HEAD>` element. The `<ISINDEX>` tag turns on searching in the browser.

2. The reader enters a string to search for at the search prompt, and hits return or selects a button (depending on how searching has been implemented in the browser).

3. The browser then requests the same URL to the CGI script, except this time the URL includes the string the user specified in the search, tacked onto the end of the URL after a question mark, like this:

   ```
   http://musite.com/cgi-bin/dosearch?ostriches
   ```

For this example, dosearch is the script, and ostriches was the string the reader typed in at the search prompt.

4. The server receives the URL and passes control on to the gateway script, using the part of the URL after the question mark as the argument (or arguments) to the script itself.

5. Your script is called a second time, but this time, since it was called with arguments, it performs a different operation, such as searching for the argument in a file and returning an HTML page indicating whether or not the argument was found.

Each part of the document-based query relies on the other parts. The script provides activation of the ISINDEX tag, which allows the query; the browser attaches the query itself to the URL, which is then passed back to the script, which uses it to perform the appropriate action, and then output a result back to the browser.

Each part of the document-based query is described in more detail in the following sections.

The Script

In document-based queries, you base what your script does on whether or not the script was called with arguments, and often based on the arguments you receive. The script will have two main results.

☐ If the script was called with no arguments, output the HTML for a default page that prompts the user for a search string.

Keep in mind that the default page is generated by a script; it's not a plain HTML file. You cannot trigger searches in this way using a plain HTML document.

☐ If the script was called with any arguments, use the arguments to perform the search, make a test, or perform the operation the script was intended to do, and then output an appropriate result.

The *ISINDEX* Tag

The <ISINDEX> tag is a special tag that goes in the <HEAD> part of the HTML file you're generating for the default page. It's one of the few tags that can go into the <HEAD> part, <TITLE> being the other obvious one. <ISINDEX> doesn't enclose any text, nor does it have a closing tag.

So what does `<ISINDEX>` do? It "turns on" searching in the browser that is reading this document. This may involve enabling a search button or reformatting the window so that it includes a prompt for a string. (Figure 12.5 shows an example.) The reader can then enter a string to search for, and then press Return or select the button for search.

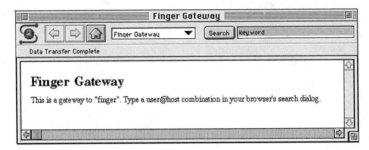

Figure 12.5. *A search prompt.*

`<ISINDEX>` is effectively what provides the user interface for the search in the browser.

The Search String and the URL

When the reader presses return or clicks a button after entering the search string, the browser calls the URL for the gateway script again, appending the value the reader typed into the search prompt to the end of the URL, with a question mark separating the name of the script and the argument. Because spaces and other special characters have a special meaning to URLs, if there are spaces in the search string, the browser converts them to the + character before the URL is called. Other special characters are similarly encoded.

On the server side, the server calls the script again and replaces the + in the argument list with spaces. This has the effect of calling the script with multiple arguments.

Exercise 12.2: Say hello.

Although document-based queries were originally intended to perform searches on databases and other documents stored on the server, you don't have to use document-based queries to actually search anything. In your gateway script, you can use the arguments passed back from the browser for any purpose you want. For example, you could use it to create a talkative browser. In this exercise you'll do just that. The main page prompts you to say "hello" to it via the search prompt. Figure 12.6 shows that main page.

Figure 12.6. *Hello, the first page.*

You can then "say" something at the search prompt. Try doing *bonjour* and sending it to the script. Figure 12.7 shows the response.

Figure 12.7. *The first response.*

Now try saying hello. You'll get the response shown in Figure 12.8.

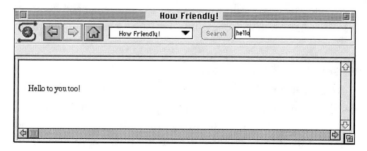

Figure 12.8. *Hello!*

Implementing this sort of script simply involves writing the script so that it tests the argument and returns the appropriate page depending on what that argument was. Next, we'll go through all the steps of writing the script so that it behaves like this.

Create the Default Page

First, you need to create the case where the script is called with no arguments; that is, the first default page. But before you even do that, you should create the basic structure of this script. First, print out the script header and the first bits of the HTML page:

```
#!/bin/sh

echo Content-type: text/html
echo

cat << EOF
    <HTML><HEAD><TITLE>
EOF
```

Now you need to test whether the script was called with arguments or not. In bourne shell scripts, the test looks like this:

```
if [ $# = 0 ]; then
...
fi
```

Put the rest of the HTML needed to create the default page inside the "if...fi" lines, like this:

```
if [ $# = 0 ]; then
    cat << EOF
    Say Hello to me</TITLE><ISINDEX></HEAD><BODY>
    <P>Say hello to me at the search prompt.
EOF
fi
```

And the end of the script finishes up the HTML file:

```
cat << EOF
</P></BODY></HTML>
EOF
```

So now, if you saved this script and ran it without arguments, you'd get the following result:

```
Content-type: text/html

    <HTML><HEAD><TITLE>
    Say Hello to me</TITLE><ISINDEX></HEAD><BODY>
    <P>Say hello to me at the search prompt.
</P></BODY></HTML>
```

The formatting is a little funny because I indented it in the actual script file, but HTML doesn't care about that; it'll get displayed as usual.

Note the <ISINDEX> tag in the appropriate spot in the <HEAD> tag; this is what activates the search feature in the browser reading this document.

Test the Arguments and Return the Appropriate Result

So now you have a basic script that works fine if there are no arguments. But when your reader types something into the search field and hits return (or presses the appropriate button), the script will be called with whatever they typed as an argument, so you'll have to add to your script to handle that argument.

Modifying the script to react differently if there are arguments is not that difficult; all you have to do is add an else to your if. However, note that in this example there can be two different results, depending on what your reader types into the search field, so just adding a single else isn't going to be enough. You're going to have to add another test to make sure the response is "hello." In the bourne shell, the structure of ifs and elses in this case would look like this:

```
if [ $# = 0 ]; then
... #the default page
else if [ $1 != "hello" ]; then
... #the not hello response
else
... #the hello response
fi
fi
```

All I've included here is the structure to create the appropriate branches, and included comments (the parts starting with #) to explain what parts go where. Now, finish up the script by adding the HTML codes in the right slots.

With the structure in place, you can add the rest of the HTML code within each section. For example, for the first section (the response to anything other than hello), you'd use the following:

```
else if [ $1 != "hello" ]; then
   cat << EOF
   Not Hello</TITLE><ISINDEX></HEAD><BODY>
   <P>Thats not a hello. Say hello to me at the search prompt.
EOF
```

Note that the <ISINDEX> tag is there again, since you're still expecting a response (and you want the right one this time!)

Finally, fill in the last slot with code to produce the "correct" page:

```
else
    cat << EOF
    How Friendly!</TITLE></HEAD><BODY>
    <P>Hello to you too!
EOF
```

And here, in the final branch, you don't need an `<ISINDEX>` tag, since you're done prompting for a response. All you're producing here is the congratulatory page, which is just plain old HTML.

So to test it, you can call the script from the command line with the appropriate arguments. The `sayhello` script with an argument of `goodbye` results in this output:

```
Content-type: text/html

    <HTML><HEAD><TITLE>
    Not Hello</TITLE><ISINDEX></HEAD><BODY>
    <P>Thats not a hello. Say hello to me at the search prompt.
</P></BODY></HTML>
```

And an argument of `hello` prints this output:

```
Content-type: text/html

    <HTML><HEAD><TITLE>
    How Friendly!</TITLE></HEAD><BODY>
    <P>Hello to you too!
</P></BODY></HTML>
```

For each response the reader gives you, there is an appropriate HTML output. You've covered all the options in separate branches.

The Complete Script

Just for reference, here's the full `sayhello` script:

```
#!/bin/sh

echo Content-type: text/html
echo

cat << EOF
    <HTML><HEAD><TITLE>
EOF

if [ $# = 0 ]; then
    cat << EOF
    Say Hello to me</TITLE><ISINDEX></HEAD><BODY>
    <P>Say hello to me at the search prompt.
EOF
```

12

287

```
else if [ $1 != "hello" ]; then
   cat << EOF
   Not Hello</TITLE><ISINDEX></HEAD><BODY>
   <P>Thats not a hello. Say hello to me at the search prompt.
EOF
else
   cat << EOF
   How Friendly!</TITLE></HEAD><BODY>
   <P>Hello to you too!
EOF
fi
fi

cat << EOF
</P></BODY></HTML>
EOF
```

Creating Special Script Output

For the majority of this chapter you've written scripts that output an actual file that is sent to the browser to be interpreted and displayed. But what if you don't want to send a new file as a result of a script's actions? What if you want to load an existing document instead? What if you just want the script to do something and not give any response back to the browser?

Fear not, you can do those things. This section explains how.

Responding by Loading Another Document

In the sayhello example in the previous section, you may have noticed that the last page you created through the script, the one that congratulated the user for saying hello, had nothing special in it that would imply it needed be constructed in the script. The other two branches had to be constructed by the script so that they could include the <ISINDEX> tag, but the last one was just an ordinary page.

Wouldn't it have been easier, rather than constructing the content of a regular page in the script (and having to go through all that cat << EOF stuff), to simply output a file that was stored on the system? Or, even better, to redirect the server to load that existing file?

What I've just described is possible with gateway scripts. To load an existing document as the output of a script, you use a line similar to the following:

```
Location: ../docs/final.html
```

The Location line is used in place of the normal output; that is, if you use Location, you do not need to use Content-type or include any other data in the output (and, in fact, you can't include any other data in the output). Like Content-type, however, you must also include a blank line after the Location line.

The path name to the file can either be a full URL, or a relative path name. This one looks for the document `final.html` in a directory called `docs` one level up from the current directory (assuming, since this is a script, that you're in the `cgi-bin` directory):

```
else
    echo Location: ../docs/final.html
      echo
fi
```

If the server can find the document you've specified in the Location line, it retrieves it and sends it back to the browser just as the output to Content-type would have been sent.

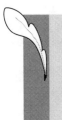

> **Note:** You cannot combine Content-type and Location output. If you want to, for example, output a standard page and then add custom content to the bottom of that same page, you'll have to use Content-type and construct both parts yourself. Note that you could use script commands to open up a local file and print it directly to the output; for example, `cat filename` instead of the `cat << EOF` the scripts in this chapter used.

So if you were using a Location line to output the last branch of the `sayhello` script, how would you modify the script to do so?

The script was originally written such that each branch of the `if` statement printed much of the same thing, so the Content-type lines and the beginning and end of the HTML file were specified outside the `if` statement. Because the final branch doesn't use these, you'll have to copy them inside the branch instead. The final modified script would look like this:

```
#!/bin/sh


if [ $# = 0 ]; then
    echo Content-type: text/html
      echo
      cat << EOF
  <HTML><HEAD><TITLE>
      Say Hello to me</TITLE><ISINDEX></HEAD><BODY>
  <P>Say hello to me at the search prompt.
      </P></BODY></HTML>
EOF
```

12

```
else if [ $1 != "hello" ]; then
    echo Content-type: text/html
    echo
    cat << EOF
  <HTML><HEAD><TITLE>
    Not Hello</TITLE><ISINDEX></HEAD><BODY>
    <P>Thats not a hello. Say hello to me at the search prompt.
    </P></BODY></HTML>
EOF
else
    echo Location: ../docs/sayhellofinal.html
    echo
fi
fi
```

No Response

Sometimes it may be appropriate for a gateway script to have no output at all. Sometimes you just want to take the information you get from the reader. You may not want to load a new document, neither by outputting the result nor by opening an existing file. The document that was on the browser's screen before should just stay there the way it was.

Fortunately, doing this is quite easy. Instead of outputting a Content-type or Location header, use the following line (with a blank line after it, as always):

```
Status: 204 No Response
```

The Status header provides status codes to the server (and to the browser). The particular status of 204 is passed on to the browser, and the browser, if it can figure out what to do with it, should do nothing.

You'll need no other output from your script, since you don't want the browser to do anything with it—just the one Status line with the blank line. Of course, your script should do something; otherwise, why bother calling the script at all?

Warning: The No Response code is a new arrival to HTTP, and many older browsers may not yet support it. If a browser doesn't support No Response, it may load a blank page or produce an error instead of remaining where it is.

Summary

Gateway scripts, sometimes called server-side scripts or CGI scripts, make it possible for programs to be run on the server, and HTML or other files to be generated on the fly.

This chapter covers the basics of how to deal with gateway programs, knowledge that you'll use tomorrow when you create forms and image maps. In particular, you've created simple scripts that run as links and worked with document queries using the ISINDEX tag.

You've also learned the three headers you can pass back to the server from your script:

- ☐ Content-type: The output following this header is a file of the type specified in this header. Content-types are MIME-based forms that include things like text/html or image/gif.

- ☐ Location: Opens and sends the specified file back to the browser; either a full URL or a relative path name.

- ☐ Status: An HTTP status code. Status is most generally used with 204 No Response, to produce no visible output from a script.

Q&A

Q What if I don't know how to program? Can I still use gateway scripts?

A If you have your access to a Web server through a commercial provider, you may be able to get help from the provider with your gateway scripts (for a fee, of course). Also, if you know even a little programming, but you're unsure of what you're doing, there are many examples available for the platform you're working on, usually as part of the server distribution, or at the same FTP location. See the documentation that came with your server; they often have pointers to further help. In fact, for the operation you want to accomplish, there may already be a script you can use with only some slight modification.

Q Can I put the <ISINDEX> tag in any HTML document?

A Well, it's legal HTML, so yes, you could put it in any HTML document. And it will turn on the searching interface in the browser when that document is read. But nothing will happen if your readers type something into the search box; they'll get an error when they try to send the results of the search.

The <ISINDEX> tag only makes sense in documents that are generated by gateway scripts that can handle the results of the query. Putting an <ISINDEX> in a regular HTML document is sort of like putting frosting and candles on an empty box.

Q Can I call my gateway script with command line options?

A You can do anything you want in your gateway script, including write it so that it will accept command line options. But how will the script ever get called with them? The only arguments your script is ever called with are those appended to the URL as part of the search query. There's no way to intercept the call to your script to include command line options; the only way they'd get added to the call would be if your reader typed them directly into the search box.

Q If you use a Location header to send a file back to the browser as a result of a script, how does the server know what kind of file it is so it can tell the browser? You don't have a Content-type line in the file, do you?

A The server "knows" what kind of file it is sending the same way it "knows" for any other file request from a browser: It maps the extension of the file name to a list of content-types it has stored internally or in a configuration file, and creates the Content-type header itself.

You only have to specifically give the server a content-type when you're feeding it output directly from a script and it doesn't have a filename extension to check.

Q What if I want to do something more complicated in my search? What if I want to include a list of ten items in the search box and have the script do something with those ten items? That's an awful lot to include in a search box.

A Yes, that is an awful lot to include in a single string, and that's precisely the reason why forms were created: to allow more extensive kinds of input back from the browser. If you can wait until tomorrow, you'll learn all about forms in Chapter 13, "Forms and Image Maps."

DAY

7

13

Forms and
Image Maps

The end of yesterday's lesson gave you the foundation you need to use the most powerful features of Web publishing yet: forms and image maps. These features make it possible for you to transform your Web pages from primarily text and graphics that your readers passively browse to interactive "toys" and presentations that can provide different options based on readers' input.

In this chapter, you learn the last of the HTML tags and do more with gateway scripts. In particular, you learn

☐ How form-based queries are different from document-based queries, including how to process the input you get from a form

☐ The basic form input elements: text fields, radio buttons, and check boxes, as well as buttons for submitting and resetting the form

☐ Other form elements: text areas, menus of options, hidden fields

☐ All about image maps and how to create them in your documents

☐ How to use the <BASE> tag to get around the strange behavior of documents linked by image maps.

Who Supports Forms?

Before you learn how to create forms, you should be aware that forms are still a new feature in the Web world, relatively speaking—"new" and "old" are measured in weeks in the Web world, since things are moving so fast. This means that you may not be able to create forms using your server on your platform, and it also means that even if you can, not all of your readers may be able to use them.

Browsers

At the time of this writing, most browsers are just beginning to support forms, and many browsers are barely supporting them. Most UNIX browsers support them, and all versions of Mosaic over 2.0 now support them, as do MacWeb on the Macintosh and Cello on Windows. Not all browsers support them equally well; I had to experiment with several browsers to find the ones that would work as advertised.

By the time you read this, it should be easier to find browsers with forms support. Nonetheless, you should examine the documentation that comes with your browser to make sure that you do have forms support. None of the examples in this chapter will work if your browser can't handle forms.

Also, some of your readers may not have forms support, so you should be sure to include, somewhere on your pages, a line that says something like "This page requires a browser that can read forms." If being compatible with all possible browsers is important to you, consider either leaving off interactivity altogether, or using document-based queries with ISINDEX instead. (ISINDEX is supported by all the browsers I've seen.)

> **Note:** I had to change browsers in order to take the pictures in this chapter; I moved from NCSA Mosaic to EINet's MacWeb. Don't be alarmed that the pictures for this chapter are different from those in other chapters; again, what you're mostly concerned about is the content of the window, not its buttons and menus.

Servers

Even if you have a browser that supports forms, you may not be able to write them. Many servers out there do not have the ability to process forms.

And once again, UNIX has come first. The CERN and NCSA HTTP servers have standardized the way they handle forms using the Common Gateway Interface (CGI), and form processing is quite stable using these servers. Because of the stability, and because much of the work in form processing on the Web is going on with UNIX-based Web servers, this chapter describes how to implement forms using those servers on UNIX systems. Despite its UNIX bias, however, you should be able to get an idea from this chapter how forms work, in general, so that you can implement them in other servers on other platforms when support is available.

How Are Form-Based Queries Different From Document-Based Queries?

Yesterday you learned how to create interactivity in your forms using ISINDEX and documents that were generated exclusively from gateway scripts. Creating interactive presentations using forms is quite similar (particularly on the server side), except it's even easier. You don't have to generate the search document from a script; you can just write one. You don't have to test whether the script is being called with arguments. Once you get the gist of working with forms, you'll never want to go back to simple document-based searches again.

Input From Searches and Forms

In a document-based query, the input to the script is in the form of whatever the reader types into the search window. If there are spaces in the input, those spaces create separate arguments in the call to the gateway script. For the most part, however, you have a limited amount of information to work with in a simple form.

In form-based queries, things are slightly different, because you can retrieve a much greater variety of information from a form. In a form, each element (for example, each text entry field or a check box) has a unique name that you assign to it when you create the form. Each element also has a value that is assigned when the reader does something with the form; the value might be whatever the reader types into the text entry box, or it might simply be "on" for a check box.

When a form is submitted, the information from the form is passed to the server as name/value pairs, with the name and the value separated by equals signs. As with document-based queries, all other special characters, including spaces, are encoded as well. Encoded form information often ends up as a string of gobbledygook something like this:

```
vitamin=on&svga=on&fish=on&theSex=female&theName=My%20Name
```

You'll learn how to decode it back into something you can understand in a later section, "Tools for Decoding Name/Value Pairs," and in the exercises in this chapter.

How the Information Gets from the Browser to the Server to the Script

Document-based searches encode the information from the reader in the URL of the script that generates the request, and then decode the results on the server side as arguments to the gateway script that was processing the request.

In form-based queries, there are two methods for submitting information to the gateway script. They are called GET and POST, after the HTTP commands of the same name (commands that the browser uses to talk to the server). When you create a form, you can choose the method with which you submit the information to your gateway script.

GET is similar to the method that document-based queries use. In a GET submission, the information in the form is encoded into the URL and then assigned to an environment

variable on the server side called QUERY_STRING. In the gateway script you can then retrieve the names and values from the form by retrieving them from the value of this variable.

POST is similar to GET, except that instead of using an environment variable, the encoded form information is passed directly to the gateway script through the standard input. No variables or arguments are assigned.

So which should you use, GET or POST? The folks at NCSA and CERN recommend that you use POST, and so do I. The problem with GET is that it goes through the shell to assign the encoded information to an environment variable. The UNIX shell has limits on the number of characters it can handle at one time, which may mean that if you use GET for some longer forms with lots of information, you'll lose some of the information (yikes!). With POST there are no limits on the amount of information you can pass back from a form. POST is the better of the two methods, and the one that I use for all the examples in this book.

The Gateway Script

The one thing that isn't different between document-based and forms-based queries is the way you send output back to the server. Everything you learned yesterday about creating gateway scripts, including the Content-type, Location, and Status headers, applies for form-based gateway scripts as well.

There is one slight difference in how it's used, however. In document-based queries, you often called a script directly as a URL, and the script returned the HTML code for the prompt. In forms-based queries, the form is an ordinary HTML document. The form is then linked to the gateway script as part of its submission process. This is much more straightforward and allows you to avoid calling scripts directly from the browser.

Tools for Decoding Name/Value Pairs

The first step in creating a gateway script to handle a form is to decode the name/value pair information that the browser sent and the server passed along into something your script can read. This involves not only breaking out the name/value pairs, but also changing any specially encoded characters (spaces, special characters, and so on) back into their original values.

Because decoding this information is a common task, there are lots of tools available on the Net in many different programming languages for doing just that. There's no reason for you to write your own decoding program unless you want to do something very unusual; the decoding programs that are out there can do a fine job, and they might

13

consider things that you haven't, such as how to avoid having your script break because someone gave your form funny input.

For decoding the form information in my gateway script, I like a program that comes with the CERN HTTPD distribution called cgiparse. It enables you to process the input from a form in many different ways without having to worry about the details of how much to read and what you need to decode. For the examples in this chapter, I use cgiparse in all the gateway scripts.

In particular, three simple lines can be used to decode the input from the form:

```
CGI=/usr/local/bin/cgiparse
eval '$CGI -init'
eval '$CGI -form'
```

So what do these lines do? They decode the information from the form submission and create a set of environment variables, one for each name in the name/value pairs, with the prefix FORM_ prepended to each name. Each value in the name/value pair is then assigned to its respective environment variable. So, for example, if you had a name in a form called "username," the resulting environment variable cgiparse created would be FORM_username.

> **Note:** The cgiparse script has a limitation in that it prefers to read its information from the QUERY_STRING environment variable. The -init option basically assigns the contents of the standard input stream (that you get from a POST method) to QUERY_STRING, and the -form option decodes the values in QUERY_STRING into individual environment variables.

Note that because you're assigning the encoded information to a shell variable, you're defeating the purpose of using the POST method in the first place—using cgiparse, if the encoded input is too long, it'll get truncated by the shell the same as if you had sent it with GET and had the server assign it to QUERY_STRING itself.

To deal with longer forms, you should look at a better decoder program that can work directly with POST form submission. But for the purposes of the examples in this chapter, cgiparse is a simple method for extracting the encoded information from the form submission.

Exercise 13.1: Tell me your name.

Now that you have a grasp of what a form is and how they're different from ISINDEX searches and other gateway scripts, let's leap forward and create a simple example. You'll find that it's easier than you think.

Figure 13.1 shows a document that has a form to prompt you for your name.

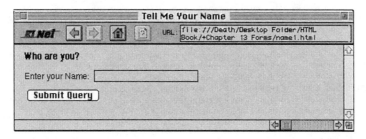

Figure 13.1. *The Tell Me Your Name form.*

You enter your name and press the Submit button (or select the Submit link, in nongraphical browsers).

> **Note:** Most browsers provide a shortcut: If there is only a form element on the page (besides Submit), you can just press Return to activate the form.

The browser then displays a hello message with your name in it (Figure 13.2).

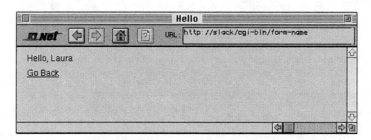

Figure 13.2. *The result of the name form.*

What if you didn't type anything at the Enter your Name prompt? You'd get the response shown in Figure 13.3.

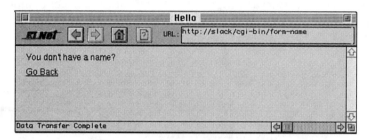

Figure 13.3. *Another result.*

The Layout

First, create the HTML code to create this form and the text that supports it.

As with all HTML documents, start with a basic framework, with just a single level two heading that says "Who Are You?"

```
<HTML><HEAD>
<TITLE>Tell Me Your Name</TITLE>
</HEAD><BODY>
<H2>Who are you?</H2>
</BODY>
</HTML>
```

Now, add the form itself.

First, use the <FORM> tag to indicate that the following content is a form. <FORM> is a two-sided tag, and all the elements of the form should be included inside the opening and closing tags. You can include multiple disparate forms in one document, but you can't nest forms—that is, you can't include a FORM tag inside another FORM.

```
<FORM METHOD="POST" ACTION="../cgi-bin/form-name">
</FORM>
```

The opening tag of the FORM element takes two elements: The METHOD and the ACTION. The METHOD attribute can be either GET or POST. For the reasons I noted in the previous section, you should almost always use POST.

The ACTION attribute indicates the script that will be called when this form is submitted. The ACTION can be specified by a relative path or by a full URL; here the script is called form-name, and it's in the cgi-bin directory (a common place to store gateway scripts).

In this example, I've specified the script as a relative URL (`../cgi-bin/form-name`), where the `cgi-bin` directory is in the directory one level up from the directory this HTML file is in. You can also specify the *ACTION* as a full URL on your server or on any other server.

The `<FORM>` tag doesn't specify the appearance and layout of the form; you'll have to use other HTML tags for that.

The first element inside the form is the text-entry area for the name. First, include the prompt, just as you would any other line of text in HTML:

```
<P>Enter your Name:
```

And then add the HTML code that indicates a text area:

```
<P>Enter your Name: <INPUT NAME="theName"></P>
```

The `<INPUT>` tag indicates a simple form element. (There are also several other form elements that use tags other than `<INPUT>`, but `<INPUT>` is the most common one). `<INPUT>` usually takes at least two attributes: `TYPE` and `NAME`.

The `TYPE` is the kind of form element this is. There are several choices, including "text" for text-entry fields, "radio" for radio buttons, and "check" for check boxes. If you leave the `TYPE` attribute out, as we've done here, the element will be a text entry field.

The `NAME` element indicates the name of this element. As I noted before, your gateway script receives the input from the form as a series of name and value pairs. The value is the actual value your reader enters; the name is the value of this attribute. You can put anything you want here, but as with all good programming conventions, it's most useful if you use a descriptive name. Here we've picked the name `theName`. (Descriptive, yes?)

Now add the final form element: the submit button (or link). Most forms require the use of a submit button; however, if you only have one text field in the form, you can leave it off. The form will be submitted when the reader presses Return.

```
<P><INPUT TYPE="submit"></P>
```

You'll use the `<INPUT>` tag for this element as well. The `TYPE` attribute is set to the special type of "submit," which creates a submit button for the form. The submit button doesn't require a name because there's no value attached to it.

It's a good practice to always include a Submit button on your form, even if there's only one text field, simply because the submit button is so common your readers may become confused if it's not there.

13

Note that each element includes tags for formatting, just as if this was text; form elements follow the same rules as text in terms for how your browser formats them. Without the <P> tags, you'd end up with all the elements on the form on the same line.

So now you have a simple form with two elements. The final HTML code to create this form looks like this:

```
<HTML><HEAD>
<TITLE>Tell Me Your Name</TITLE>
</HEAD>
<BODY>
<H2>Who are you?</H2>

<FORM METHOD="POST" ACTION="../cgi-bin/form-name">
<P>Enter your Name: <INPUT NAME="theName"></P>
<P><INPUT TYPE="submit"></P>
</FORM>
</BODY></HTML>
```

The Script

Once you have a form in an HTML document, you need a gateway script on the server side to process the form. Like the gateway scripts you learned about in this last chapter, the output from the script will be passed back to the server, so everything you learned about the Content-type headers and generating HTML output applies to forms scripts as well.

The first step in a form script is to decode the information that was passed to your script through the POST method. As I noted in the last section, there are several publicly available programs that will do this, so you won't have to do it yourself (making writing these scripts a *lot* easier—why reinvent the wheel?) Here, I'll use one called cgiparse, part of the CERN HTTP server distribution. These three lines use cgiparse to decode the name /value pairs received from the form into individual environment variables with the same names as the NAME attributes, except with the letters FORM_ prefixed. So, for example, the theName name would become FORM_theName.

```
CGI=/usr/local/bin/cgiparse
eval '$CGI -init'
eval '$CGI -form'
```

Note: If I were doing a better job of programming this example, I would test the return status of the cgiparse program to make sure it worked before going on with the rest of the script. But for the purposes of this example, let's assume that cgiparse will always get good values.

Now, output the usual headers and HTML code to begin the page:

```
echo Content-type: text/html
echo

cat << EOF
    <HTML><HEAD>
    <TITLE>Hello</TITLE>
    <BODY>
    <P>
EOF
```

Now comes the meat of the script. You have two branches here, one to say hello with the same name that was input in the script, and one to accuse the reader of not entering a name.

The value of the theName variable is contained in the FORM_theName environment variable. Using a simple bourne shell test (-z), you can see whether this environment variable is empty or not, and include the appropriate response in the output:

```
if [ ! -z "$FORM_theName" ]; then
        echo "Hello, "
        echo $FORM_theName
else
        echo "You don't have a name?"
fi
```

Finally, add on the last bit of HTML code to add the "go back" link. This link points back to the original form.

```
cat << EOF
    </P>
    <P><A HREF="../lemay/name1.html">Go Back</A><P>
    </BODY></HTML>
EOF
```

Et voilà. You now know just about all you need to know to handle forms and their interaction with gateway scripts. That wasn't bad at all, was it?

13

Simple Form Layout

So now that you've got the basics down, you'll want to know exactly what kind of nifty interface elements you can put in a form. Let's waste no more time.

Each of the elements described in this section go inside a <FORM>...</FORM> tag, which you learned about in the previous exercise (here, the form calls a script called test-cgi, which does nothing except return the values it is given). They're also various forms of the <INPUT> tag; you'll learn about the other available form elements later in this chapter.

The Submit Button

Each form can have one, and only one, submit button (or link in nongraphical browsers; for the sake of simplicity, let's just call them buttons). To create a Submit button, use "submit" as TYPE attribute in an <INPUT> tag:

```
<INPUT TYPE="SUBMIT">
```

You can change the text of the button by using the VALUE attribute:

```
<INPUT TYPE="SUBMIT" VALUE="Submit Query">

<FORM METHOD=POST ACTION="../cgi/bin/test-cgi">
<INPUT TYPE="SUBMIT">
</FORM>

<FORM METHOD=POST ACTION="../cgi/bin/test-cgi">
<INPUT TYPE="SUBMIT" VALUE="Press Here">
</FORM>
```

Figure 13.4. *The output in Mosaic.*

Figure 13.5. *The output in Lynx.*

Text Fields

Text elements enable your reader to type text into a single-line field. (For multiple-line fields, use the `<TEXTAREA>` element, described later in this chapter.)

To create a text-entry field, you can either use `TYPE="text"` in the `<INPUT>` tag, or leave off the `TYPE` specification all together. (The default `TYPE` for the `INPUT` tag is text.) You must also include a `NAME` attribute; `NAME` indicates the name of this field as passed to the gateway script processing the form.

```
<INPUT TYPE="text" NAME="myText">
```

You can also include the attributes `SIZE` and `MAXLENGTH` in the `<INPUT>` tag. `SIZE` indicates the length of the text-entry field, in characters; the field is 20 characters by default. Your readers can enter as many characters as they want; the field will scroll horizontally as your reader types. Try to keep the `SIZE` under 50 characters so that it will fit on most screens.

```
<INPUT TYPE="text" NAME="longText" SIZE="50">
```

`MAXLENGTH` enables you to limit the number of characters that your reader can type into a text field (refusing any further characters). If `MAXLENGTH` is less than `SIZE`, browsers will sometimes draw a text field as large as `MAXLENGTH`.

Included in the NCSA examples for creating forms, but not listed in the official HTML 2.0 specification, is also the "password" type. Password text fields are identical to ordinary text fields, except that all the characters typed are echoed back in the browser as asterisks or bullets. (See Figure 13.6.)

```
<INPUT TYPE="PASSWORD" NAME="passwd">
```

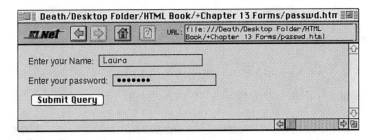

Figure 13.6. *Password fields.*

Note: Despite the masking of characters in the browser, password fields are not secure as the password is sent to the server in clear text; that is, anyone could intercept the password and be able to read it. The masking is simply a convenience.

```
<FORM METHOD=POST ACTION="../cgi/bin/test-cgi">
Enter your Name: <INPUT TYPE="TEXT" NAME="theName"><BR>
Enter your Age:
<INPUT TYPE="TEXT" NAME="theAge" SIZE="3" MAXLENGTH="3"><BR>
Enter your Address:
<INPUT TYPE="TEXT" NAME="theAddress" SIZE="80" ><BR>
</FORM>
```

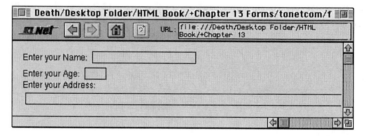

Figure 13.7. *The output in Mosaic.*

```
Enter your Name: _____
Enter your Age: ___
Enter your Address:
_____

_____


Commands: Use arrow keys to move, '?' for help, 'q' to quit, '<-' to go back
```

Figure 13.8. *The output in Lynx.*

Radio Buttons

Radio buttons indicate a list of items, of which only one can be chosen. If one radio button in a list is selected, all the other radio buttons in the same list are deselected.

Radio buttons use "radio" for their TYPE attribute. You indicate groups of radio buttons using the same NAME for each one. In addition, radio buttons must each have a unique VALUE attribute, indicating the selection's value.

```
<OL>
<INPUT TYPE="radio" NAME="theType" VALUE="animal">Animal<BR>
<INPUT TYPE="radio" NAME="theType" VALUE="vegetable">Vegetable<BR>
<INPUT TYPE="radio" NAME="theType" VALUE="mineral">Mineral<BR>
</OL>
```

You can use multiple, independent groups of radio buttons by using different names for each group:

```
<OL>
<INPUT TYPE="radio" NAME="theType" VALUE="animal">Animal<BR>
    <OL>
    <LI><INPUT TYPE="radio" NAME="theAnimal" VALUE="cat">Cat
    <LI><INPUT TYPE="radio" NAME="theAnimal" VALUE="dog">Dog
    <LI><INPUT TYPE="radio" NAME="theAnimal" VALUE="fish">fish
    </OL>
<INPUT TYPE="radio" NAME="theType" VALUE="vegetable">Vegetable<BR>
<INPUT TYPE="radio" NAME="theType" VALUE="mineral">Mineral<BR>
</OL>
```

When the form is submitted, a single name/value pair for the group of buttons is passed to the script. That pair includes the NAME attribute for each group of radio buttons and the VALUE attribute of the button that was currently selected.

```
<FORM METHOD=POST ACTION="../cgi/bin/test-cgi">
<OL>
<LI><INPUT TYPE="radio" NAME="theType" VALUE="animal">Animal<BR>
    <OL>
    <LI><INPUT TYPE="radio" NAME="theAnimal" VALUE="cat">Cat
    <LI><INPUT TYPE="radio" NAME="theAnimal" VALUE="dog">Dog
    <LI><INPUT TYPE="radio" NAME="theAnimal" VALUE="fish">fish
    </OL>
    <LI><INPUT TYPE="radio" NAME="theType" VALUE="vegetable">Vegetable
    <LI><INPUT TYPE="radio" NAME="theType" VALUE="mineral">Mineral
    </OL>
</FORM>
```

13

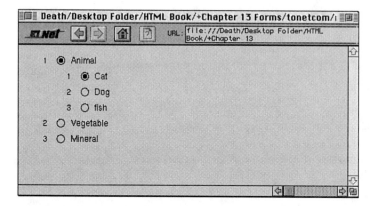

Figure 13.9. *The output in Mosaic.*

```
   1. <■►>Animal
        1. (*)Cat
        2. ( )Dog
        3. ( )fish
   2. ( )Vegetable
   3. ( )Mineral
```

(Checkbox Field)   Use right-arrow or <return> to toggle.

Figure 13.10. *The output in Lynx.*

Check Boxes

Check boxes make it possible for multiple nonexclusive items in a list to be chosen, as many as the reader wants to choose. Each check box can either be "on" or "off."

Check boxes use `"checkbox"` as their TYPE attribute:

```
<UL>
<LI><INPUT TYPE="checkbox" NAME="red">Red
<LI><INPUT TYPE="checkbox" NAME="green">Green
<LI><INPUT TYPE="checkbox" NAME="blue">Blue
</UL>
```

When the form is submitted, only the name/value pairs for each selected check box are submitted. By default, each name/value pair for a check box has a value of ON. You can also use the VALUE attribute to indicate the value you would rather see in your script:

```
<UL>
<LI><INPUT TYPE="checkbox" NAME="red" VALUE="checked">Red
<LI><INPUT TYPE="checkbox" NAME="green" VALUE="checked">Green
<LI><INPUT TYPE="checkbox" NAME="blue" VALUE="checked">Blue
</UL>
```

You can also implement check box lists such that elements have the same NAME attribute, similarly to radio buttons. Note, however, that this means you may end up with several name/value pairs with the same name (each check box that is selected will be submitted to the script), and you'll have to take that into account when you process the input in your script.

```
<FORM METHOD=POST ACTION="../cgi/bin/test-cgi">
<P>Profession (choose all that apply): </P>
<UL>
<LI><INPUT TYPE="checkbox" NAME="doctor">Doctor
<LI><INPUT TYPE="checkbox" NAME="lawyer">Lawyer
<LI><INPUT TYPE="checkbox" NAME="teacher">Teacher
<LI><INPUT TYPE="checkbox" NAME="nerd">Programmer
</UL>
</FORM>
```

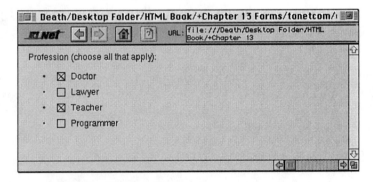

Figure 13.11. *The output in Mosaic.*

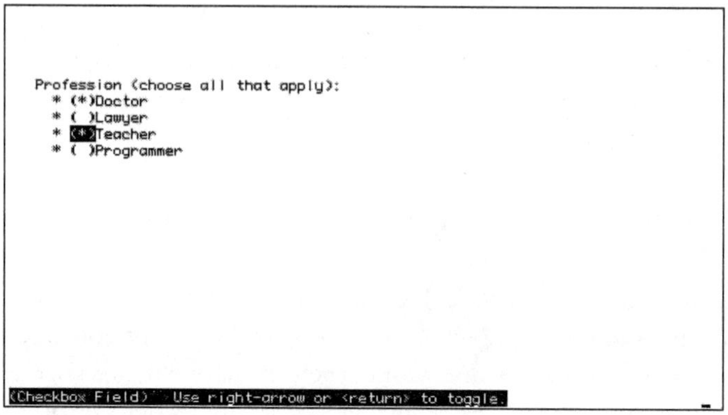

Figure 13.12. *The output in Lynx.*

Setting And Resetting Default Values

Each form element can have a default value that is entered or selected when the form is viewed:

☐ For text fields, use the VALUE attribute with a string for the default value. The VALUE is entered in the box automatically when the form is displayed.

☐ For check boxes and radio buttons, the attribute CHECKED selects that element by default.

In addition to the default values for each element, you can include a Reset button, similar to the Submit button, on your form; the Reset button clears all selections or entries your reader has made and resets them to their default values. Also like Submit, a VALUE attribute indicates the label for the button.

```
<INPUT TYPE="RESET" VALUE="Reset Defaults">
```

Exercise 13.2: The Surrealist census.

The Surrealist Society of America has decided to conduct a small census, via an interactive form on the World Wide Web. Figure 13.13 shows an example of the form they want you to create for the census.

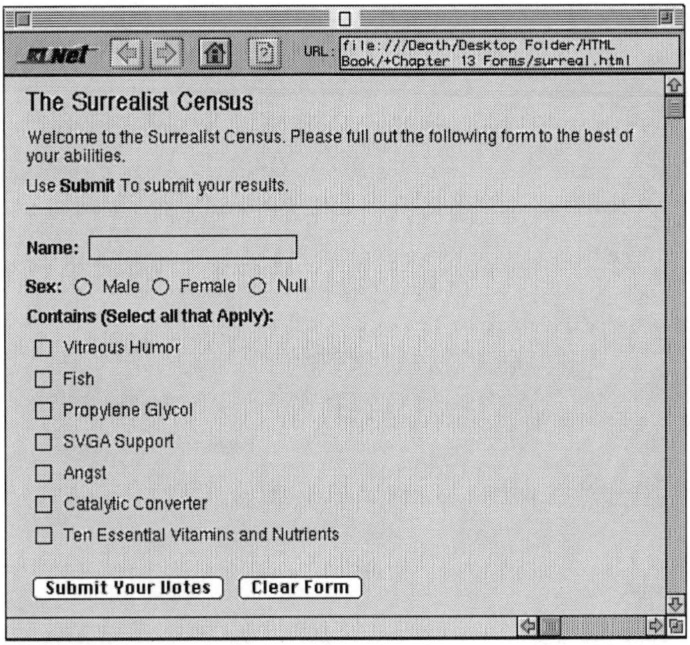

The Surrealist Census

file:///Death/Desktop Folder/HTML
Book/+Chapter 13 Forms/surreal.html

The Surrealist Census

Welcome to the Surrealist Census. Please full out the following form to the best of your abilities.

Use **Submit** To submit your results.

Name: [   ]

Sex: ○ Male ○ Female ○ Null

Contains (Select all that Apply):

☐ Vitreous Humor

☐ Fish

☐ Propylene Glycol

☐ SVGA Support

☐ Angst

☐ Catalytic Converter

☐ Ten Essential Vitamins and Nutrients

[**Submit Your Uotes**] [**Clear Form**]

Figure 13.13. *The Surrealist Society's census form.*

After the reader fills out the form and presses Submit Your Votes, your gateway script for the form should process the input and return a formatted report of the votes the reader has made, as shown in Figure 13.14.

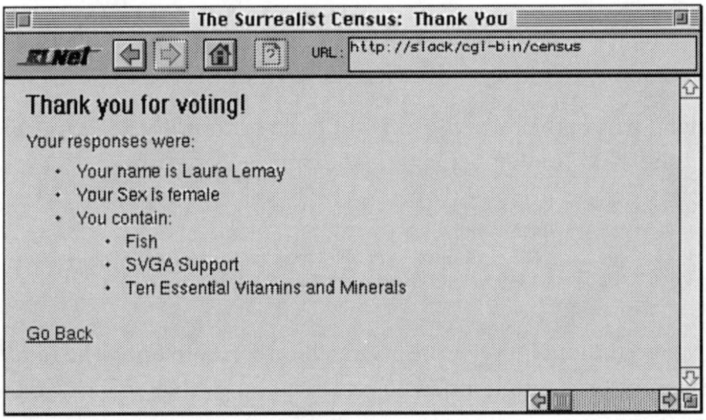

The Surrealist Census: Thank You

http://slack/cgi-bin/census

Thank you for voting!

Your responses were:

- Your name is Laura Lemay
- Your Sex is female
- You contain:
    - Fish
    - SVGA Support
    - Ten Essential Vitamins and Minerals

Go Back

Figure 13.14. *The result of the census.*

13

In this exercise, you go through the steps of creating both the form and the script to process it.

The Form

The form to create the census falls roughly into three parts: the name field, the radio buttons for sex, and the check boxes for the things your reader contains.

Start with the basic structure, as with all HTML documents:

```
<HTML><HEAD>
<TITLE>The Surrealist Census<TITLE>
</HEAD><BODY>
<H1>The Surrealist Census</H1>
<P>Welcome to the Surrealist Census. Please fill out the following
form to the best of your abilities.</P>
<P>Use <STRONG>Submit</STRONG> To submit your results.
<HR>
<FORM METHOD="POST" ACTION="../cgi-bin/census">

</FORM>
<HR>
</BODY></HTML>
```

I've included the tags for `<FORM>` here as part of the basic structure, with the `POST` method and the name of my script (a script called `census` in, once again, the `cgi-bin` directory)

Note also that I've included rule lines before and after the form. Because the form is a discrete element on the page, it makes sense to visually separate it from the other parts of the page. This is especially important if you have multiple forms on the same page; separating them with rule lines visually divides them.

Now, let's add the name element. This is essentially the same element that we used in the previous example:

```
<P><STRONG>Name: </STRONG><INPUT TYPE="TEXT" NAME="theName"></P>
```

The second part of the form is a series of radio buttons for "Sex." There are three: Male, Female, and Null (remember, this is the Surrealist Census):

```
<P><STRONG>Sex: </STRONG>
<INPUT TYPE="radio" NAME="theSex" VALUE="male">Male
<INPUT TYPE="radio" NAME="theSex" VALUE="female">Female
<INPUT TYPE="radio" NAME="theSex" VALUE="null">Null
</P>
```

Note that even though they were arranged on separate lines, the radio button elements are formatted on a single line. Always remember that form elements do not imply formatting; you have to include other HTML tags to arrange them in the right spots.

Now, add the last part of the form: the list of "Contains" check boxes:

```
<P><STRONG>Contains (Select all that Apply): </STRONG><BR>
<INPUT TYPE="checkbox" NAME="humor">Vitreous Humor<BR>
<INPUT TYPE="checkbox" NAME="fish">Fish<BR>
<INPUT TYPE="checkbox" NAME="glycol">Propylene Glycol<BR>
<INPUT TYPE="checkbox" NAME="svga">SVGA Support<BR>
<INPUT TYPE="checkbox" NAME="angst">Angst<BR>
<INPUT TYPE="checkbox" NAME="catcon">Catalytic Converter<BR>
<INPUT TYPE="checkbox" NAME="vitamin">Ten Essential Vitamins and Nutrients<BR>
</P>
```

Note that each name is unique; this will be important later when you write the script to process the form.

Finally, add the submit button so that the form can be submitted to the server. A nice touch is to also include a "Reset Form" button. Both buttons have special labels specific to this form:

```
<P><INPUT TYPE="SUBMIT" VALUE="Submit Your Votes">
<INPUT TYPE="RESET" VALUE="Clear Form"></P>
```

Whew! With all the elements in place, here's what the entire HTML file for the form looks like:

```
<HTML><HEAD>
<TITLE>The Surrealist Census<TITLE>
</HEAD><BODY>
<H1>The Surrealist Census</H1>
<P>Welcome to the Surrealist Census. Please fill out the following
form to the best of your abilities.</P>
<P>Use <STRONG>Submit</STRONG> To submit your results.
<HR>
<FORM METHOD="POST" ACTION="../cgi-bin/census">
<P><STRONG>Name: </STRONG><INPUT TYPE="TEXT" NAME="theName"></P>
<P><STRONG>Sex: </STRONG>
<INPUT TYPE="radio" NAME="theSex" VALUE="male">Male
<INPUT TYPE="radio" NAME="theSex" VALUE="female">Female
<INPUT TYPE="radio" NAME="theSex" VALUE="null">Null
</P>
<P><STRONG>Contains (Select all that Apply): </STRONG><BR>
<INPUT TYPE="checkbox" NAME="humor">Vitreous Humor<BR>
<INPUT TYPE="checkbox" NAME="fish">Fish<BR>
<INPUT TYPE="checkbox" NAME="glycol">Propylene Glycol<BR>
<INPUT TYPE="checkbox" NAME="svga">SVGA Support<BR>
<INPUT TYPE="checkbox" NAME="angst">Angst<BR>
<INPUT TYPE="checkbox" NAME="catcon">Catalytic Converter<BR>
<INPUT TYPE="checkbox" NAME="vitamin">Ten Essential Vitamins and Nutrients<BR>
</P>
<P><INPUT TYPE="SUBMIT" VALUE="Submit Your Votes">
<INPUT TYPE="RESET" VALUE="Clear Form"></P>
</FORM>
<HR>
</BODY></HTML>
```

13

The Script

And now, write the script to process the form you've just created. The output of the script essentially just prints the values from the form in a nice bulleted list. This script will look real similar to the script you created in the last example, so we'll start with a copy of that script, modified slightly to fit the output we want to create from this form:

```
#!/bin/sh

CGI=/usr/local/bin/cgiparse

eval '$CGI -init'
eval '$CGI -form'

echo Content-type: text/html
echo

cat << EOF
   <HTML><HEAD>
   <TITLE>The Surrealist Census: Thank You</TITLE>
   <BODY>
   <H1>Thank you for voting!</H1>
   <P>Your responses were:</P>
   <UL>
EOF


if [ ! -z "$FORM_theName" ]; then
        echo "<LI>Your name is "
        echo $FORM_theName
else
        echo "<LI>You don't have a name."
fi
```

That `if` statement there should look real familiar; it's basically the same thing as the last example. Now, add a bullet for the sex the reader entered. For the `theSex` name/value pair, you don't have to test to see if `theSex` is empty; the radio button structure means at least one value must be submitted with the form, so all you really have to do for the Sex element is print the value:

```
echo "<LI>Your Sex is "
echo $FORM_theSex
```

And now, add the list of Contains elements in a nested list. Because you don't know which of the check boxes were submitted, you'll have to test all of those variables—their values will be "on" if they were selected, and create output for the ones that were submitted, like this:

```
echo "<LI>You contain:"
echo "<UL>"

if [ "$FORM_humor" = "on" ]; then
```

```
            echo "<LI>Vitreous Humor"
fi
if [ "$FORM_fish" = "on" ]; then
        echo "<LI>Fish"
fi
```

I'll only include the `if` statements for the first two tests here; the other five look exactly the same. You can check the script at the end of this section if you're really interested.

> **Note:** If I were a better bourne shell programmer, I'm sure I could make the tests for each variable much more efficient, but it works, so I'm not going to worry too much about it.

Finally, finish up the script with a link back to the form. You should always provide some way out of the HTML files you generate from forms; although going back to some known spot (such as the home page) would make more sense, even going back to the form is better than nothing:

```
cat << EOF
    </UL></UL>
    <P><A HREF="../lemay/census.html">Go Back</A><P>
    </BODY></HTML>
EOF
```

Here's the full script for processing the census form:

```
#!/bin/sh

CGI=/usr/local/bin/cgiparse

eval '$CGI -init'
eval '$CGI -form'

echo Content-type: text/html
echo

cat << EOF
    <HTML><HEAD>
    <TITLE>The Surrealist Census: Thank You</TITLE>
    <BODY>
    <H1>Thank you for voting!</H1>
    <P>Your responses were:</P>
    <UL>
EOF

if [ ! -z "$FORM_theName" ]; then
        echo "<LI>Your name is "
        echo $FORM_theName
else
```

```
            echo "<LI>You don't have a name."
fi

echo "<LI>Your Sex is "
echo $FORM_theSex
echo "<LI>You contain:"
echo "<UL>"

if [ "$FORM_humor" = "on" ]; then
        echo "<LI>Vitreous Humor"
fi
if [ "$FORM_fish" = "on" ]; then
        echo "<LI>Fish"
fi
if [ "$FORM_glycol" = "on" ]; then
        echo "<LI>Propylene Glycol"
fi
if [ "$FORM_svga" = "on" ]; then
        echo "<LI>SVGA Support"
fi
if [ "$FORM_angst" = "on" ]; then
        echo "<LI>Angst"
fi
if [ "$FORM_catcon" = "on" ]; then
        echo "<LI>Catalytic Converter"
fi
if [ "$FORM_vitamin" = "on" ]; then
        echo "<LI>Ten Essential Vitamins and Minerals"
fi

cat << EOF
   </UL></UL>
   <P><A HREF="../lemay/name1.html">Go Back</A><P>
   </BODY></HTML>
EOF
```

More Forms Layout

Besides the <INPUT> tag with its many options, there are also two other tags that create form elements: TEXTAREA, for blocks of text entry, and SELECT, which has the capability to create pull-down menus and scrolling lists.

This section describes these other two tags and also explains how to create "hidden" elements—form elements that don't actually show up on the page, but exist in the form nonetheless.

Selections

Selections enable the reader of a form to select one or more items from a menu or a scrolling list. They're similar to radio buttons or check boxes, in a different form.

Selections are indicated by the <SELECT> tag, and individual options within the selection by the <OPTION> tag. The <SELECT> tag also contains a NAME attribute to hold its value when the form is submitted.

<SELECT> and <OPTION> work much like lists do, with the entire selection surrounded by the opening and closing <SELECT> tags, and each option beginning with a single-sided <OPTION, like this:

```
<P>Select a hair color:
<SELECT NAME="hcolor">
<OPTION>Black
<OPTION>Blonde
<OPTION>Brown
<OPTION>Red
<OPTION>Blue
</SELECT></P>
```

When the form is submitted, the value selection is the text that follows the selected <OPTION> tag—in this case, Brown, Red, Blue, and so on. You can also use the VALUE attribute to the <OPTION> tag to use a different value.

Selections of this sort are generally formatted in graphical browsers as pop-up menus, as shown in Figure 13.15.

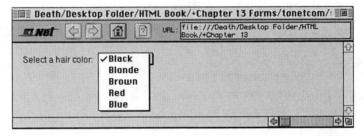

Figure 13.15. *Selections.*

You can set the default item to be initially selected using the SELECTED attribute, part of the OPTION tag:

```
<P>Select a hair color:
<SELECT NAME="hcolor">
<OPTION>+Black
<OPTION>Blonde
<OPTION SELECTED>Brown
<OPTION>Red
<OPTION>Blue
</SELECT></P>
```

By default, selections act like radio buttons; that is, only one item can be selected at once. You can change the behavior of selections to allow multiple options to be selected by using the MULTIPLE attribute, part of the SELECTION tag:

```
<P>Shopping List:
<SELECT NAME="shopping" MULTIPLE>
<OPTION>Butter
<OPTION>Milk
<OPTION>Flour
<OPTION>Eggs
<OPTION>Cheese
<OPTION>Beer
<OPTION>Pasta
<OPTION>Mushrooms
</SELECT></P>
```

Note: The browser determines how the reader makes multiple choices. Usually, the reader must hold down a key while making multiple selections, but that particular key may vary from browser to browser.

The optional <SELECT> attribute SIZE is in several of the NCSA form examples, but is not in the HTML 2.0 specification. When <SIZE> is used, the selection is rendered as a scrolling list in graphical browsers, with the number of elements in the SIZE attribute visible on the form itself. (Figure 13.16 shows an example.)

```
<P>Shopping List:
<SELECT NAME="shopping" MULTIPLE SIZE="5">
<OPTION>Butter
<OPTION>Milk
<OPTION>Flour
<OPTION>Eggs
<OPTION>Cheese
<OPTION>Beer
<OPTION>Pasta
<OPTION>Mushrooms
</SELECT></P>
```

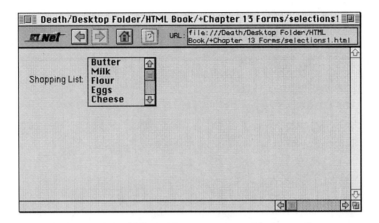

Figure 13.16. *Selections with* SIZE.

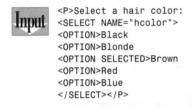
```
<P>Select a hair color:
<SELECT NAME="hcolor">
<OPTION>Black
<OPTION>Blonde
<OPTION SELECTED>Brown
<OPTION>Red
<OPTION>Blue
</SELECT></P>
```

Figure 13.17. *The output in Mosaic.*

13

```
Select a hair color:
(  ) Black
( ) Blonde
(*) Brown
( ) Red
( ) Blue
```

Figure 13.18. *The output in Lynx.*

Text Areas

Text areas are fields in which the reader can type text. Unlike text input fields (`<INPUT TYPE="text">`), text areas can contain multiple lines of text, making them extremely useful for forms that require extensive input. For example, if you wanted to create a form that enabled readers to compose electronic mail, you might use a text area for the body of the message.

To include a text area element in a form, use the `<TEXTAREA>` tag. `<TEXTAREA>` includes three attributes:

- ☐ `NAME`: The name to be sent to the gateway script when the form is submitted.
- ☐ `ROWS`: The height of the text area element, in rows of text.
- ☐ `COLS`: The width of the text area element in columns (characters).

For example:

```
<TEXTAREA NAME="theBody" ROWS="14" COLS="50">
<TEXTAREA NAME="vt100" ROWS="24" COLS="80">
```

The text in a text area is generally formatted in a fixed-width font such as Courier. Text that exceeds the width of the box wraps to the next line, and text that exceeds the number of rows in the box causes the box to scroll—and, in fact, many browsers may render a text area with a scroll bar.

```
<P>Enter any Comments you have about this Web page here:
<TEXTAREA NAME="comment" ROWS="30" COLS="60">
</P>
```

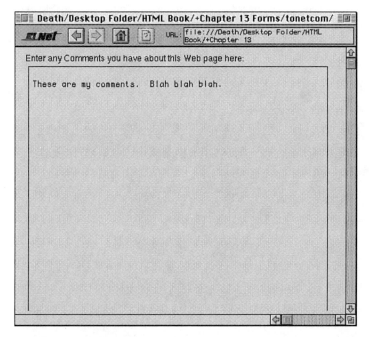

Figure 13.19. *The output in Mosaic.*

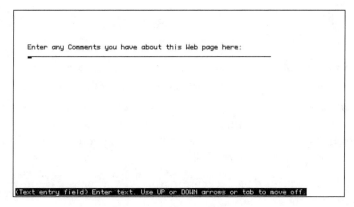

Figure 13.20. *The output in Lynx.*

13

323

Hidden Fields

One value for the TYPE attribute to the INPUT tag I haven't mentioned is "hidden." Hidden fields do not appear on the actual form; they are invisible in the browser display, but not hidden if someone decides to look at the HTML code for your page. Hidden input elements look like this:

```
<INPUT TYPE="HIDDEN" NAME="theName" VALUE="TheValue">
```

So why would you want to create a hidden form element? If it doesn't appear on the screen and the reader can't do anything with it, what's the point?

Let's take a hypothetical example. You create a simple form. In the script that processes the first form, you create a second form based on the input from the first form. The script to process the second form takes the information from both the first and second forms and creates a reply based on that information. Figure 13.21 shows how all this flows:

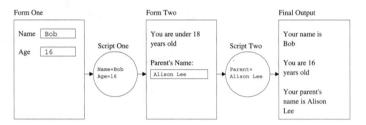

Figure 13.21. *Form to Form to Reply.*

How would you pass the information from the first form to the script that processes the second form? You can do one of two things:

☐ Write the information from the first form out to a temporary file and read that file back in again when the second form starts up.

☐ In the first script that constructs the second form, create hidden fields in the form with the appropriate information in NAME and VALUE fields. Then those names and values will be passed automatically to the second script when the reader submits the second form.

See? Hidden elements do make sense, particularly when you get involved in generating forms from forms.

What Is an Image Map?

In Chapter 7, "Including Images on Your Web Pages," you learned how to create an image that doubles as a link, simply by including the <IMG> tag inside a link (<A>) tag. By doing this, the entire image becomes a link; you could click on the image, the background, or the border, and the same effect would occur.

In image maps, different parts of the image activate different links (Figure 13.22). Using image maps, you could create a visual hyper-linked map that linked you to pages describing the regions you click. Or you could create visual metaphors for the information you're presenting: a set of books on a shelf or a photograph in which each person in the picture is individually described.

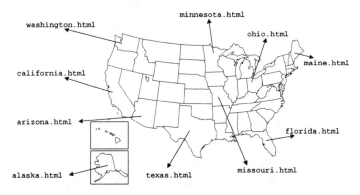

Figure 13.22. *Image maps: different places, different links.*

Image Maps and Text-Only Browsers

Because of the inherently graphical nature of image maps, they can only work on graphical browsers. In fact, if you try to view a document with an image map on it in a text-only browser such as Lynx, you don't even get an indication that the image exists, yet you won't be able to navigate the presentation without it.

If you do decide to create a Web page with an image map on it, it is doubly important that you also create a text-only equivalent so that readers with text-only browsers can use your page. The use of image maps can very effectively lock out readers with text-only browsers; have sympathy and allow them at least some method for viewing your content.

13

Creating Image Maps

There are three general steps to creating a clickable image map:

- ☐ Selecting an appropriate image
- ☐ Creating a "map file"—a text file indicating the coordinates of various areas on the image and mapping those areas to URLs to load when a hit within that area is detected
- ☐ Connecting the image, the map file, and the gateway script to process it all by placing the image in an HTML file and indicating that it's a map

Sounds easy, doesn't it? Well, there's a wrinkle in the process: There is no standard process for creating image maps across servers, not even between the CERN and NCSA servers.

This section explains how to construct clickable images in both the NCSA and CERN servers. If you're using another server, you're on your own—it's likely that they are using still another method for creating image maps.

Getting an Image

To create an image map, you'll need an image. The image that serves as the map is most useful if it has several discrete visual areas that can be individually selected; for example, images with several symbolic elements, or images that can be easily broken down into polygons. Photographs make difficult image maps because their various "elements" tend to blend together or are of unusual shapes. Figures 13.23 and 13.24 show examples of good and bad images for image maps.

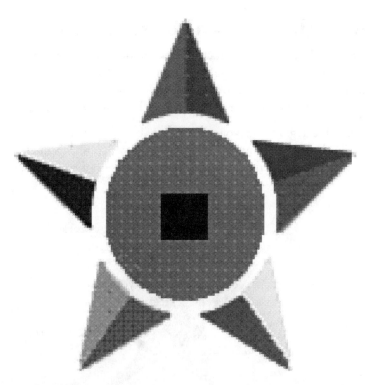

Figure 13.23. *A good image map.*

Figure 13.24. *A not-so-good image map.*

13

Sketch the Clickable Regions

The heart of the image map structure is a map file, which is essentially a description of the various regions in the image that should be clickable, and the links that they point to when they're selected. The first step to creating a map file is to sketch out the locations of the clickable areas on your image, and to find out the coordinates of those images.

The clickable regions on your image can be of several shapes: circles, rectangles, arbitrarily-shaped polygons, and (for NCSA's server), points. Sometimes it helps to print out your image and to draw the significant regions on the page (Figure 13.25).

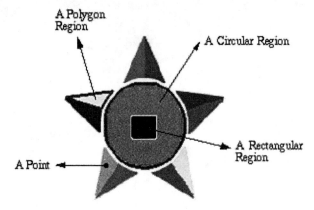

Figure 13.25. *Sketching mappable regions.*

Your regions can overlap; you'll decide in your map file which region will be selected first. You goal is to cover as many of the meaningful portions of the image as you can.

Find the Coordinates of the Regions

Once you've got a vague idea of where the regions in your map will go, you'll need to figure out what the coordinates for the endpoints of those regions are. (See Figure 13.26.)

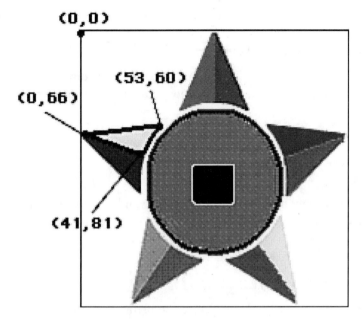

Figure 13.26. *Get the coordinates.*

For circle regions, note the coordinates of the center point and the radius, in pixels.

For rectangular regions, note the top left and bottom right corners.

For polygons, note the coordinates of each corner.

For points, note the point.

> **Note:** The 0,0 origin is at the top left-hand corner of the image, and positive Y is down.

Many image-editing programs enable you to find the coordinates of a given point within an image. There are also applications for "map-making" that will help you do this as well. (See Appendix A, "Sources for Further Information," for sites.)

I've found that the best way to keep track of all this is just to note it on paper: the region and its coordinates, and roughly where on the image this region corresponds to.

You're more than halfway there. Your last step is to come up with a set of URLs to link to for each region or point that is selected with the URL. You can have multiple regions pointing to the same URL, but each region must have only one link.

With all your regions, coordinates and URLs noted, you can now write a map file for your particular server. Move on to the section that applies to your server: CERN or NCSA.

Creating Image Maps: CERN HTTPD

This section describes how to take the regions and coordinates from the last section and create CERN-specific map files and link the image with the map file with the gateway to process it all.

Creating a Map File

Map files for the CERN HTTPD look something like this:

```
default URL
circle (x,y) r URL
rectangle (x,y) (x,y) URL
polygon (x1,y1) (x2,y2) ... (xN,yN) URL
```

Substitute the values for the coordinates you noted in the previous section in each of the x or y positions (or x1, y1, and so on). You must include the parentheses, and the r (in the circle line) is the radius for the circle region.

The URLs you specify must be either full URLs (starting with http or ftp or some other protocol), or full path names to the files you are linking to; that is, everything that you could include after the host name in a URL. You cannot specify relative path names in the image map file.

Here's a sample of a CERN map file:

```
circle (10,15) 20 /lemay/mapping.html
circle (346,23) 59 /lemay/mapping.html
polygon (192,3) (192,170) (115,217) /lemay/test/orange.html
rectangle (57,57) (100,210) /lemay/pencil.html
default /lemay/nopage.html
```

 Note: CERN's map files do not include individual points.

The order of regions in the map file is relevant; the further up a region is in the file, the higher precedence it has for mouse clicks. If a part of the region is selected that occurs on overlapping regions, the first region listed in the map file is the one that is activated.

Finally, the CERN map file includes a "default" region, with no coordinates, just a URL. Default is used when a point that is not inside a region is selected; it provides a "catch all" for the parts of the image that do not point to a specific link.

Save your map file with a descriptive name (say, `books.map`), and put it somewhere in your central repository of scripts. I have a map directory that holds all my maps at the same level as my `cgi-bin` directory. Note that `/lemay` is at this level as well:

```
/home/www/cgi-bin/
/home/www/maps/books.map
/home/www/lemay/
```

Specifying a Clickable Image in Your Web Document with CERN

Now you can link everything together. You'll be relieved to know that you don't have to write a gateway script to handle the image map; one has been provided for you with the CERN distribution called `htimage`.

Note: You may have to install the `htimage` program into your `cgi-bin` directory.

Now, all that's left to do is to link it all together. In your HTML document that contains the image map, you'll use both the `<A>` and `<IMG>` tags together to create the effect of the clickable image:

```
<A HREF="../cgi-bin/htimage/maps/books.map">
<IMG SRC="image.gif" ISMAP>
</A>
```

Note several things about this link. First of all, the link to the gateway script (`htimage`) is indicated the way you would expect, but then the path to the map file is appended onto the end of it. The path to the map file should be a full path name from the root of your Web directory, in this case, `/maps/books.map`.

The second part of the map is the `ISMAP` attribute to the `<IMG>` tag. This is a simple attribute that indicates to the browser and the server to communicate individual mouse-click coordinates to the gateway script for processing.

13

And now, try it out! You should be able to select various bits of the image using the mouse and have the coordinates sent as part of the URL to the htimage script, which in turn uses the map file to find an appropriate action for each region.

Creating Image Maps: NCSA HTTPD

This section describes how to take the regions and coordinates you defined in the section "Find the Coordinates of the Regions," create NCSA-specific map files, and link the image with the map file with the gateway to process it all.

Creating a Map File

The form of an NCSA image map file is roughly the same as CERN's, but the elements are in a different order. NCSA Map files look like this:

```
default URL
circle URL x,y r
rect URL x,y x,y
poly URL x1,y1 x2,y2 ... xN,yN
point URL x,y
```

Substitute the values for the coordinates you noted in the previous section in each of the x or y positions (or x1,y1, and so on). The r (in the circle line) is the radius for the circle region.

The URLs you specify must be either full URLs (starting with http or ftp or some other protocol), or full path names to the files you are linking to; that is, everything that you could include after the host name in a URL. You cannot specify relative path names in the image map file.

Here's a sample of an NCSA map file:

```
circle /lemay/mapping.html 10,15 20
circle /lemay/mapping.html 346,23 59
poly /lemay/test/orange.html 192,3 192,170 115,217
rect /lemay/pencil.html 57,57 100,210
point /lemay/pencil.html 100,100
point /lemay/orange.html 200,200
```

Points, in NCSA maps, allow you to specify that a given mouse click, if it doesn't land directly on a region, will activate the nearest point. Points are useful for photographs or other images with nondiscrete elements, or for a finer granularity than just "everything not in a region."

Finally, the NCSA map can also include a "default" region, with no coordinates, just a URL. Default is used when a point that is not inside a region is selected; it provides a "catch all" for the parts of the image that do not point to a specific link. Note that if you include default in your map file, you shouldn't include any points. The existence of point elements precludes that of default.

```
default /lemay/nopage.html
```

The order of regions in the map file is relevant; the further up a region is in the file, the higher precedence it has for mouse clicks. If a part of the region is selected that occurs on overlapping regions, the first region listed in the map file is the one that is activated.

Save your map file with a descriptive name (say, books.map), and put it somewhere in your central repository of scripts. I have a map directory that holds all my maps at the same level as my cgi-bin directory. Note that /lemay is at this level as well:

```
/home/www/cgi-bin/
/home/www/maps/books.map
/home/www/lemay/
```

Specifying a Clickable Map in Your Web Document: NCSA

One you have an image and a map file, you can link those elements together with the imagemap program, a gateway program that handles all the interaction between mouse clicks on the image and the map file.

By far the easiest way to set up image maps in NCSA is to make sure you have the latest version of the imagemap gateway script. The version that comes with the NCSA httpd 1.3 distribution is not the newest version; look for a version with comments in the header later than August 1994. (Don't go by the version number at the top of the file.) I found the most recent version in http://hoohoo.ncsa.uiuc.edu/docs/setup/admin/imagemap.txt, and renamed it to imagemap.c after I had downloaded it.

Once you have the newest version, compile it and install it in your cgi-bin directory. Toss out the old imagemap program.

Now, all that's left to do is to link the image to the map file to the gateway. In your HTML document that contains the image map, you'll use both the <A> and <IMG> tags together to create the effect of the clickable image:

```
<A HREF="../cgi-bin/imagemap/maps/books.map">
<IMG SRC="image.gif" ISMAP>
</A>
```

Note several things about this link. First of all, the link to the gateway script (imagemap) is indicated the way you would expect, but then the path to the map file is appended onto the end of it. The path to the map file should be a full path name from the root of your Web directory—in this case, /maps/books.map.

The second part of the map is the ISMAP attribute to the <IMG> tag. This is a simple attribute that indicates to the browser and the server to communicate individual mouse-click coordinates to the gateway script for processing.

> **Note:** If you don't have the newest version of imagemap.c, when you try to select portions of your image using this forms you will get errors that imagemap "Cannot Open Configuration file." Previous methods of implementing clickable images in the NCSA Web server involved an extra configuration file; if you are using the newest version of imagemap and setting up your clickable images in the way I've described above, you won't need that file. Double-check that you have compiled and installed the right version of imagemap.c.

Exercise 13.3: A clickable bookshelf.

Image maps can get pretty hairy, particularly since the map files are prone to error if you don't have your areas clearly outlined. In this exercise, we'll take a simple image and create an entry for both the CERN and NCSA map files for an area of an image so you can get a feel for what the map files look like and how to create them.

The image we'll use here is a simple color image of a bunch of books (Figure 13.27). You can't see the colors here, but from left to right, they are red, blue, yellow, and green.

Figure 13.27. *The bookshelf image.*

First, let's define the regions that will be clickable on this image. Because of the angular nature of the books, it's most appropriate to create polygon-shaped regions. Figure 13.28 shows an example of the sort of region it makes sense to create on the image, this one for the leftmost (red) book. You can define similar regions for each of the books in the stack. (Draw on the figure itself. I won't mind.)

13

Figure 13.28. *The bookshelf with areas defined.*

With an idea of the areas for each region, now let's find the coordinates of the corners. This will be difficult for you, since all you have is the printed version, but I'll show you what I've done. I used Adobe Photoshop to find the coordinates using the "Info" window, and came up with the coordinates shown in Figure 13.29. If you had the file, you could also find coordinates for each of the polygon regions on each of the books as well.

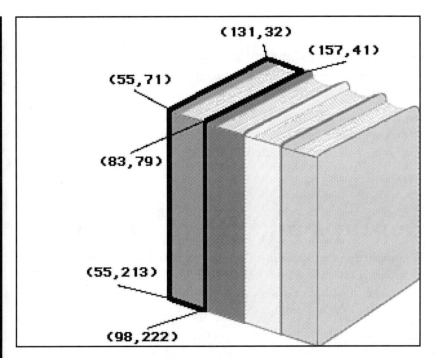

Figure 13.29. *The bookshelf with coordinates.*

With regions and a list of coordinates, all you need now are documents to jump to when the appropriate book is selected. These can be any documents, or they can be scripts; anything you can call from a browser you can use as a document to jump to. For this example, I've created a document called redbook.html in my Web directory (/lemay from the top of the Web root). This is the document that we'll define as the document to jump to when the red book is selected.

All that's left is to create the entry in the map file. In the CERN map file, it would look like this:

```
polygon (78,0) (0,37) (0,183) (27,192) (27,48) (103,9)
/lemay/redbook.html
```

And in NCSA's map file, the same information looks like this:

```
poly /lemay/redbook.html 78,0 0,37 0,183 27,192 27,48 103,9
```

13

Note that the URLs in the map file have to be absolute path names from the top of the Web root (not from the top of the file system). They cannot be relative URLs from the map file; image maps don't work like that. In this case, my `lemay` directory is at the Web root, and the `redbook.html` file is in that directory, so the URL for the purposes of the map file is `/lemay/redbook.html`

Now that you've done it for the red book, you can create identical examples for the other books in the image (blue, yellow, green). Don't forget to include a default line in the map file to map mouse clicks that don't hit any books:

```
default /lemay/notabook.html
```

Image Maps and Relative Links

There is a problem with image map links: sometimes, following a link through an image map will suddenly cause the relative links within that document to become invalid. This happens most often with the CERN image map server as it mucks with the URL of the document to get to the link from the image.

To understand how relative links work, you have to understand how browsers understand them. When the browser requests a document from a server, it constructs a URL pointing to that document. If the link is a relative URL, the browser builds a complete URL from the information it has. If your browser has a capability for viewing the URL of the current document, you can get a feel for what the browser is doing when it builds URLs. (See Figure 13.30.)

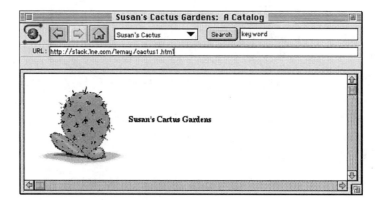

Figure 13.30. *URL built by browsers.*

Within an HTML document, all the relative links are not necessarily relative to that document itself (as I've been implying throughout this book), but they are relative to the URL of the document—or rather, the browser's current idea of what that URL is.

Most of the time this isn't a big issue, because the URL the browser builds is usually accurate. However, you'll note that sometimes when you navigate to a document using an imagemap, the URL of the current document as shown by the browser ends up being not the URL of the current document, but the actual map information instead. The following two URLs point to the same document, but only the latter is the "real" URL:

```
http://slack/cgi-bin/htimage/maps/books.map?45,73
http://slack/lemay/bluebook.html
```

Because navigating using image maps creates these funny URLs, all the relative links you've been so careful to include in that document won't work because your browser will be trying to navigate to those document relative to the wrong URL.

If you're having this problem, there's an easy way to fix it: it's called the <BASE> tag, and you put it in the <HEAD> element of your HTML file. <BASE> is used to indicate the full URL (protocol, system name, path name) of the current document, like this:

```
<HEAD>
<TITLE>This is a document</TITLE>
<BASE HREF="http://myserver.com/docs/document.html">
</HEAD>
```

Then, when your browser reads a document with BASE in it, it'll use that URL as its default URL, and use it to find all the relative links in that document instead of the one that it thinks belongs to the document.

Warning: Be careful when using <BASE>. It may seem like a clever way of making sure all your relative links always work, but it also reduces the portability of your documents. Should you change directories or servers, you'll have to go in and redo all those BASE elements. Only use BASE when it's necessary to get around problems with relative URLs.

13

Summary

Forms and image maps are two of the most interesting innovations that have been added in recent times to Web publishing. With the advent of these features, the Web changed from being a publishing medium with hypertext links to a fully interactive environment with the potential for being something entirely new.

In this chapter, you've learned how to lay out form elements in HTML as well as how to process the results on the server when that form is submitted. You should now know the difference between GET and POST and be able to explain why one is better. And you know the difference between a CERN and NCSA image map, how to create both of them, and how to connect clickable images, map files, and gateway scripts on the appropriate servers.

In addition, you've learned about the remaining tags defined by the current version of HTML—those that define the elements of a form. Table 13.1 presents a quick summary of all the tags and attributes you've learned about in this chapter.

Table 13.1. HTML Tags from Chapter 13.

Tag	Use
<FORM>...</FORM>	A form. You can have multiple forms within a document, but forms cannot be nested.
METHOD	An attribute of the <FORM> tag, indicating the method with which the form input is given to the script that processes the form. Possible values are GET and POST.
ACTION	An attribute of the <FORM> tag indicating the script to process the form input. Contains a relative path or URL to the script.
<INPUT>	A form element.
TYPE	An attribute of the <INPUT> tag indicating the type of form element. Possible values are SUBMIT, RESET, TEXT, RADIO, CHECKBOX and HIDDEN.
	SUBMIT creates a button to submit the form to the script which processes the input.
	RESET creates a button which resets the default values of the form, if any.
	TEXT creates a single-line text field.
	RADIO creates a radio button.

Tag	Use
	CHECKBOX creates a check box
	HIDDEN creates a form element that is not presented but has a name and a value that can then be passed onto the script that processes the form input.
NAME	An attribute of the <INPUT>, <SELECT>, and <TEXTAREA> tags. Indicates the name of the variable which holds the eventual value of this element, as submitted to the script.
VALUE	An attribute of the <INPUT> tag, indicating the default value for the form element, if any, or the value submitted with the NAME to the script. For SUBMIT and RESET buttons, VALUE indicates the label of the button.
SIZE	An attribute of the <INPUT> tag used only when TYPE is TEXT. Indicates the size of the text field, in characters.
MAXLENGTH	An attribute of the <INPUT> tag used only when TYPE is TEXT. Indicates the maximum number of characters this text field will accept.
CHECKED	An attribute of the <INPUT> tag used only when TYPE is CHECKBOX or RADIO. Indicates that this element is selected by default.
<SELECT>	A menu or scrolling list of items. Individual items are indicated by the <OPTION> tag.
MULTIPLE	An attribute of the <SELECT> tag indicating that multiple items in the list can be selected.
SIZE	An attribute of the <SELECT> tag which causes the list of items to be displayed as a scrolling list with the number of items indicated by SIZE visible.
<OPTION>	Individual items within a <SELECT> element.
SELECTED	An attribute of the <OPTION> tag indicating that this item is selected by default.
<TEXTAREA>	A text-entry field with multiple lines.
ROWS	An attribute of the <TEXTAREA> tag indicating the height of the text field, in rows.
COLS	An attribute of the <TEXTAREA> tag indicating the width of the text field, in characters.

13

Q&A

Q Is there any time when I should be using the GET method in my forms?

A It's a better idea to use POST, since processing the input from POST isn't much more complicated and allows you to create forms of any length. Once you've learned how to deal with the POST method, GET is just different and doesn't offer any features that POST does.

If you're really interested in using GET, see the CGI documentation that came with your server.

Q Where can I got those tools for processing form input from POST?

A I've included a few addresses for scripts and programs in Appendix A.

Q You used cgiparse in all your scripts in your chapter. Have you noticed that if you use cgiparse on a set of name/value pairs that include multiple names that only the last value is used? All the others are discarded.

A Yes (she said, with an embarrassed smile). This is a drawback with cgiparse that I didn't realize until I was three-quarters through writing this chapter, and at that point I decided I'd rather explain it here than change everything else in the chapter.

You can get around this problem in one of two ways:

☐ Don't implement your forms to use multiple identical NAME attributes. Make sure each NAME is unique.

☐ Use something other than cgiparse to process the input of POST. Again, I've included sources for various processing tools in Appendix A.

Q My image maps aren't working.

A Here are a couple things you can look for:

☐ Make sure that the URLs in your map file are absolute path names from the top of your root Web directory to the location of the file you want to link to. You cannot use relative path names in the map file.

☐ Make sure that when you append the path of the map file to the gateway script (htimage or imagemap) that you also use an absolute path name.

☐ If you're using NCSA httpd, make sure you're using the newest version of imagemap.c. Requests to the new imagemap gateway script should not look for configuration files.

Q I saw an example of a form that used an `<INPUT>` with `TYPE="IMAGE"`.
It looked like another way to do image maps.

A You're right, it is another way to do image maps, part of the NCSA forms
package. Using image maps in forms is especially cutting edge at this point. In
fact, I couldn't find more than one browser that would reliably support them.
So I decided to describe the "old" method of doing image maps instead.
Perhaps when it comes time to write *Teach Yourself Web Publishing with
HTML in a Week: The Second Edition*, image maps within forms will be better
supported by the browsers on the market.

13

14

HTML Assistants: Editors and Converters

HTML Assistants: Editors and Converters

After the enormous amount of information presented in the last chapter, you're probably wondering what other terrors I have left to describe in this last chapter. Fear not; to finish up on this last day I'm not going to describe any more HTML tags or illustrate any more difficult technical concepts. In this chapter you'll just learn about tools that are designed to make writing HTML documents easier.

Writing HTML documents by hand in a text editor is probably the most difficult way to write HTML. You have to type in all the tags , and you have to remember what the tags are. (I can never remember whether it's a SELECT or a SELECTION you use to create selection lists.) And you have to remember to close your two-sided tags and include closing quotes on attributes. With all that to remember, it sometimes becomes difficult to remember what you're actually writing *about.*

On the other hand, if you go looking for a full-featured HTML editor that lets you quickly see the result of your work, insert links and anchors and inline graphics quickly and easily, or build a form using element widgets you can drag from a toolbox, you'll be looking for a very long time.

Which is not to say that tools for writing HTML files don't exist; on the contrary, there are lots of them, and there are even more converters and filters available that allow you to work in a tool you're familiar with and then output HTML later on. But none of these tools really works to create a really good environment for working in HTML. A truly excellent HTML environment has yet to be produced.

In this chapter, you learn about

- ☐ Tag editors—text editors that help you create HTML files by inserting tags or managing links
- ☐ WYSIWYG editors for HTML
- ☐ Converters—programs that let you convert files created by popular word processing programs or other formats to HTML
- ☐ The advantages and disadvantages of using a converter or of working directly in HTML

This chapter is by no means a complete list of the available editors and converters for HTML, only a sample of some of the more popular tools. Also, this is a rapidly growing field of development, and by the time you read this it is likely that there will be newer, better, and more powerful tools for HTML development available. For this reason, Appendix A, "Sources for Further Information," provides some pointers to lists of editors and filters. These lists are being constantly updated and are the best source for finding tools that may not be described in this chapter.

Tag Editors

A *tag editor* is a term I'll use to describe a simple standalone text editor or an extension to an existing text editor that helps you write HTML documents by inserting the tags for you. Tag editors generally provide shortcuts to creating HTML files—instead of trying to remember whether selections in forms are specified by the `<SELECT>` tag or the `<SELECTION>` tag, or having to type both the opening and closing parts of a long tag by hand, tag editors usually provide windows or buttons with meaningful names that insert the tag into the text for you at the appropriate spot. You're still working with text, and you're still working directly in HTML, but tag editors take away a lot of the drudgery involved in creating HTML documents.

For Microsoft Windows

If you use Windows to develop HTML files, you have no shortage of tag editors: HTML Assistant, HTMLed, HTML HyperEdit, and HTML Writer provide text editor and HTML capabilities.

HTML Assistant

HTML Assistant is one of the more popular tag editors for Windows, enabling you to insert tags by clicking buttons in a toolbar and to preview your work with your favorite browser.

One of its best features is the capability to collect URLs from hotlists generated by Mosaic and Cello and to enable you to create links to those URLs. With this feature, you may never have to type a URL into your HTML documents.

The FAQ (Frequently Asked Questions) for HTML Assistant is at `ftp://ftp.cs.dal.ca/htmlasst/htmlafaq.html`. (You can get to the actual program from that file as well.)

HTMLed

HTMLed is similar to HTML Assistant in that it enables you to insert tags using buttons from a toolbar. It also provides a method for converting existing text by automatically placing tags at the beginnings and ends of lines; for example, to convert a plain document to HTML.

You can obtain a copy of HTMLed from the URL: `http://pringle.mta.ca/~peterc/htmed11.zip`.

HTML HyperEdit

HTML HyperEdit enables you to insert tags using buttons. If you select a portion of text, both the opening and closing tags are added to the beginning and end of the selection. With HTML HyperEdit you can also convert plain text to HTML, convert special characters to their respective character entities, and convert HTML back to text. Unlike HTML Assistant, HTML HyperEdit does not have the capability to launch a browser to preview your HTML documents.

You can find out more about HTML HyperEdit at `http://www.curtin.edu.au/curtin/dept/cc/packages/htmledit/home.html`.

HTML Writer

With HTML Writer, you can insert tags using a variety of methods: menus, toolbars, and keyboard shortcuts. Unlike many other tag editors, it can load and manage really big documents and also supports form tags. Like HTML Assistant, it has a Test (preview) button that loads Mosaic or Cello to preview your work.

See `http://wwf.et.byu.edu/~nosackk/html-writer/index.html` for more information.

For Macintosh

If you're developing HTML files on the Macintosh, HTML.edit provides a single environment for inserting HTML tags into text files and managing related documents. If you're used to working on a more full-featured text editor such as Alpha or BBEdit, there are also HTML extensions for both these packages.

HTML.edit

HTML.edit is a HyperCard-based HTML tag editor, but it does not require HyperCard to run. It provides menus and buttons for inserting HTML tags into text files, as well as features for automatic indexing (for creating those hyperlinked table-of-contents lists) and automatic conversion of text files to HTML.

Its most interesting feature, however, is its Index page, which enables you to collect a set of related HTML documents, sort of like a project in THINK C or a bookfile in FrameMaker. Once a file is listed on the Index page, that file appears in a list of files that you can link to, so you can create navigation links between related files quickly and easily.

You can get information about HTML.edit from `http://nctn.oact.hq.nasa.gov/tools/HTMLedit/HTMLedit.html`.

HTML Extensions for Alpha and BBEdit

Alpha and BBEdit are two of the more popular shareware text editors available for the Macintosh. Both provide mechanisms for adding in extensions for working in particular languages and writing text to conform to a particular style. Extensions exist for both Alpha and BBEdit to help with writing HTML tags.

There are advantages to using a standard text editor with extensions as opposed to using a dedicated HTML tag editor. For one thing, general text editors tend to provide more features for general text editing, including search and replace and spell checking, that a simple HTML text editor does not. Also, if you're used to working in a standard text editor, being able to continue to use that text editor for your HTML development means that you don't have to take the time to learn a new program in order to get your work done.

If you use the Alpha editor, versions after 5.92b include the HTML extensions in the main distribution. You can get Alpha and its HTML extensions from `ftp://cs.rice.edu/public/Alpha/`.

There are actually two extension packages for HTML development in BBEdit: the first, called simply HTML Extensions for BBEdit, was written by Carles Bellver. You can get information about this package from `http://www.uji.es/bbedit-html-extensions.html`.

The second package, HTML BBEdit Tools, was based on Carles Bellver's extensions, and includes some additional features. You can get more information about it at `http://www.york.ac.uk/~ld11/BBEditTools.html`.

For UNIX

tkHTML is a nice graphical HTML tag editor for the X11 Window System that uses the tcl language and the tk toolkit. It enables you to not only insert tags into text files, but to also convert existing text easily to HTML, and to automatically preview your HTML files using a WWW browser called WWwish. You can get more information about tkHTML from `http://alfred1.u.washington.edu:8080/~roland/tkHTML/tkHTML.html`, or download the source directly from `ftp://ftp.u.washington.edu:/public/roland/tkHTML`.

If you prefer to work in Emacs, the popular text editor-slash-kitchen sink, you have three HTML mode packages to choose from:

- [ ] html-mode, the original, available at `ftp://ftp.ncsa.uiuc.edu/Web/elisp/html-mode.el`.

☐ html-helper-mode, an enhanced version of the above. You can get information about it at `http://www.santafe.edu/~nelson/tools/`.

☐ hm—html-menus is also based on html-mode, but provides additional features for Lucid Emacs (now called Xemacs) and GNU Emacs 19. Information is available at `http://www.tnt.uni-hannover.de/data/info/www/tnt/soft/info/www/html-editors/hm—html-menus/overview.html`. (Whew!)

WYSIWYG Editors

The concept of a true WYSIWYG editor for HTML files is a bit of a fallacy, since (as I've harped on throughout this book) each browser formats HTML documents in different ways, and most allow the reader to configure their browser to use their favorite fonts to use to view documents. The closest an editor could come to WYSIWYG would be if it allowed you to select the browser that would be viewing your document—and you could look at your document under Lynx, then under Mosaic for X, then under Cello.

There are some editors that purport to be WYSIWYG, or, more correctly, WYSIWYGIM (What You See Is What You Get In Mosaic). This section describes a few.

For Microsoft Windows

For near-WYSIWYG HTML editing under Windows, you have essentially two choices: any of a number of template packages for Microsoft Word 2.0 or 6.0, and SoftQuad HoTMetaL.

Template Packages for MS Word

If you like Microsoft Word Version 2.0 or Version 6.0, several template packages exist that enable you to create HTML documents from directly within Word, assigning styles as you would in any Word document and selecting HTML features (such as links and inline images) from a toolbar. All also enable you to export the files you've written to HTML format. Note, however, that if you make changes to the HTML document you've exported, you cannot import it back into Word.

There are three template packages:

☐ CU_HTML (from Chinese University of Hong Kong, hence the CU). Information is available at `http://www.cuhk.hk/csc/cu_html/cu_html.htm`.

☐ GT_HTML (from Georgia Tech Research Institute). See the information at `http://www.gatech.edu/word_html/release.htm`.

☐ ANT_HTML (by Jill Smith; according to an information file that comes with the package, "the acronym is a secret"). You can retrieve the entire package from `ftp://ftp.einet.net/einet/pc/ANT_HTML.ZIP`.

SoftQuad HoTMetaL

SoftQuad HoTMetaL is an excellent standalone editor that allows very near-WYSIWYG capabilities without trying to hide the fact that you're still working in HTML. You still work with tags in HoTMetaL, and you can only insert tags where they are legally permissible. (You can't, for example, put regular paragraphs into a `<HEAD>` section.) This is a good thing; it means that if you use HoTMetaL you cannot write an HTML document that does not conform to correct HTML style.

HoTMetaL is freeware for the basic version; there is also a commercial version available with more features. Information about HoTMetaL and SoftQuad's other SGML-based tools is available at `http://www.sq.com/`.

For Macintosh

HTML Editor is a wonderful application that enables you to both insert tags into your file and see the result in a WYSIWYG fashion—at the same time. The tags are shown in a lighter color than the surrounding text, and the text itself looks like it would look in Mosaic, although you can change the appearance of any style and apply it across the document. There are options to hide the tags in your document to get the full effect, and you can also preview the document using your favorite browser. Until HoTMetaL is ported to the Mac (and even if it is), HTML Editor is your best choice for developing HTML documents.

The documentation for HTML Editor is available at `http://dragon.acadiau.ca:1667/~giles/HTML_Editor/Documentation.html`. You can get the actual package from `ftp://cs.dal.ca/giles/HTML_Editor_1.0.sit.hqx`.

For UNIX

Three WYSIWYG tools are available for UNIX systems running X: SoftQuad HoTMetaL, tkWWW, and htmltext.

SoftQuad HoTMetal

SoftQuad's HoTMetaL HTML editor, described in the section on Windows editors, is also available for Sun SPARC workstations running X11 (Motif). See `http://www.sq.com/` for more information.

tkWWW

tkWWW is a World Wide Web browser and editor that runs using the tcl language and tk toolkit under X. Because it is both an editor and browser, it can rightfully claim WYSIWYG-ness if you use tkWWW as your only browser. In tkWWW, you choose items and styles from menus, and correct HTML is produced when you save the document. This is nice if you can't stand looking at HTML tags—using tkWWW, you never have to see one.

tkWWW requires tcl and tk. An overview of its features is available at `http://uu-gna.mit.edu:8001/tk-www/help/overview.html`; you can retrieve the package itself from `ftp://ftp.aud.alcatel.com:/tcl/extensions`.

htmltext

htmltext is an HTML editor similar to tkWWW in that it hides the tags from you, so you can work entirely in a WYSIWYG environment that looks an awful lot like Mosaic for X.

htmltext was written using the Andrew Toolkit, and if you have Andrew installed on your system, you can use htmltext almost as a full-fledged word processor. Also, if you compile it from source, you'll also need to get the Andrew Toolkit. A precompiled binary for SunOS 4.1.x is available.

See `http://web.cs.city.ac.uk/homes/njw/htmltext/htmltext.html` for more information.

Converters

What if you'd prefer not to work in HTML at all—you have your own tool or language that you're familiar with, and you'd prefer to work in that? Many programs exist that will convert different formats into HTML. This section describes many of those converters.

For Windows

Converters for Windows are available for two of the most popular word processing systems: Microsoft Word and WordPerfect.

Microsoft Word

The CU_HTML, ANT_HTML, and GT_HTML packages, by virtue of the fact that they are templates for Word, can be used to convert Word documents to HTML. See the section about these packages earlier in this chapter for information.

Microsoft Word can also export files in RTF (Rich Text Format), which can then be converted to HTML using the RTFTOHTM filter for Windows. You can get more information about this filter from `http://info.cern.ch/hypertext/WWW/Tools/RTFTOHTM.html`.

WordPerfect

WPTOHTML is a set of WordPerfect macros that convert WordPerfect 5.1 and 6.0 for DOS files to HTML. WordPerfect can also export RTF files, enabling you to use the RTF converter mentioned in the previous section on Microsoft Word.

The WPTOHTML macros are described at `gopher://black.ox.ac.uk/h0/ousu_dir/.html-stuff/wptohtml.html`.

For Macintosh

Not much work has gone on with converters on the Macintosh; however, there is an excellent RTF to HTML converter. Since many popular word processing and desktop publishing programs can export RTF (including Microsoft Word, PageMaker, Quark Express, and FrameMaker), this may be the only converter you need.

You can get information about rtftohtml at `ftp://ftp.cray.com/src/WWWstuff/RTF/rtftohtml_overview.html`.

Also, if you have access to a UNIX system, there are converters for FrameMaker MIF files and Quark Express tagged text available that you could use after moving your Mac-generated files to that UNIX system.

For UNIX

UNIX, of course, has all the good converters. Many of these are written in the Perl language, however, which means that if you have a port of Perl for your system these converters may work there as well.

Here's a quick rundown of the more popular converters.

Plain Text

If you have files in plain text format that you want to convert to HTML quickly and easily, there are two simple filters that will do it for you, both called txt2html. See either `http://www.seas.upenn.edu/~mengwong/txt2html.html` or `http://www.cs.wustl.edu/~seth/txt2html/` for more information.

RTF (Rich Text Format)

Although RTF is a more popular format for desktop word processors, the filter mentioned under Macintosh converters also exists for UNIX systems. That URL, once again, is `ftp://ftp.cray.com/src/WWWstuff/RTF/rtftohtml_overview.html`.

LaTeX

For converting LaTex files to HTML, you can use latex2html. latex2html is quite enthusiastic in its conversion, including converting equations into GIF files for inclusion in the HTML document. You can get latex2html at `http://cbl.leeds.ac.uk/nikos/tex2html/doc/latex2html/latex2html.html`.

FrameMaker

Several filters to convert FrameMaker files exist for UNIX.

☐ Frame2HTML from Norwegian Telecom does an excellent job of converting whole books to HTML, including preserving inter-document HyperText links as HTML tags and also converting internal graphics into GIF files with the GhostScript and PBM filter packages installed. See `http://info.cern.ch/hypertext/WWW/Tools/fm2html.html` for more information.

☐ WebMaker is a similar package for converting FrameMaker documents to HTML. It is available in binary form for several popular platforms including SunOS, Solaris, HPUX and IRIX. You can get more information from `http://www.cern.ch/WebMaker/`.

☐ MifMucker is a simple program for converting MIF (Maker Interchange Format) files to HTML and other formats. Although its not as fully featured as Frame2HTML or WebMaker for converting to HTML, it does provide filters to several other formats, and I like the name. See `http://www.oac.uci.edu/indiv/ehood/mifmucker.doc.html` for more information.

Quark Express

Quark Express files themselves cannot yet be converted to HTML, but Quark can output tagged text that can then be converted to HTML. More information is contained at `http://the-tech.mit.edu/~jeremy/qt2www.html`.

PostScript

Information about a general-purpose PostScript to HTML converter can be found at `http://stasi.bradley.edu/ftp/pub/ps2html/ps2html-v2.html`. You will need Ghostscript to use this converter.

Working Directly in HTML versus Using a Converter

With all the converters from common word processing programs to HTML available, it may seem tempting to do most of your HTML development in those programs and deal with converting the files to HTML at the last minute. And for many projects, this may be the way to go.

Consider the advantages of working in a converter:

- ☐ Authors do not have to keep track of tags. Having to memorize and know the rules of how tags work is a major issue if all one wants to do is write.

- ☐ Fewer errors end up in HTML documents (misspellings, forgetting to close tags, using overlapping tags). Because the HTML is generated, there's less chance of "operator error" in the final output.

- ☐ Authors can use a tool they're familiar with. If they know MS Word and live and die by MS Word, they can work in MS Word.

On the other hand, working in a converter is not a panacea. There are pitfalls, which include:

- ☐ No tools can provide all the features of HTML, particularly with links to external documents. Some handworking of the final HTML files will generally be required after you convert.

- ☐ The split-source issue. Once you convert your files from their original form to HTML, you have two sources you are going to have to keep track of. To make changes after you do the conversion, you will either have to change the original and regenerate the HTML (wiping out any hand-massaging you did to those files), or you'll have to make sure you make the change to BOTH the original source and the HTML documents. For large projects, splitting the source at any point in time except the very last minute can create enormous headaches for everyone involved.

14

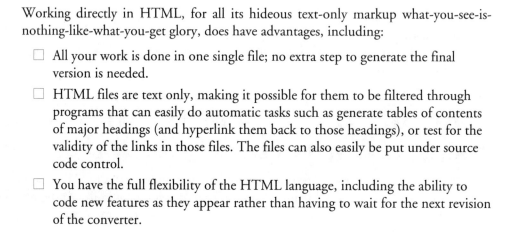

Working directly in HTML, for all its hideous text-only markup what-you-see-is-nothing-like-what-you-get glory, does have advantages, including:

- [ ] All your work is done in one single file; no extra step to generate the final version is needed.

- [ ] HTML files are text only, making it possible for them to be filtered through programs that can easily do automatic tasks such as generate tables of contents of major headings (and hyperlink them back to those headings), or test for the validity of the links in those files. The files can also easily be put under source code control.

- [ ] You have the full flexibility of the HTML language, including the ability to code new features as they appear rather than having to wait for the next revision of the converter.

Summary

To wind down in the last chapter of the last day, I've simply provided some simple lists of HTML editors and converters to help you in your HTML development. After everything you've learned in the last week, the prospect of tools to help you must come as a welcome relief. Consider using one or more of the tools mentioned in this chapter; they can help enormously in producing HTML documents.

Congratulations! Upon completing this chapter, you have learned most of the publishing concepts available on the World Wide Web today. You know everything from the HTML tag to create a level three heading to how to create a map file for clickable images. And I hope that somewhere along the line you've picked up some ideas for designing and structuring your documents so that they can be read and navigated quickly and easily and serve the demands of your readers.

Good luck with your Web development.

A

Sources for Further Information

Haven't had enough yet? In this appendix you'll find the URLs for all kinds of information about the World Wide Web, HTML, developing Web presentations, and locations of tools to help you write HTML documents. With this list you should be able to find just about anything you need on the Web.

> **NOTE:** Some of the URLs in this section refer to FTP sites. Some of these sites may be very busy during business hours, and you may not be able to immediately access the files. Try again during non-primetime hours.
>
> Also, some of these sites, for mysterious reasons, may be accessible through the FTP program itself, but not through Web browsers. If you are consistently getting refused from these sites using a browser, and you have access to FTP, try that program instead.

Collections of HTML Development Information

The Virtual Library
Linkname: Virtual Library/CyberWeb: WWW Development
URL: `http://www.charm.net/~web/Vlib/`

Netspace HTML Developer Information
Linkname: Developing HTML Documents and WWW Servers
URL: `http://netspace.org/netspace/wwwdoc.html`

The Developer's JumpStation
Linkname: JHU/APL's WWW & HTML Developer's JumpStation—
Version 1.4 (April 6)
URL: `http://oneworld.wa.com/htmldev/devpage/dev-page.html`

The Repository
Linkname: Subjective Electronic Information Repository
URL: `http://cbl.leeds.ac.uk/nikos/doc/repository.html`

Yahoo's WWW Section
Linkname: Computers: World Wide Web
URL: `http://akebono.stanford.edu/yahoo/Computers/World_Wide_Web/`

WWW in General

The Home of the WWW Consortium
Linkname: The World Wide Web Organization
URL: `http://www.w3.org/hypertext/WWW/Organization/Consortium/W3OSignature.html`

Home of the World Wide Web
Linkname: World Wide Web Home
URL: `http://info.cern.ch/`

WWW Indexes

ALIWEB, a great Web index
Linkname: ALIWEB
URL: `http://web.nexor.co.uk/aliweb/doc/aliweb.html`

The Web Crawler
Linkname: The WebCrawler
URL: `http://www.biotech.washington.edu/WebCrawler/WebCrawler.html`

Yahoo (my favorite index)
Linkname: Yahoo—A Guide to WWW
URL: `http://akebono.stanford.edu/yahoo/`

The Web Worm
Linkname: WWWW—the WORLD WIDE WEB WORM
URL: `http://www.cs.colorado.edu/home/mcbryan/WWWW.html`

An Index of Indexes
Linkname: Web Indexes
URL: `http://www.biotech.washington.edu/WebCrawler/WebIndexes.html`

Another list of indexes and catalogs
Linkname: Virtual Library/CyberWeb: Catalogs
URL: `http://www.charm.net/~web/Vlib/Users/Catalogs.html`

Browsers

A general list
Linkname: WWW Client Software products
URL: http://info.cern.ch/hypertext/WWW/Clients.html

NCSA Mosaic (X, Windows, Mac)
Linkname: NCSA Mosaic Home Page
URL: http://www.ncsa.uiuc.edu/SDG/Software/Mosaic/
NCSAMosaicHome.html

AIR Mosaic (Spry)
Linkname: AIR Mosaic FREE Offer
URL: http://www.spry.com/airfree.html

Spyglass Enhanced Mosaic
Linkname: Mosaic from Spyglass Home Page
URL: http://www.spyglass.com/mos_home.htm

Web Explorer (OS/2)
URL: ftp://ftp.ibm.net/pub/WebExplorer/web.exe
(Also available as part of the OS/2 Warp commercial package.)

Netscape (X, Windows, Mac)
Linkname: Questions About Netscape
URL: http://home.mcom.com/home/faq_docs/faq_client.html

Lynx (UNIX and DOS)
Linkname: About Lynx Ver. 2.2
URL: http://www.cc.ukans.edu/about_lynx/lynx2_2.html

Cello (Windows)
Linkname: FAQ FOR CELLO (PART 1)
URL: http://www.law.cornell.edu/cello/cellofaq.html

WinWeb (Windows)
Linkname: EINet WinWeb
URL: http://www.einet.net/EINet/WinWeb/WinWebHome.html

MacWeb (Macintosh)
Linkname: EINet MacWeb
URL: http://www.einet.net/EINet/MacWeb/MacWebHome.html

Arena (X)
Linkname: Welcome to Arena
URL: http://info.cern.ch/hypertext/WWW/Arena/

Amiga Mosaic
Linkname: Amiga Mosaic Home
URL: http://insti.physics.sunysb.edu/AMosaic/

Chimera (for X)
Linkname: Chimera Home Page
URL: http://www.unlv.edu/chimera/

Specifications for HTML, URLs, HTTP, etc.

The HTML Level 2 specification
Linkname: HTML Specification Review Materials
URL: http://www.hal.com/users/connolly/html-spec/index.html

The original HTML specification
Linkname: Hypertext Markup Language (HTML)
URL: http://info.cern.ch/hypertext/WWW/MarkUp/HTML.html

The HTML+ (HTML Level 3) draft specification (HTML)
Linkname: HTML+ (Hypertext markup format)
URL: http://info.cern.ch/hypertext/WWW/MarkUp/HTMLPlus/
htmlplus_1.html

The HTML+ (HTML Level 3) draft specification (in PostScript)
Linkname: HTML+ Specification (draft)
URL: http://www.ics.uci.edu/WWWdocs/papers/
draft-raggett-www-html-00.ps.gz

The HTTP specification
Linkname: HTTP: A protocol for networked information
URL: http://info.cern.ch/hypertext/WWW/Protocols/HTTP/HTTP2.html

Pointers to URL, URN, and URI information and specifications
Linkname: UR* and The Names and Addresses of WWW objects
URL: http://info.cern.ch/hypertext/WWW/Addressing/
Addressing.html

Tools for Images

Some good information about transparent GIFs
Linkname: Transparent Background Images
URL: `http://melmac.harris-atd.com/transparent_images.html`

giftrans
Linkname: source for giftrans
URL: `ftp://ftp.rz.uni-karlsruhe.de/pub/net/www/tools/giftrans.c`

Linkname: DOS executable for giftrans
URL: `ftp://ftp.rz.uni-karlsruhe.de/pub/net/www/tools/giftrans.exe`

Transparency (Macintosh)
URL: `ftp://sumex-aim.stanford.edu/info-mac/grf/util/transparency-10b4.hqx`

Sumex-aim is often busy, so try a mirror site instead, for example:

URL: `http://hyperarchive.lcs.mit.edu/HyperArchive/Archive/grf/util/transparency-10b4.hqx`

(The actual file name may have changed if there is a newer version available.)

Sound and Video

SOX (UNIX and DOS sound Converter)
URL: `ftp://ftp.cs.ruu.nl/pub/MIDI/PROGRAMS`

WAVany (Windows sound converter)
URL: `ftp.netcom.com:/pub/neisius/wvany10.zip`

WHAM (Windows sound converter)
URL: `file://ftp.ncsa.uiuc.edu/Mosaic/Windows/viewers/wham131.zip`

SoundAPP (Macintosh sound converter)
URL: `ftp://sumex-aim.stanford.edu/info-mac/snd/util/sound-app-131.hqx`

Sumex-aim is often busy, so try a mirror site instead, for example:

URL: `http://hyperarchive.lcs.mit.edu/HyperArchive/Archive/snd/util/sound-app-131.hqx`

FastPlayer (Macintosh Quicktime "flattener")
URL: `ftp://sumex-aim.stanford.edu/info-mac/grf/util/fast-player-110.hqx`

Sumex-aim is often busy, so try a mirror site instead, for example:

URL: `http://hyperarchive.lcs.mit.edu/HyperArchive/Archive/grf/util/fast-player-110.hqx`

QFlat (Windows QuickTime "flattener")
URL: `ftp://venice.tcp.com/pub/anime-manga/software/viewers/qtflat.zip`

Sparkle (MPEG player and converter for Macintosh)
URL: `ftp://sumex-aim.stanford.edu/info-mac/grf/util/sparkle-215.hqx`

Sumex-aim is often busy, so try a mirror site instead, for example:

URL: `http://hyperarchive.lcs.mit.edu/HyperArchive/Archive/grf/util/sparkle-215.hqx`

XingCD (AVI to MPEG converter)
Send mail to xing@xingtech.com or call 805/473-0145

AVI-Quick (Macintosh converter for AVI to Quicktime)
URL: `ftp://sumex-aim.stanford.edu/info-mac/grf/util/avi-to-qt-converter.hqx`

Sumex-aim is often busy, so try a mirror site instead, for example:

URL: `http://hyperarchive.lcs.mit.edu/HyperArchive/Archive/grf/util/avi-to-qt-converter.hqx`

SoundCap (Windows Quicktime and AVI Converter)
URL: `ftp://ftp.intel.com/pub/IAL/Indeo_video/smartc.exe`

The MPEG FAQ
Linkname: MPEG Moving Picture Expert Group FAQ
URL: `http://www.crs4.it/~luigi/MPEG/mpegfaq.html`

Information on making MPEG movies
Linkname: How to make MPEG movies
URL: `http://www.arc.umn.edu/GVL/Software/mpeg.html`

Servers

CERN HTTPD
Linkname: CERN Server User Guide
URL: http://info.cern.ch/httpd_3.0/

NCSA HTTPD
Linkname: NCSA httpd Overview
URL: http://hoohoo.ncsa.uiuc.edu/docs/Overview.html

NCSA HTTPD for Windows
Linkname: NCSA httpd for Windows
URL: http://www.alisa.com/win-httpd/

MacHTTP
Linkname: MacHTTP Info
URL: http://www.uth.tmc.edu/mac_info/machttp_info.html

Web Providers

An index from HyperNews
Linkname: Leasing a Server
URL: http://union.ncsa.uiuc.edu/www/leasing.shtml

Gateway Scripts and the Common Gateway Interface (CGI)

The original NCSA CGI documentation
Linkname: The Common Gateway Interface
URL: http://hoohoo.ncsa.uiuc.edu/cgi/

The spec for CGI
Linkname: The Common Gateway Interface Specification
URL: http://hoohoo.ncsa.uiuc.edu/cgi/interface.html

Information about CGI in CERN HTTPD
Linkname: CGI/1.1 script support of the CERN Server
URL: http://info.cern.ch/hypertext/WWW/Daemon/User/CGI/
Overview.html

A library of C programs to help with CGI deveopment
Linkname: EIT's CGI Library
URL: http://wsk.eit.com/wsk/dist/doc/libcgi/libcgi.html

An index to HTML-related programs written in Perl
Linkname: Index of Perl/HTML archives
URL: http://www.seas.upenn.edu/~mengwong/perlhtml.html

An archive of CGI Programs at NCSA
Linkname: CGI sample scripts
URL: ftp://ftp.ncsa.uiuc.edu/Web/httpd/Unix/ncsa_httpd/cgi

Un-CGI, a program to decode form input
Linkname: Un-CGI Version 1.2
URL: http://www.hyperion.com/~koreth/uncgi.html

Forms and Image Maps

The original NCSA forms documentation
Linkname: The Common Gateway Interface: FORMS
URL: http://hoohoo.ncsa.uiuc.edu/cgi/forms.html

Mosaic form support documenation
inkname: Mosaic for X Version 2.0 Fill-Out Form Support
URL: http://www.ncsa.uiuc.edu/SDG/Software/Mosaic/Docs/
fill-out-forms/overview.html

Image maps in CERN HTTPD
Linkname: Clickable image support in CERN Server
URL: http://info.cern.ch/hypertext/WWW/Daemon/User/CGI/
HTImageDoc.html

Image maps in NCSA
Linkname: Graphical Information Map Tutorial
URL: http://wintermute.ncsa.uiuc.edu:8080/map-tutorial/
image-maps.html

Some Perl scripts to manage forms
Linkname: CGI Form Handling in Perl
URL: http://www.bio.cam.ac.uk/web/form.html

Mapedit: A tool for Windows and X11 for creating Imagemap map files
Linkname: mapedit 1.1.2
URL: `http://sunsite.unc.edu/boutell/mapedit/mapedit.html`

HyperMap Edit (Macintosh map creator)
URL: `ftp://sumex-aim.stanford.edu/info-mac/comm/tcp/`
`hyper-map-edit-hc.hqx`
URL: `http://hyperarchive.lcs.mit.edu/HyperArchive/Archive/comm/tcp/`
`hyper-map-edit-hc.hqx`

HTML Editors and Converters

A list of converters, updated regularly
Linkname: HTML converters
URL: `http://info.cern.ch/hypertext/WWW/Tools/Filters.html`

A better list of converters
Linkname: Computers:World Wide Web:HTML Converters
URL: `http://akebono.stanford.edu/yahoo/Computers/World_Wide_Web/`
`HTML_Converters/`

A great list of editors
Linkname: Computers:World Wide Web:HTML Editors
URL: `http://akebono.stanford.edu/yahoo/Computers/World_Wide_Web/`
`HTML_Editors/`

A general list of tools and editors
Linkname: Browsers, Viewers and HTML Preparation Software
URL: `http://www.utirc.utoronto.ca/HTMLdocs/intro_tools.html`

Other

Tim Berners-Lee's style guide
Linkname: Style Guide for Online Hypertext
URL: `http://info.cern.ch/hypertext/WWW/Provider/Style/`
`Overview.html`

Some good information on registering and publicizing your Web page
Linkname: A guide to publishing on the World Wide Web
URL: `http://www.cl.cam.ac.uk/users/gdr11/publish.html`

A great index of the newsgroups and mailing lists that talk about the WWW

Linkname: World Wide Web Mailing Lists

URL: http://www.leeds.ac.uk/ucs/WWW/WWW_mailing_lists.html

A

B

A Summary of HTML Commands

This appendix is a reference to the HTML tags you can use in your documents, according to the HTML 2.0 Specification (October 25, 1994).

> **Note:** A few of the tags in this section have not been described in the body of the book. If a tag is mentioned here that you haven't seen before, don't worry about it; that means that the tag is not in active use or is for use by HTML-generating and -reading tools, and not for general use in HTML documents.

Basic HTML Tags

Comments

```
<!-- ... -->
```

Structure Tags

`<HTML>...</HTML>`
Encloses the entire HTML document.
Can Include: `<HEAD>`, `<BODY>`

`<HEAD>...<HEAD>`
Encloses the head of the HTML document.
Can Include: `<TITLE> <ISINDEX> <BASE> <NEXTID> <LINK>`
Allowed Inside: `<HTML>`

`<BODY>...</BODY>`
Encloses the body (text and tags) of the HTML document.
Can Include: `<H1> <H2> <H3> <H4> <H5> <H6> <P> <UL> <OL> <DIR> <MENU> <DL> <PRE> <BLOCKQUOTE> <FORM> <ISINDEX> <HR> <ADDRESS>`
Allowed Inside: `<HTML>`

`<BASE>`
Indicates the full URL of the current document.
Attributes: `HREF="..."`; the full URL of this document
Allowed Inside: `<HEAD>`

`<ISINDEX>`

Indicates that this document is a gateway script that allows searches.

Allowed Inside: `<BLOCKQUOTE>` `<BODY>` `<DD>` `<FORM>` `<HEAD>` `<LI>`

`<LINK>`

Indicates the relationship between this document and some other document. Generally used only by HTML-generating tools.

Attributes:

`HREF="..."`

`REL="..."`

`REV="..."`

`URN="..."`

`TITLE="..."`

`METHODS="..."`

Allowed Inside: `<HEAD>`

`<NEXTID>`

Indicates the "next" document to this one (as might be defined by a tool to manage HTML documents in series).

Attributes: `N="..." >`

Allowed Inside: `<HEAD>`

Title and Headings

`<TITLE>...</TITLE>`

Indicates the title of the document.

Allowed Inside: `<HEAD>`

All the headings have the following characteristics:

Can Include: `<A>` `<IMG>` `<BR>` `<EM>` `<STRONG>` `<CODE>` `<SAMP>` `<KBD>` `<VAR>` `<CITE>` `<TT>` `<B>` `<I>`

Allowed Inside: `<BLOCKQUOTE>` `<BODY>` `<FORM>`

`<H1>`

A first-level heading.

`<H2>`

A second-level heading.

`<H3>`

A third-level heading.

```
<H4>
```
A fourth-level heading.

```
<H5>
```
A fifth-level heading.

```
<H6>
```
A sixth-level heading.

Paragraphs

```
<P>...</P>
```
A plain paragraph. According to the Level 2.0 specification, the closing tag (</P>) is optional.

Can Include: `<A>` `<IMG>` `<BR>` `<EM>` `<STRONG>` `<CODE>` `<SAMP>` `<KBD>` `<VAR>` `<CITE>` `<TT>` `<B>` `<I>`

Allowed Inside: `<BLOCKQUOTE>` `<BODY>` `<DD>` `<FORM>` `<LI>`

Links

```
<A>...</A>
```
With the HREF attribute, creates a link to another document or anchor; with the NAME attribute, creates an anchor which can be linked to.

Attributes:

```
HREF="..."
```

```
NAME="..."
```

Can Include: `<IMG>` `<BR>` `<EM>` `<STRONG>` `<CODE>` `<SAMP>` `<KBD>` `<VAR>` `<CITE>` `<TT>` `<B>` `<I>`

Allowed Inside: `<ADDRESS>` `<B>` `<CITE>` `<CODE>` `<DD>` `<DT>` `<EM>` `<H1>` `<H2>` `<H3>` `<H4>` `<H5>` `<H6>` `<I>` `<KBD>` `<LI>` `<P>` `<PRE>` `<SAMP>` `<STRONG>` `<TT>` `<VAR>`

Lists

```
<OL>...</OL>
```
An ordered (numbered) list.
Can Include: `<LI>`
Allowed Inside: `<BLOCKQUOTE>` `<BODY>` `<DD>` `<FORM>` `<LI>`

`<UL>...</UL>`
An unordered (bulleted) list.
Can Include: `<LI>`
Allowed Inside: `<BLOCKQUOTE>` `<BODY>` `<DD>` `<FORM>` `<LI>`

`<MENU>...</MENU>`
A menu list of items.
Can Include: `<LI>`
Allowed Inside: `<BLOCKQUOTE>` `<BODY>` `<DD>` `<FORM>` `<LI>`

`<DIR>...</DIR>`
A directory listing; items are generally smaller than 20 characters.
Can Include: `<LI>`
Allowed Inside: `<BLOCKQUOTE>` `<BODY>` `<DD>` `<FORM>` `<LI>`

`<LI>`
A list item for use with `<OL>`, `<UL>`, `<MENU>` or `<DIR>`
Can Include: `<A>` `<IMG>` `<BR>` `<EM>` `<STRONG>` `<CODE>` `<SAMP>` `<KBD>` `<VAR>` `<CITE>`
`<TT>` `<B>` `<I>` `<P>` `<UL>` `<OL>` `<DIR>` `<MENU>` `<DL>` `<PRE>` `<BLOCKQUOTE>`
Allowed Inside: `<DIR>` `<MENU>` `<OL>` `<UL>`

`<DL>...</DL>`
A definition or glossary list. The COMPACT attribute specifies a formatting that takes
less whitespace to present.
Attributes: COMPACT
Can Include: `<DT>` `<DD>`
Allowed Inside: `<BLOCKQUOTE>` `<BODY>` `<DD>` `<FORM>` `<LI>`

`<DT>`
A definition term, as part of a definition list.
Can Include: `<A>` `<IMG>` `<BR>` `<EM>` `<STRONG>` `<CODE>` `<SAMP>` `<KBD>` `<VAR>` `<CITE>`
`<TT>` `<B>` `<I>`
Allowed Inside: `<DL>`

`<DD>`
The corresponding definition to a definition term, as part of a definition list.
Can Include: `<A>` `<IMG>` `<BR>` `<EM>` `<STRONG>` `<CODE>` `<SAMP>` `<KBD>` `<VAR>` `<CITE>`
`<TT>` `<B>` `<I>` `<P>` `<UL>` `<OL>` `<DIR>` `<MENU>` `<DL>` `<PRE>` `<BLOCKQUOTE>` `<FORM>`
`<ISINDEX>`
Allowed Inside: `<DL>`

Character Formatting

All the character formatting tags have these features:

Can Include: `<A>` `<IMG>` `<BR>` `<EM>` `<STRONG>` `<CODE>` `<SAMP>` `<KBD>` `<VAR>` `<CITE>` `<TT>` `<B>` `<I>`

Allowed Inside: `<A>` `<ADDRESS>` `<B>` `<CITE>` `<CODE>` `<DD>` `<DT>` `<EM>` `<H1>` `<H2>` `<H3>` `<H4>` `<H5>` `<H6>` `<I>` `<KBD>` `<LI>` `<P>` `<PRE>` `<SAMP>` `<STRONG>` `<TT>` `<VAR>`

Attributes:

`<EM>`...`</EM>` Emphasis (usually italic)

`<STRONG>`...`</STRONG>` Stronger emphasis (usually bold)

`<CODE>`...`</CODE>` Code sample (usually Courier)

`<KBD>`...`</KBD>` Text to be typed (usually Courier)

`<VAR>`...`</VAR>` A variable or placeholder for some other value

`<SAMP>`...`</SAMP>` Sample text

`<DFN>`...`<DFN>` (Proposed) A definition of a term

`<CITE>`...`</CITE>` A citation

`<B>`...`</B>` Boldface text

`<I>`...`</I>` Italic text

`<TT>`...`</TT>` Typewriter font

Other Elements

`<HR>`

A horizontal rule line.

Allowed Inside: `<BLOCKQUOTE>` `<BODY>` `<FORM>` `<PRE>`

`<BR>`

A line break.

Allowed Inside: `<A>` `<ADDRESS>` `<B>` `<CITE>` `<CODE>` `<DD>` `<DT>` `<EM>` `<H1>` `<H2>` `<H3>` `<H4>` `<H5>` `<H6>` `<I>` `<KBD>` `<LI>` `<P>` `<PRE>` `<SAMP>` `<STRONG>` `<TT>` `<VAR>`

`<BLOCKQUOTE>`... `</BLOCKQUOTE>`

Used for long quotes or citations.

Can Include: `<BLOCKQUOTE>` `<H1>` `<H2>` `<H3>` `<H4>` `<H5>` `<H6>` `<P>` `<UL>` `<OL>` `<DIR>``<MENU>` `<DL>` `<PRE>` `<BLOCKQUOTE>` `<FORM>` `<ISINDEX>` `<HR>` `<ADDRESS>` `</BLOCKQUOTE>`

Allowed Inside: `<BLOCKQUOTE>` `<BODY>` `<DD>` `<FORM>` `<LI>`

`<ADDRESS>...</ADDRESS>`

Used for signatures or general information about a document's author.

Can Include: `<A>` `<IMG>` `<BR>` `<EM>` `<STRONG>` `<CODE>` `<SAMP>` `<KBD>` `<VAR>` `<CITE>` `<TT>` `<B>` `<I>`

Allowed Inside: `<BLOCKQUOTE>` `<BODY>` `<FORM>`

Images

`<IMG>`

Insert an inline image into the document.

Attributes:

`SRC="..."` The URL of the image.

`ALT="..."` A text string that will be displayed in browsers that cannot support images.

`ALIGN="..."` How the text before and after the image will be aligned vertically with the image. Possible values are `TOP`, `MIDDLE`, `BOTTOM`.

`ISMAP` This image is a clickable image map.

Allowed Inside: `<A>` `<ADDRESS>` `<B>` `<CITE>` `<CODE>` `<DD>` `<DT>` `<EM>` `<H1>` `<H2>` `<H3>` `<H4>` `<H5>` `<H6>` `<I>` `<KBD>` `<LI>` `<P>` `<SAMP>` `<STRONG>` `<TT>` `<VAR>`

Forms

`<FORM>...</FORM>`

Indicates a form.

Attributes:

`ACTION="..."` The URL of the script to perform to process this form input.

`METHOD="..."` How the form input will be sent to the gateway on the server side. Possible values are `GET` and `POST`.

`ENCTYPE="..."` Only one value right now: application/x-www-form-urlencoded.

Can Include: `<H1>` `<H2>` `<H3>` `<H4>` `<H5>` `<H6>` `<P>` `<UL>` `<OL>` `<DIR>` `<MENU>` `<DL>` `<PRE>` `<BLOCKQUOTE>` `<ISINDEX>` `<HR>` `<ADDRESS>` `<INPUT>` `<SELECT>` `<TEXTAREA>`

Allowed Inside: `<BLOCKQUOTE>` `<BODY>` `<DD>` `<LI>`

`<INPUT>`

An input widget for a form.

Attributes:

TYPE="..." The type of input widget this is. Possible values are CHECKBOX, HIDDEN, RADIO, RESET, SUBMIT, TEXT, or IMAGE.

NAME="..." The name of this item, as passed to the gateway script as part of a name/value pair.

VALUE="..." For a text or hidden widget, the default value; for a check box or radio button, the value to be submitted with the form; for Reset or Submit buttons, the label for the button itself.

SRC="..." The source file for an image.

CHECKED For checkboxes and radio buttons, indicates that the widget is checked.

SIZE="..." The size, in characters, of a text widget.

MAXLENGTH="..." The maximum number of characters that can be entered into a text widget.

ALIGN="..." For images in forms, determines how the text and image will align (same as with the <IMG> tag).

Allowed Inside: <FORM>

<TEXTAREA>...</TEXTAREA>

Indicates a multiline text entry widget.

Attributes:

NAME="..." The name to be passed to the gateway script as part of the name/value pair.

ROWS="..." The number of rows this text area displays.

COLS="..." The number of columns (characters) this text area displays.

Allowed inside: <FORM>

<SELECT>...</SELECT>

Creates a menu or scrolling list of possible items.

Attributes:

NAME="..." The name that is passed to the gateway script as part of the name/value pair.

SIZE="..." The number of elements to display. If SIZE is indicated, the selection becomes a scrolling list. If no SIZE is given, the selection is a pop-up menu.

MULTIPLE Allows multiple selections from the list.

Can Include: <OPTION>

Allowed Inside: <FORM>

```
<OPTION>
```
Indicates a possible item within a `<SELECT>` widget.

Attributes:

`SELECTED` With this attribute included, the `<OPTION>` will be select by default in the list.

`VALUE="..."` The value to submit if this `<OPTION>` is selected when the form is submitted.

Allowed Inside: `<SELECT>`

Character Entities

Table B.1 contains the possible numeric and character entities for the ISO-Latin-1 (ISO8859-1) character set. Where possible, the character is shown.

Note: Not all browsers can display all characters, and some browsers may even display different characters from those that appear in the table. Newer browsers seem to have a better track record for handling character entities, but be sure and test your HTML files extensively with multiple browsers if you intend to use these entities.

Table B.1. ISO-Latin-1 character set.

Character	Numeric Entity	Character Entity (if any)	Description
	&#00;-&#08;		Unused
	&#09;		Horizontal tab
	&#10;		Line feed
	&#11;-&#31;		Unused
	&#32;		Space
!	&#33;		Exclamation mark
"	&#34;	&quot;	Quotation mark

continues

Table B.1. continued

Character	Numeric Entity	Character Entity (if any)	Description
#	&#35;		Number sign
$	&#36;		Dollar sign
%	&#37;		Percent sign
&	&#38;	&amp;	Ampersand
‘	&#39;		Apostrophe
(	&#40;		Left parenthesis
)	&#41;		Right parenthesis
*	&#42;		Asterisk
+	&#43;		Plus sign
,	&#44;		Comma
-	&#45;		Hyphen
.	&#46;		Period (fullstop)
/	&#47;		Solidus (slash)
0-9	0 - 9		Digits 0-9
:	&#58;		Colon
;	&#59;		Semi-colon
<	&#60;	&lt;	Less than
=	&#61;		Equals sign
>	&#62;	&gt;	Greater than
?	&#63;		Question mark
@	&#64;		Commercial at
A-Z	A-Z		Letters A-Z
[	&#91;		Left square bracket
\	&#92;		Reverse solidus (backslash)
]	&#93;		Right square bracket
^	&#94;		Caret
—	&#95;		Horizontal bar
`	&#96;		Grave accent

Character	Numeric Entity	Character Entity (if any)	Description
a-z	a-z		Letters a-z
{	&#123;		Left curly brace
|	&#124		Vertical bar
}	&#125;		Right curly brace
~	&#126;		Tilde
	&#127;-		Unused
¡	&#161;		Inverted exclamation
¢	&#162;		Cent sign
£	&#163;		Pound sterling
¤	&#164;		General currency sign
¥	&#165;		Yen sign
¦	&#166;		Broken vertical bar
§	&#167;		Section sign
¨	&#168;		Umlaut (dieresis)
©	&#169;		Copyright
ª	&#170;		Feminine ordinal
‹	&#171;		Left angle quote, guillemotleft
¬	&#172;		Not sign
-	&#173;		Soft hyphen
®	&#174;		Registered trademark
¯	&#175;		Macron accent
°	&#176;		Degree sign
±	&#177;		Plus or minus
²	&#178;		Superscript two
³	&#179;		Superscript three
´	&#180;		Acute accent
µ	&#181;		Micro sign
¶	&#182;		Paragraph sign

Table B.1. continued

Character	Numeric Entity	Character Entity (if any)	Description
·	&#183;		Middle dot
¸	&#184;		Cedilla
¹	&#185;		Superscript one
º	&#186;		Masculine ordinal
›	&#187;		Right angle quote, guillemotright
1/4	&#188;		Fraction one-fourth
1/2	&#189;		Fraction one-half
3/4	&#190;		Fraction three-fourths
¿	&#191;		Inverted question mark
À	&#192;	&Agrave;	Capital A, grave accent
Á	&#193;	&Aacute;	Capital A, acute accent
Â	&#194;	&Acirc;	Capital A, circumflex accent
Ã	&#195;	&Atilde;	Capital A, tilde
Ä	&#196;	&Auml;	Capital A, dieresis or umlaut mark
Å	&#197;	&Aring;	Capital A, ring
Æ	&#198;	&AElig;	Capital AE dipthong (ligature)
Ç	&#199;	&Ccedil;	Capital C, cedilla
È	&#200;	&Egrave;	Capital E, grave accent
É	&#201;	&Eacute;	Capital E, acute accent
Ê	&#202;	&Ecirc;	Capital E, circumflex accent

Character	Numeric Entity	Character Entity (if any)	Description
Ë	&#203;	&Euml;	Capital E, dieresis or umlaut mark
Ì	&#204;	&Igrave;	Capital I, grave accent
Í	&#205;	&Iacute;	Capital I, acute accent
Î	&#206;	&Icirc;	Capital I, circumflex accent
Ï	&#207;	&Iuml;	Capital I, dieresis or umlaut mark
Ш	&#208;	&ETH;	Capital Eth, Icelandic
Ñ	&#209;	&Ntilde;	Capital N, tilde
Ò	&#210;	&Ograve;	Capital O, grave accent
Ó	&#211;	&Oacute;	Capital O, acute accent
Ô	&#212;	&Ocirc;	Capital O, circumflex accent
Õ	&#213;	&Otilde;	Capital O, tilde
Ö	&#214;	&Ouml;	Capital O, dieresis or umlaut mark
×	&#215;		Multiply sign
Ø	&#216;	&Oslash;	Capital O, slash
Ù	&#217;	&Ugrave;	Capital U, grave accent
Ú	&#218;	&Uacute;	Capital U, acute accent
Û	&#219;	&Ucirc;	Capital U, circumflex accent
Ü	&#220;	&Uuml;	Capital U, dieresis or umlaut mark
Y	&#221;	&Yacute;	Capital Y, acute accentfi

B

Table B.1. continued

Character	Numeric Entity	Character Entity (if any)	Description
Þ	&#222;	&THORN;	Capital THORN, Icelandic
■	&#223;	&szlig;	Small sharp s, German (sz ligature)
à	&#224;	&agrave;	Small a, grave accent
á	&#225;	&aacute;	Small a, acute accent
â	&#226;	&acirc;	Small a, circumflex accent
ã	&#227;	&atilde;	Small a, tilde
ä	&#228;	&aauml;	Small a, dieresis or umlaut mark
å	&#229;	&aring;	Small a, ring
æ	&#230;	&aelig;	Small ae dipthong (ligature)
ç	&#231;	&ccedil;	Small c, cedilla
è	&#232;	&egrave;	Small e, grave accent
é	&#233;	&eacute;	Small e, acute accent
ê	&#234;	&ecirc;	Small e, circumflex accent
ë	&#235;	&euml;	Small e, dieresis or umlaut mark
ì	&#236;	&igrave;	Small i, grave accent
í	&#237;	&iacute;	Small i, acute accent
î	&#238;	&icirc;	Small i, circumflex accent
ï	&#239;	&iuml;	Small i, dieresis or umlaut mark
≡	&#240;	&eth;	Small eth, Icelandic
ñ	&#241;	&ntilde;	Small n, tilde
ò	&#242;	&ograve;	Small o, grave accent

Character	Numeric Entity	Character Entity (if any)	Description
ó	&#243;	&oacute;	Small o, acute accent
ô	&#244;	&ocirc;	Small o, circumflex accent
õ	&#245;	&otilde;	Small o, tilde
ö	&#246;	&ouml;	Small o, dieresis or umlaut mark
÷	&#247;		Division sign
ø	&#248;	&oslash;	Small o, slash
ù	&#249;	&ugrave;	Small u, grave accent
ú	&#250;	&uacute;	Small u, acute accent
û	&#251;	&ucirc;	Small u, circumflex accent
ü	&#252;	&uuml;	Small u, dieresis or umlaut mark
ý	&#253;	&yacute;	Small y, acute accent
▪	&#254;	&thorn;	Small thorn, Icelandic
ÿ	&#255;	&yuml;	Small y, dieresis or umlaut mark

C

The Netscape Extensions to HTML

This appendix describes the support for additional HTML tags that Netscape Communications Corporation has added to its Web browser, the Netscape Navigator (as of version 1.0). Most of these tags are currently used and supported *only* by Netscape, although for the most part they will not prevent your documents from being viewed in other browsers (most will just be ignored). If you choose to use these tags in your Web pages keep in mind that when those pages are viewed by a browser that does not support them, your pages may look considerably different. As always, test your pages in multiple browsers to be sure of the effect.

For more information about these extensions and how to use them, see the Netscape documents "Extensions to HTML" (`http://http://home.netscape.com/home/services_docs/html-extensions.html`) and "How to Create High-Impact Documents" (`http://home.netscape.com/home/services_docs/html-extensions.html`).

Centering Text

`<CENTER>...</CENTER>`
Allows you to center a block of text on the page (which can include paragraphs, headings, and so on).

Lists

`<UL>`
Additional Attributes:
`TYPE="..."` The bullet used to mark each list item. Possible values are `DISC` (solid bullet), `CIRCLE` (hollow bullet), or `SQUARE` (square hollow bullet)

`<OL>`
Additional Attributes:
`TYPE="..."` The numbering scheme used for this list. Possible values are `A` (capital letters), `a` (small letters), `I` (large Roman numerals), `i` (small Roman numerals, or `1` (numbers; the default).
`START="..."` The number to start the list from. The default is `1`.

`<LI>`
Additional Attributes:
`TYPE="..."` The type of list item, depending on whether this is a numbered or bulleted list. Possible values are `DISC`, `CIRCLE`, `SQUARE`, `A`, `a`, `I`, `i`, `1`. Setting the type of a list item changes this item and all subsequent items.

VALUE="..." (within <OL> only) Indicates the value of this list item, and restarts the numbering of subsequent items from this value.

Images

<IMG>
Additional Attributes:
ALIGN="..." In addition to the standard TOP, MIDDLE, and BOTTOM values to this attribute, there are also several additions, described below.
HSPACE="..." The space, in pixels, between the image and the text on either side of it.
VPSACE="..." The space, in pixels, between the image and the text above and below it.
BORDER="..." The width of the border surrounding an image.
WIDTH="...", HEIGHT="..." The width and height of the image, in pixels. If these numbers are the actual width and height of the image, the page will load faster (due to Netscape being able to position the image within the text accurately without having to read the image first). If WIDTH and HEIGHT are different numbers than the actual image size, Netscape scales the image to fit.
LOWSRC="..." The file name of an alternate image which is loaded before the image indicated in SRC. This attribute can be used to load a smaller or lower resolution image into the document at the first pass; the final image then replaces this image after all the initial LOWRC images are complete.

<IMG ALIGN>
Additional Values:
LEFT Aligns the image on the left margin, and wraps any text following that image alongside it.
RIGHT Same as ALIGN=LEFT, except that the image is aligned on the right margin, and text wraps to the left of the image.
TEXTTOP Aligns the top of the image with the tallest text in the line (which may or may not be different from the result given by ALIGN=TOP).
ABSMIDDLE Aligns the middle of the image with the middle of the line of text (unlike ALIGN=MIDDLE, which often aligns the middle of the image with the baseline of the text).
BASELINE Aligns the bottom of the image with the baseline of the text (same as ALIGN=BOTTOM)
ABSBOTTOM Aligns the bottom of the image with the lowest text in the line (which may be lower than the baseline).

Line Breaks

`<BR>`
Additional Attributes:

`CLEAR="..."` Where text and images have been aligned next to each other, the CLEAR attribute causes a new line to start below the image; that is, back to the original margin. Possible values are LEFT (break to a clear left margin), RIGHT (break to a clear right margin), and ALL (break to a full clear line).

`<NOBR>...</NOBR>`
The text within the `<NOBR>` tag does not wrap to the next line.

`<WBR>`
Indicates an appropriate breaking point within a word or phrase, which Netscape will use only if appropriate. Can also be used within a `<NOBR>` section to indicate a line break.

Rule Lines

`<HR>`
Additional Attributes:

`SIZE="..."` The vertical thickness, in pixels, of the rule line.
`WIDTH="..."` The horizontal width of the rule line. Can either be an exact pixel width or a percentage (the latter is indicated by a percent sign: 25%, 50%, and so on).
`ALIGN="..."` The alignment of the horizontal rule (in cases where the rule line is smaller than the width of the screen). Possible values are LEFT, RIGHT, and CENTER.
`NOSHADE="..."` Netscape rule lines have a drop shadow by default. This attribute shows the rule line as a solid bar.

Font Sizes

`<FONT>`
Specifies either the default font size or a size relative to the size of the surrounding text.
Attributes:

`SIZE="..."` (required) The size of the font, with values between 1 and 7 (3 is the default). You can also specify font changes relative to the base font size (as indicated by the `<BASEFONT>` tag) by using a + or - before the number itself (for example, `<FONT SIZE="+2">`).

`<BASEFONT>`

Changes the default (base) size of the font. All relative font changes are based on this value.

Attributes:

`SIZE="..."` (required) The size of the default font, with values between 1 and 7 (3 is the default).

Other Extensions

`<ISINDEX>`

Additional Attributes:

`PROMPT"..."` The search prompt that appears instead of the default when a document containing `<ISINDEX>` is displayed.

`&reg; &copy;`

Entities for registered trademark and copyright, respectively.

`<BLINK>...</BLINK>`

Causes the enclosed text to have a blinking effect (which varies in different versions of Netscape). `<BLINK>` was included in Netscape as an undocumented "Easter egg," but has since become popular on the Web at large. Note that blinking is extremely annoying to many people, and in some versions of Netscape it is possible to turn off blinking entirely. Use `<BLINK>` sparingly, if at all, and be sure to provide some other form of emphasis in blinking text (for example, boldface) for browsers that cannot or will not display it.

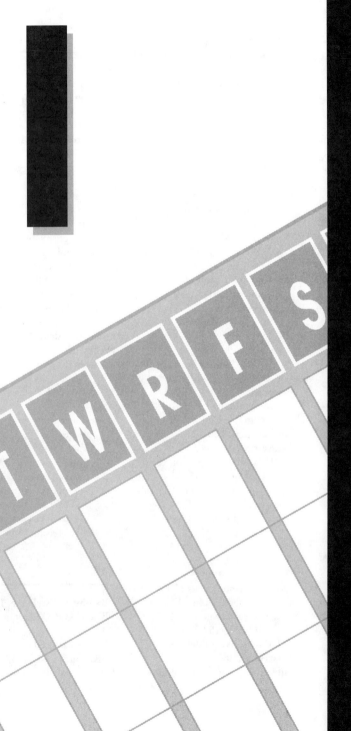

GIF format

Quark Express

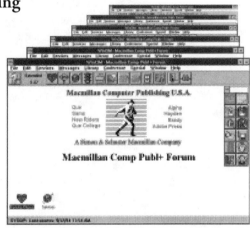

Add to Your Sams Library Today with the Best Books for Programming, Operating Systems, and New Technologies

The easiest way to order is to pick up the phone and call
1-800-428-5331
between 9:00 a.m. and 5:00 p.m. EST.
For faster service please have your credit card available.

ISBN	Quantity	Description of Item	Unit Cost	Total Cost
0-672-30617-4		The World Wide Web Unleashed	$35.00	
0-672-30466-X		The Internet Unleashed	$44.95	
0-672-30627-1		Plug-n-Play Mosaic	$29.99	
0-672-30459-7		Curious About the Internet?	$14.99	
0-672-30519-4		Teach Yourself the Internet: Around the World in 21 Days	$25.00	
0-672-30485-6		Navigating the Internet, Deluxe Edition	$29.95	
0-672-30520-8		Your Internet Consultant: The FAQs of Life Online	$25.00	
0-672-30530-5		The Internet Business Guide: Riding the Information Superhighway to Profit	$25.00	
0-672-30595-X		Education on the Internet	$25.00	
0-672-30599-2		Tricks of the Internet Gurus	$35.00	
0-672-30464-3		Teach Yourself UNIX in a Week	$28.00	
0-672-30001-X		Learning UNIX	$39.95	
		Shipping and Handling: See information below.		
		TOTAL		

O 3 ½" Disk

O 5 ¼" Disk

Shipping and Handling: $4.00 for the first book, and $1.75 for each additional book. Floppy disk: add $1.75 for shipping and handling. If you need to have it NOW, we can ship product to you in 24 hours for an additional charge of approximately $18.00, and you will receive your item overnight or in two days. Overseas shipping and handling adds $2.00 per book and $8.00 for up to three disks. Prices subject to change. Call for availability and pricing information on latest editions.

201 W. 103rd Street, Indianapolis, Indiana 46290

1-800-428-5331 — Orders   1-800-835-3202 — FAX   1-800-858-7674 — Customer Service

Book ISBN 0-672-30667-0

PLUG YOURSELF INTO...

The MCP Internet Site

Free information and vast computer resources from the world's leading computer book publisher—online!

Find the books that are right for you!

A complete online catalog, plus sample chapters and tables of contents give you an in-depth look at *all* our books. The best way to shop or browse!

- ✦ **Stay informed** with the latest computer industry news through discussion groups, an online newsletter, and customized subscription news.

- ✦ **Get fast answers** to your questions about MCP books and software.

- ✦ **Visit** our online bookstore for the latest information and editions!

- ✦ **Communicate** with our expert authors through e-mail and conferences.

- ✦ **Play** in the BradyGame Room with info, demos, shareware, and more!

- ✦ **Download software** from the immense MCP library:
  - Source code and files from MCP books
  - The best shareware, freeware, and demos

- ✦ **Discover hot spots** on other parts of the Internet.

- ✦ **Win books** in ongoing contests and giveaways!

Drop by the new Internet site of Macmillan Computer Publishing!

To plug into MCP:

World Wide Web: http://www.mcp.com/
Gopher: gopher.mcp.com **FTP:** ftp.mcp.com

GOING ONLINE DECEMBER 1994!

Summary of HTML Tags

Structure Tags - Chapter 3

`<HTML>...</HTML>`	Encloses the entire HTML document.
`<HEAD>...<HEAD>`	Encloses the head of the HTML document.
`<BODY>...</BODY>`	Encloses the body (text and tags) of the HTML document.
`<BASE>`	Indicates the full URL of the current document.
`<ISINDEX>`	Indicates that this document is a gateway script that allows searches.
`<LINK>`	Indicates the relationship between these document and some other document. Generally used only by HTML-generating tools.
`<NEXTID>`	Indicates the "next" document to this one (as might be defined by a tool to manage HTML documents in series).

Title and Headings - Chapter 3

`<TITLE>... </TITLE>`	Indicates the title of the document.
`<H1>`	A first-level heading.
`<H2>`	A second-level heading.
`<H3>`	A third-level heading.
`<H4>`	A fourth-level heading.
`<H4>`	A fifth-level heading.
`<H6>`	A sixth-level heading.

Paragraphs - Chapter 3

`<P>...</P>`	A plain paragraph. According to the Level 2.0 specification, the closing tag (`</P>`) is optional.

Links - Chapter 4

`<A>... </A>`	With the HREF attribute, creates a link to another document or anchor; with the NAME attribute, creates an anchor which can be linked to.